RED SCARE RACISM AND COLD WAR BLACK RADICALISM

UNIVERSITY OF
WINCHESTER

Martial Rose Library
Tel: 01962 827306

WITHDRAWN FROM
THE LIBRARY

UNI...
WINCHES...

To be returned on or before the day marked above, subject to recall.

Race, Rhetoric, and Media Series
Davis W. Houck, General Editor

RED SCARE RACISM AND COLD WAR BLACK RADICALISM

James Zeigler

University Press of Mississippi / Jackson

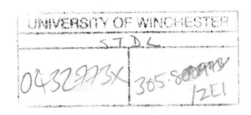

www.upress.state.ms.us

The University Press of Mississippi is a member
of the Association of American University Presses.

First printing 2015

∞

Library of Congress Cataloging-in-Publication Data

Zeigler, James.
Red scare racism and Cold War Black radicalism / James Zeigler.
pages cm. — (Race, rhetoric, and media series)
Includes bibliographical references and index.
ISBN 978-1-4968-0238-5 (cloth : alk. paper) — ISBN 978-1-4968-0239-2 (ebook) 1. Anticommunist movements—United States—History—20th century. 2. Racism—Political
aspects—United States—History. 3. African Americans—Politics and government—20th
century. 4. United States—Race relations—History—20th century. 5. United States—
Politics and government—1945–1989. I. Title.
E743.5.Z44 2015
305.800973'0904—dc23   2015005898

British Library Cataloging-in-Publication Data available

For Vicki

Contents

Acknowledgments

I have received a humbling amount of assistance for this book. Writing it required more time than I care to recall. Family, friends, colleagues, and students made possible my dedication to the task. I am fortunate to have this chance to register my gratitude, however overdue and insufficient it is relative to my debts. First thanks go to my folks, John and Patricia Hilger Zeigler, for their abiding support and confident expectations. Thanks also to Sara, Phil, Aileen, and Hunter: my encouraging sisters and brothers-in-law.

The kind, brilliant guidance of J. Hillis Miller, Michael Davidson, and Steven Mailloux prepared me to start work on this book. Hillis remains an inspiration. The intelligence and grace with which he teaches are complementary to his voluminous, influential publications. Despite extensive commitments, Michael volunteered his counsel to my initial investigations of Cold War culture. It has been my privilege in recent years to feature his impeccable *Guys Like Us* in my graduate seminars. The introduction to this book indicates Steve's definitive influence on my rhetorical approach to literary and cultural studies, and I hope that all my professional undertakings are a credit to his example. I am grateful to professors, colleagues, staff, and friends in the Departments of English and Comparative Literature at UC Irvine, which in my experience was a rare place for rigorous, playful, smart inquiry in good company.

Short-term colleagues and long-term friends from the Department of English at SMU were generous with cheer and good suggestions when I debuted ideas that prompted this book. Thanks especially to Suzanne Bost, Dennis Foster, Michael Householder, Nina Schwartz, Lisa Siraganian, and Steven Weisenburger.

For thoughtful remarks and encouraging words in response to various presentations of the work-in-progress, thanks also to Myka Tucker-Abramson, Seyla Benhabib, Walter Biggins, Joseph Darda, Barbara Foley,

Philip Goldstein, Farah Griffin, Mariam Lam, Debra Ligorsky, Shannon Madden, Gregory Meyerson, Tim Murphy, Jeffrey Nealon, Tracey Nicholls, Aldon Nielsen, Vorris Nunley, Donald Pease, Joanna Rapf, Russell Reising, Anthony Stewart, Linda Wagner-Martin, Daniel Waterman, Kerry Webb, Thomas Wells, Jenny Williams, and Kirt Wilson.

Thanks to colleagues, students, and staff in the Department of English at the University of Oklahoma. From the moment I arrived for an interview, Ron Schleifer has provided sage counsel, unyielding support, and a constant example of how to enjoy the work. I appreciate the ministrations of David Mair, Catherine John, and Daniela Garofalo, successive chairs of the department during my time so far. Thanks to Catherine and Francesca Sawaya for our regular talks and their occasional interventions. Francesca provided rapid, incisive, and encouraging feedback on long sections of the book-in-progress. Dan Cottom did the same for the entire manuscript, much of it twice. The eloquence of his writing made his confidence in my work especially persuasive at a time when I could use convincing. Alex Bain's remarks on an early draft were pivotal, and Henry McDonald was always up for a chat about Foucault. Joshua Nelson and David Anderson provided models of professional conduct when contending with the uncertainty of a first book. Chris Carter used his acute sense of diplomacy to assist me with those key documents that represent the book without being part of it. Indelible conversations with civil rights historian Dave Chappell oriented and emboldened my understanding of Martin Luther King Jr.'s radicalism. Emily Rook-Koepsel refined my appreciation of the persistent importance of decolonization. Graduate students in my seminars on "The Rhetorical Culture of the Cold War" and "Cold War Sexualities, Queer Theory, and Cultural Rhetoric Studies" were hard-working partners for investigating the sundry ways anticommunism colors public culture. OU's Office of the Vice President for Research, Office of the Provost, College of Arts and Sciences, and Department of English provided funding for archival research, a semester's leave from teaching, and permissions.

Many thanks to my editor Vijay Shah and the entire team at the University Press of Mississippi. Thanks also to Anthony Dawahare and an anonymous reader for preparing reports that rewarded my hard work with praise while offering conscientious recommendations for improvement. I am appreciative and proud that Davis Houck chose my book for UPM's series Race, Rhetoric, and Media. Thanks to Brian Dolinar for introducing me to Dr. Helma Harrington, and thanks to her for allowing me to include a political cartoon by her late husband, Ollie Harrington. Excerpts from C. L. R. James's unpublished correspondence appear with the permission of the Estate of C. L. R. James and the kind assistance of Robert Hill.

Most importantly, thanks to my wife, Victoria Sturtevant, and our children. Wiley and Marlo were still just great ideas when I began research for this book. In the intervening years, their rapid achievements and noisy joy have been an irrepressible, daily spur to finish work and resume play. However diverting their father's big project may have seemed to their precocious sensibilities, it became for me increasingly a labor of love for them. Even as we doubled our numbers at home and her career advanced through three promotions, Vicki helped make time for me to write. And we both owe thanks to my parents and sisters, Jim and Rosalie Sturtevant, Bill and Sandra Pinter, Sharon and Bill Schneider, Cornelia Lambert, and Marni Vincent, whose caring for our kids was essential to our balance of work and family obligations. Vicki's respectful and affectionate suggestions for revision made this a better book—much as her partnership adds significance to everything I know and am.

PREFACE

Fear of a Black and "Red" President

Let me begin with an unbelievable story. President Barack Obama is not the son of the Kenyan citizen for whom he is named. Their relationship was contrived in a secret pact to hide the fact that his biological father is actually Frank Marshall Davis. A radical poet and journalist who, in the 1930s, was part of the famous South Side Writers Group in Chicago, Davis was also a member of the Communist Party of the United States of America (CPUSA). He joined in Chicago during World War II and remained a member after moving to Hawaii in 1948. It was there some years later that he became friends with President Obama's grandfather, Stanley Dunham. Or so he thought. Dunham was not, however, the furniture salesman he appeared to be; that career was a cover for his real work as a field agent for the Central Intelligence Agency (CIA). Becoming familiar with Davis was a tactic for gathering information about the CPUSA's operations in Hawaii. This initial pretense of friendship brought Davis into the orbit of Dunham's family and led to the scandal that prompted the two men to set aside their contrary political loyalties in order to collude privately in a deception that was of mutual interest and is now of world historical significance.

Davis's politics were not the only problem with his paternity, though the cover-up was necessary for Dunham to protect his job with the CIA. Revelations about his daughter's sexual relationship with a Communist would have ruined his career. Other concerns were more sordid. Davis was thirty-seven years older than Stanley Ann Dunham, who was only a teenager when he seduced her. He was black, and she was white. Interracial relationships may have been more acceptable in multicultural Hawaii than in much of the continental United States, but race was still a site of social tension. He was also married and already had five children with his wife. And he was a freelance pornographer. Ann posed nude for photos Davis sold to magazines. The illicit, salacious relationship motivated her father to take advantage of another of his CIA assignments: coordinating students brought to the University of Hawaii

by "Africa Airlift," which promoted American values internationally by providing opportunities to study at US universities. Dunham bribed a student of
his acquaintance from Kenya, Barack Hussein Obama, to enter a sham marriage in order to give his daughter's pregnancy legitimacy and to disguise the
fact that his grandchild was a red-diaper baby. After a respectable interval,
the senior Obama and his wife divorced, their marriage supposedly undone
by the professional ambitions that drove him to pursue graduate studies at
Harvard, leaving Ann and his "son" behind. For her part, Ann complied with
the plan in exchange for her father's financial support while she and her baby
lived in Seattle so that she could enroll at the University of Washington.

Until he was twelve years old, according to this story, President Obama
remained innocent of how his grandfather, Davis, and his young mother
arranged his identity. On the cusp of adolescence, he became a willing accomplice to the conspiracy that with his election to the Presidency in 2008 became
a fraud perpetrated against the American people. As Obama acknowledges in
his 1995 autobiography *Dreams from My Father*, he first met "a poet named
Frank" through his grandfather, who encouraged him to seek the older man's
counsel on what it means to be black in America.[1] What his book does not
admit is that it took him only a few months to discern that "Gramps" and Frank
shared a secret. Rummaging through papers stored in his grandparents' home,
he discovered that his birth certificate listed his father as "unknown." When he
demanded an explanation, his grandfather admitted that Davis was his actual
father. Confronted by the young Obama with this revelation, Davis confessed
the truth, swore his son to maintain the ruse of Kenyan heritage for its exotic
appeal in the United States, and began a more deliberate, regular tutorial over
several years to inculcate in Obama the un-American aspirations of the Cold
War–era Communist Party to which Davis had dedicated his life. Initially
shocked by his discovery, Obama became happy in his close collaboration with
his real father. He applied himself to learning a Marxist vision of history that
Davis taught him was complementary to the black nationalist view that Western modernity was a euphemism for white supremacy. Obama grew to accept
that communism is necessary to "neuter" the white man. This family legacy of
Obama's off-the-record schooling was the basis for the un-American political
philosophy that his administration did its best to impress on US policy from
the time of his inauguration in 2009. Contrary to popular opinion, the election
of the first African American president of the United States was not a hard-won
triumph of the civil rights movement's long struggle against anti-black racism.
The true color of the Obama administration was Communist red.

The source of this fantastic story is a film, *Dreams from My Real Father:
A Story of Reds and Deception*.[2] It was released on DVD in late July 2012 just

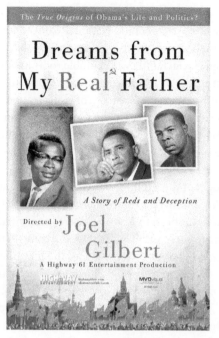

1. Advertising poster for *Dreams from My Real Father* (Highway 61 Entertainment 2012)

weeks before the national conventions of the Republican and Democratic parties confirmed the contest for the Presidency would be between Governor Mitt Romney and President Obama. Approximately four million residences in "swing states" received free copies in the mail. Promotions in major newspapers and on nationally syndicated radio programs advertised the film's major revelation and its availability for purchase. The documentary fabricates its conspiracy theory with the pretense that its discoveries are the result of two years of painstaking investigative journalism by producer, director, and writer Joel Gilbert. He claims his private inquiry into Obama's genealogy began when he noticed that photographs of the president are unlike pictures of his father but resemble images of Davis. The film opens by displaying photographs of all three men as if to suggest that the discrepancies and similarities are ocular proof that something is amiss in the president's biography. Obama, the presentation teaches, simply looks suspicious.

With a voiceover that impersonates Obama's distinctive sound, the film proceeds to narrate in first-person an alternative autobiography to the public record of the president's life story. In a script that mixes citations from *Dreams from My Father* with inventions of fact and opinion, the narrator

"Obama" admits how the personal story he first addressed to the nation from the podium of the 2004 Democratic National Convention was a lie embellished strategically to become a myth with powerful political appeal. Born into an international, interracial family with humble roots in both Kenya and Kansas, Obama was an exemplary American success story after the achievements of the civil rights movement and for an era of globalization. The contradictory account displayed so emphatically by the film's promotional materials is that the real story of his origins is a tale of "Reds and Deception," not "Race and Inheritance" as the subtitle of his book claims. In lieu of the Kenyan landscape depicted on the cover of Obama's memoir, the poster for the film shows a crowd marching within sight of the Kremlin carrying dozens of the now defunct flag of the former Soviet Union. Like the vociferous protestations of the "birthers" who insisted Obama was born in Kenya, Gilbert's conspiracy theory purports to demonstrate his presidency is illegitimate. Conceding that Obama was born in the United States to two American citizens, the film nonetheless intimates that a red diaper baby raised in a secret alliance with his Communist father is even more decisively un-American than if he were born outside the country. More than foreign, Gilbert's Obama is a US citizen nurtured into an enemy of the state in order to realize a dream authored in the middle of the last century by the despotic leaders of a nation-state that no longer exists.

Among the countless ways of degrading Obama's person and presidency that circulated after 2008 to the delight and outrage of audiences already persuaded he was an un-American usurper, stories affiliating him with the deceased Communist Davis were especially vivid efforts to delimit the significance of the election of the first African American president.[3] The allegations that Davis mentored Obama recall a tradition of countersubversive cultural politics and policing that assumes African American political agency that demands equal rights regardless of race must take its impetus not from a thoughtful rejection of discrimination and oppression but instead from the outside influence of Communists who make cynical use of race to undermine America.[4] The tales of Davis advising the future president also recycle wholesale the Federal Bureau of Investigation's (FBI) monolithic account of communism during the early years of the Cold War. Not a political philosophy, Communism—always with a capital C in the minds of the FBI—was an international criminal conspiracy controlled absolutely by the USSR and enacted by people of deficient character seeking to deny humanity the value of democracy. With his insistence on Obama's family connection to the CPUSA, Gilbert's film reiterates the trope of black-is-Red and then amplifies the criminal identity of Communism by animating its involvement in the election of the first African American president with racist conceits about the sexuality of black men. The portrait of Davis as Obama's father adds to the un-American plot a subtext of sexual violence. Gilbert's Davis was a predator who ruined Obama's white mother, conceiving the future president in adulterous sexual congress that in most American jurisdictions today would qualify as statutory rape. And in keeping with the perverse, age-old logic that says sexual violence perpetrated against a white woman by a black man robs her of innocence and may twist her sexuality unnaturally, the allegations that Obama's mother was victimized do not deter the film from the further suggestion that she was also to blame for Davis's violations. Her initial interest in him, the film suggests, means she had an unwholesome sexual appetite that became more elaborate and depraved under Davis's tutelage. Invoking the specter of black male virility, Gilbert purports to reveal that the president's unacknowledged father was at least twice a criminal while his young mother was averse to the kind of moral guidance that would have protected her from Davis. Guilty of rape and treason, Davis is the key, Gilbert insists, to understanding the worldview that informed Obama's plans for the United States. The use of Davis to impugn Obama exemplifies the discursive strategy of employing anticommunism to perpetuate anti-black racism while pretending to be concerned solely with national security. The film associates the president with a myth of African American men's sexual violence and an exaggerated history of un-American treachery, implicating Obama in his parents' turpitude by virtue of his supposedly abiding fidelity to Davis's Communist party dreams.

To be perfectly clear, let me say that Gilbert's film is unbelievable because it is not true. Needless to say, it is offensive. Adhering to the conventions of the conspiracy theory genre, it is also impervious to refutation.[5] From within the logic of the film's argument, to dispute its so-called findings is to be cast as a member of that constituency that was gullible enough in the first place to fall for Obama's trickery. The implicit depiction of the electorate in the film is unflattering. For all of the intricacy in the masterful plan to parlay the fiction of Obama's origins into control over the most powerful individual position in the world, Gilbert, recall, spotted the problem by perusing a few photographs. His appeal, then, is not for everyone. Despite being timed to coincide with the contest for president, the film is an invitation not to the electorate but to an elect: a fortunate few devoted to a civil religion of American nationalism that must soldier on despite having lost command of its government to an insurrection that the rest of us, nominally citizens, lacked the insight and temerity to acknowledge.

The credulous audience addressed by Gilbert's film, like those imagined for all of the various productions and publications that propose to identify the precise source and character of Obama's duplicity, is not a political constituency joined by formal affiliation to a party or an organization. Nor does the film attempt to occult its approving viewers into a strict community of belief. One can participate in the discussion of Obama's un-American character and treasonous leadership without attending meetings or services. The Republican party that sought to unseat him could, as a consequence, avail itself of Red Scare vocabulary while insisting it was just talking tough, not endorsing the concrete accusations dog-whistling through its rhetoric. The appeals of the conspiracy theories, while limited, are indeterminate. Gilbert's film hails any viewer with expressions of resentment and suspicion about Obama, and then it offers those bad feelings and doubts a narrative form. After 2008 such stories served as points of connection and solidarity between relative strangers who went forth to enjoin each other by keeping their alternative reality of the American state in circulation while responding in kind to others' signs of also being in on the secret and persuaded that the revelations must be repeated until finally everyone accedes. Influence spread and stuck together, which emboldened the demarcations between them and us unsuspecting, somnambulist others. The virtual constituency I am describing fashioned itself as if it were the citizenry, but those subscribing to the idea that Obama's presidency was essentially a deception by America's enemies composed a counterpublic.

As Michael Warner acknowledges in the title essay of *Publics and Counterpublics*, these virtual entities are challenging to define, circumscribe, and command. "Publics," he writes, "have become an essential fact of the social landscape; yet it would tax our understanding to say exactly what they are."[6] Not identical to *the* public designated in electoral politics as the social totality that opinion polling chops into demographic stratifications that then provide a pie-chart calculus of what "we" want, nor a concrete audience routinely addressed en masse in political oration, stand-up comedy, or even a sporting event, the concept of a public that concerns Warner and informs my argument in this book refers to a personified, collective subject that "comes into being only in relation to texts and their circulation."[7] Publics, in this sense, are substantially discursive and entail interactions of address and response, though merely paying attention may be sufficient entry to membership, which in every case is provisional. No state or outside agency organizes a public; self-organizing, these publics bring strangers into social relation by virtue of their mutual participation. Counterpublics are the same with a key exception.[8] They come together with the greater intensity of being subordinate and, likely, at least a little strange relative to those publics that do not strain or agitate social conventions so generally agreeable that they are habitual. That hard work may change habits is cause for counterpublics to persist with optimism about extending their influence. If that is an alarming thought in the case of the anticommunist contingency arrayed in contempt for the first African American president, consider that the civil rights movement was a counterpublic mobilization forced to impress itself on public life in the United States. For more than half of Frank Marshall Davis's life, publics in America, including the national public, lacked consensus opposition to racial apartheid. As I write, structural racism may have sundry means of support, but only counterpublics marginalized in the extreme accommodate outspoken nostalgia for Jim Crow rules or the romantic plenitude of plantation life.

To forecast my debt to Warner, the dichotomy in my title, *Red Scare Racism and Cold War Black Radicalism*, refers first to a public beholden in the long 1950s to conceits of anticommunism that facilitated the perpetuation of systemic racism in the United States. Engaging in Red Scare cultural practices was a public means, even in the privacy of one's home, for voluntary service in a network dedicated to securing American nationalism against ideas deemed anathema to human freedom. Cold War black radicalism, in contrast, signifies concerted efforts by intellectuals—a term inclusive of activists and artists—in the two decades following World War II to keep alive for the black freedom struggle the kinds of anticapitalist, leftist ideas rightly affiliated with Marxism that the postwar Red Scare targeted not only as treasonous but also as pathological. Considering the prevalence and popularity of Red Scare tropes, narratives, arguments, and images in public culture, Cold War black radicals had to keep their bearings and sharpen their critiques by forging counterpublics in which their ideas and ostensibly un-American activities remained possible without the stigma of betrayal and madness. Counterpublics of black radicalism in the Cold War years prior to *Brown v. Board of Education* in 1954 afforded the combination of anticapitalist and anti-racist ideas and initiatives some protection from unreasoning critique and persecution, but Cold War black radical intellectuals were nevertheless often compelled into exile. This disparity between an American public residing comfortably at home while counterpublics concerned with conditions in the United States had to strain for connection from far away hints at one of the key features of Warner's discrimination: counterpublics are defined, in part, by vulnerability.[9]

Not much recommends a comparison of the Red Scare counterpublics incited by the election of Obama and the counterpublics of Cold War black radicalism. Certainly, Gilbert and other conspiracy theorists were marginalized in the theater of electoral politics, but only from inside their anti-Obama, black-is-Red perspective could they be imagined to suffer vulnerabilities for their ideas such as the surveillance, censorship, unemployment (by blacklisting), personal intimidation, public interrogations, incarceration, expulsion, and violence, often lethal, that was carried out against the black left. These two counterpublic formations do, however, share a quality of being idiosyncratic relative to the common-sense parameters of political culture of their times; for each, their difference tended to make them illegible to US public culture, though a resourceful feature of counterpublics in Warner's understanding is that they aspire to public status. Although located more in the circulation of texts than in physical space, counterpublics are venues in which to work collaboratively to translate particular, as yet isolating terms of value into those normative frameworks through which a public exercises unique agency in regard to institutions that govern and reproduce modern social life. A counterpublic lacks such agency but seeks it by endeavoring to become public. This dynamic by which a counterpublic might communicate its identity into a more public disposition makes Gilbert's film worth watching out for in my view. US public culture may not have admitted his ugly narrative of Obama's real black Communist father and sexually aberrant mother into the normative discourse of electoral politics in 2012, but the impossible scenario resonated with the impressive variety of ways that Obama was called un-American by candidates for office at every level of government, including numerous incumbents.

Of course, calling political opponents un-American has been standard practice since long before and ever after the founding of the House Un-American Activities Committee in 1938. The John Birch Society had the nerve and bad moral luck to leaflet Dallas with flyers calling President Kennedy a Communist in the days just prior to his assassination. Speculations about his Roman Catholic obligations to the Pope also pretended to raise a practical difficulty about sovereignty in order to imply that his American identity was marred with alien loyalties, though I trust we can agree that suggesting Obama's upbringing made him a stranger to American culture carried a weightier connotation of racial difference. Regardless of their denials to the contrary, Obama's race is a problem for his opponents from all sides. Whether or not they have racist feelings or intentions toward him is incidental to my point, which is that no president before Obama symbolized at one time the sovereignty of the American people and the achievement of African Americans and their allies to wrest democratic franchise from a body politic that only relinquished it under duress. The first African American president could not help but have his legitimacy enjoy additional dignity bestowed by association with the civil rights movement that, in its long history, made his election possible.

Impugning Obama either for a belated, secret allegiance to America's Cold War opponent or for simply a witless devotion to ideas supposedly proven bankrupt by the USSR's record of atrocities and inevitable dissolution, the anticommunist attacks on his presidency sought to attribute to him un-American connections that mean he was not a legacy of the civil rights movement. Incorporated predominantly through the figure of Martin Luther King Jr. and featuring excerpts of soaring oratory and aspirational images from events such as the March on Washington in 1963, the civil rights movement is now recognized as part of American national identity. Its virtue is incontrovertible. And while the movement is made monumental and sanitary for school curricula and the ritual commemorations that mark the Martin Luther King Jr. Holiday, there is no question that US public culture now has the normative expectation that the history of the civil rights movement must be treated with respect. That imperative does not deter its being used for political advantage or profit, but even appropriations that run so contrary to the movement's values must be couched in deferential terms.

The efforts to paint "Red" the first black president in order to disaffiliate him from the freedom struggles that helped win franchise for so many US citizens were ironic for what they wanted forgotten. In that memorialized decade of the movement's greatest visibility, stretching from the Montgomery bus boycott to the Selma marches, civil rights organizations and activists were maligned, investigated, threatened, and punished for allegedly taking directions from the CPUSA. Reacting to President Obama's authority by recalling Cold War accusations of un-American activities put him in good company with the very people the Red Scare complaints invoked to claim that he was a traitor to their cause and country. Also missing from these portraits of the civil rights movement that were leveraged against Obama was a record of influence that the nationalist celebrations of the King years cannot abide either. As this book endeavors to demonstrate, anticapitalist convictions, varieties of small-c communism, were integral to the black freedom struggle. The influence of these ideas was salutary. They were no less essential when their purveyors were card-carrying Communists such as Frank Marshall Davis, who understood that the black liberation movement in allegiance with other initiatives for social equality must pursue two forms of redress at once: political recognition and socioeconomic redistribution. Revisiting Davis and other Cold War black radicals without the impediment of their Red Scare caricatures is a chance to recognize their prescient observation that the residue of Jim Crow rule would not really be swept away unless white privilege were dispossessed of its unearned assets.[10] Such a transformation of value cannot be undertaken in accordance with the confines of a late capitalism that came into its own under the cover of American publics that Cold War black radicals tried and, it must be said, failed to persuade about the damaging coordination of race and class facilitated by anticommunism.

A contribution to scholarship and literature that audits the harm caused by the impositions of anticommunism on and against the black freedom struggle in the early years of the Cold War, *Red Scare Racism and Cold War Black Radicalism* takes the return of Red Scare aspersions aimed at the first African American president as an occasion to consider the importance of anticapitalist convictions for both the achievements and the incomplete aspirations of the civil rights movement. The polemical inference to consider after completing this book is that US public culture will not have the history of anticommunism right until the term communist conveys no necessary connotations of treason, madness, or depravity. Such reckoning will also hold the civil rights movement in truer esteem.

RED SCARE RACISM AND COLD WAR BLACK RADICALISM

INTRODUCTION

Cold War Civil Rights and Cultural Rhetoric Studies

A cultural rhetoric study of how the discourse of anticommunism has influenced the politics of race in the United States, this book observes that the Cold War Red Scare contributed to the end of state-sanctioned racial segregation in the American South but provided for the survival of systemic anti-black racism in the United States after the supposed death of Jim Crow.[1] Identifying the relationship between the postwar Red Scare and the civil rights movement as a pernicious ambivalence that ultimately harmed the black freedom struggle, I describe how Cold War anticommunism worked to render US public culture oblivious to the fundamental convergence of racial discrimination and class exploitation. The termination of *de jure* Jim Crow segregation in the American South may have been a necessity for the success of the United States in global propaganda battles with the USSR, but the pervasive influence of Red Scare rhetoric throughout the country divided the struggle for civil rights from the pursuit of the kinds of social reparations that would make legal recognition equally valuable to all citizens regardless of race. While eventually endorsing the gradual delegitimation of overt, intentional policies and acts of racism, the discourse of Cold War anticommunism affixed to complaints about class inequality an un-American connotation. The uncanny return of Red Scare invective in reaction to the election of President Obama is further evidence of the rhetorical power anticommunism has commanded in US public culture, especially in response to the political agency of African Americans. Red Scare rhetoric has proven a durable, hyperbolic resource to discredit as un-American efforts to explain and redress socioeconomic inequality with reference to racialized structural disadvantages.

In addition to reconstructing how the normative discourse of Cold War anticommunism was an asset to African American claims for civil rights but an impediment to demands for socioeconomic reparations, this book examines how intellectuals working in a tradition of black radicalism informed by

Marxism were nonetheless able to engage critically with the culture of Cold War America to show how anti-racist political initiatives would only succeed if they were informed by anticapitalist convictions and activism. A corollary to black radical criticisms of domestic anticommunism was the characterization of postwar US foreign policy as a threat to the national liberation struggles against European colonialism throughout Africa, Asia, and the Americas. Anticommunism's exclusive concern for the Cold War opposition of West against East obscured the more significant re-institution of a geopolitical division between the North Atlantic powers and the global South, which after the Bretton Woods accord of 1944 was coordinated primarily by the United States' informal empire of military and commercial sway. To proffer demands against socioeconomic inequality and US imperialism during the two decades following World War II (i.e., the long 1950s), radicals dedicated to black freedom struggles had to cross the boundary between civil and "un-American" political speech; such transgression saw the free expression of political ideas twisted into heresy or, worse, treason. Like labor unions, the Hollywood film industry, and government agencies, during the early years of the Cold War the NAACP and other major organizations of the civil rights movement were zealous in expelling anticapitalist influences from their ranks.[2] As a consequence, intellectuals and activists schooled in Marxism had to work from the periphery of the civil rights movement in order to keep the black freedom struggle in the United States in touch with the kinds of critiques of capitalism that had been integral to anti-racist activism prior to WWII and that animated postwar decolonization efforts overseas.[3] Translated into the discourse of Cold War anticommunism in the public culture of the United States during the long 1950s, black radical objections to the dyad of racism and capitalism were mischaracterized and then maligned as mad rants inspired or dictated by the Communist party's overseers in the USSR.

Historians of the relationship between the Cold War and the black freedom struggle including Mary Dudziak, Gerald Horne, Manning Marable, Ellen Schrecker, Penny Von Eschen, and others have demonstrated that the policing of African American dissent by J. Edgar Hoover's FBI, the House Committee on Un-American Activities (HUAC), the Senate Subcommittee on Internal Security, the Senate Permanent Subcommittee on Investigations of the Committee on Government Operations (Senator McCarthy's committee), and the dozens of "little HUACs" and other tribunals that investigated un-Americanism at the state and local levels, all contributed to a fearful atmosphere of repression that narrowed the scope of legitimate deliberations within institutions that influenced and authored government policy, including major civil rights organizations. There is no doubt that the postwar Red

Scare was an effective program of political repression coordinated between state, commercial, and civil institutions, but my cultural rhetoric studies approach accompanies the findings of these historians by concentrating less on what was forbidden and more on how the discourse of Cold War anticommunism was a formidable pedagogy for the US public.[4] The knowledge ordinary citizens acquired in and out of school about the Red Scare meant that Cold War black radicals faced an inordinately difficult challenge when they sought to instruct the American public about anticapitalist ideas that were anathema to an emerging common sense in which democracy was identified with capitalism and the mere use of Marxist terms was dismissed as a symptom of mental derangement. In Cold War anticommunist discourse's most prevalent and influential formulations, the innate rectitude attributed to US citizens in neat opposition to depraved, un-American communists was bolstered with the further portrayal of American national identity as the culmination of Western modernity. The promise of the postwar United States was the final realization of the European Enlightenment, and the USSR was the last significant obstacle to the so-called end of history.

In defiance of anticommunist strictures against political dissent inspired by critiques of capitalism, the black radical intellectuals I consider insisted presciently that the foreign policy and domestic culture of "containment" would facilitate the leading role of the United States in transforming the mid-century promise of decolonization in Africa, Asia, and the Americas (including the US) into the enduring impositions of neocolonialism. In its function as a popular heuristic in the United States, the Cold War dichotomy of West against East was an imaginary geography that effectively elided decolonization, assimilating scenes of anti-colonial revolution across Europe's colonies into a Cold War frame that treated demands for national autonomy as if they were merely assertions of affiliation with one side or the other. Focusing on texts of social protest occasioned by the confluence of the Cold War and the black freedom struggle, I study efforts to contest the validity of Red Scare tropes, arguments, narratives, and images when addressing audiences schooled to use anticommunist discourse to make sense of everything from remote episodes of international crisis, to electoral politics, to the national security subtext of ordinary activities in local schools, churches, and community groups. For their troubles, with the exception of Martin Luther King Jr. who came (back) to Cold War black radicalism late in his career, each of the intellectuals I consider was compelled to leave the continental United States. Richard Wright moved to Paris in 1947, admitting later that he chose permanent exile rather than return to a public culture of anticommunism and a likely subpoena from HUAC. Many of his nonfiction writings of the 1950s

dwell on the Cold War's disorienting effects on the national liberation struggles of decolonization. A long contest with immigration authorities forced
C. L. R. James to return to England, where he continued for some years to
correspond with his coterie of Marxist intellectuals in Detroit. Pressured by
the un-American investigations in Chicago and drawn to Hawaii's ethnic and
racial diversity, Frank Marshall Davis relocated there in 1948 but committed
his journalism to fighting the Red Scare as it made its way to the islands from
the mainland.[5] Although their departures are representative of how successful Cold War anticommunism was at expelling both critics and critiques of
late capitalism from the public culture of the United States, this book argues
that, in their confrontations with the Cold War national security state, these
intellectuals crafted singular and incisive black radical responses to anticommunism. They warned that Cold War cultural politics would ensure that the
termination of *de jure* segregation would be insufficient to redress socioeconomic inequalities that would, in turn, reproduce systemic racism. With
transnational perspectives, exiles from America such as Wright, James, and
Davis essayed to disrupt the stupefying, parochial consequences of Red Scare
rhetoric; staying closer to home, King made a comparable effort when the
failures of desegregation impressed on him the synchronicity between postwar US imperialism and the underdevelopment of African Americans.

Reconstructing Anticommunist Discourse

As I endeavor in this book to appraise the harm of Cold War anticommunism and the ingenuity of black radical responses that together constitute an
archive of historical possibilities lost to the Red Scare, I make a case for the
value of cultural rhetoric studies. This approach to textual interpretation is
effective for discerning how public culture communicates normative expectations that constrain political possibilities and for identifying idiosyncratic
texts or other symbolic acts that expose how those constraints invite critique
and, despite their apparent persuasiveness, need not be regarded as necessary.
While this approach generates compelling interpretations of particular texts
and new knowledge about the interaction of Cold War anticommunism and
the black left in the long 1950s, it also facilitates the application of my historical findings to explain the return of Red Scare rhetoric that characterized the
politics of race in the United States after the election of President Obama.
Cold War anticommunism may have insulated US public culture from the
most vital ideas of black radicalism. But revisiting impressive, unfulfilled
efforts to pair anti-racism and anticapitalism during the long 1950s is, I hope,

promising instruction for sustaining aspirations for social equality when confronted by the inauspicious circumstance in which liberty is cited regularly to misrepresent and license deprivation. Critical and inventive responses to punishing social norms may not be sufficient to effect change, but Cold War black radicals expected that disrupting anticommunist habits of thought would be instrumental for cultivating the political imagination required to contend against what is to this day late capitalism's greatest trick: insisting there is no alternative.

Although I frequently call attention to the Cold War state's exercise of sovereign and capricious authority, my priority in examining the power of the postwar Red Scare refers more commonly to the ways in which public instruction about communism's dangerous ideas supplemented ordinary habits, conventional wisdom, and unspoken common sense with feelings of national security. Identifying Cold War anticommunism as a discourse of "power/knowledge" in Foucault's sense, I consider the ways it instilled in its practitioners a constellation of truisms that rewarded them with the capacity to act socially in the domestic United States. A well-disciplined understanding of the nature, intentions, activities, and risks that were supposed to define the character of any Communist was compulsory to enjoy influence among like-minded people and within those prominent, non-governmental institutions of social life that over the first two decades of the Cold War married vigilance against suspected Communists and the ideas of communism to their primary objectives of cultivating faith, commerce, education, entertainment, charity, journalism, or community relations. Red Scare social skills were a must in most walks of public life in the United States. Needless to say, for government employment they were an absolute obligation, as Truman's introduction of the federal employee loyalty program drove home in 1947.[6]

Readers of Foucault will know that his counter-intuitive account of power is scattered throughout a number of his writings, lectures, and interviews. I take my most direct cues from several well-known pages in the "Method" chapter of *The History of Sexuality* in which he presents a set of propositions about his conception of power.[7] It is not a property to be wielded over others, which means he distinguishes it from direct violence or force. It is exercised in relation with others, and is always informed by other kinds of relationships that seem to be not about power, such as schooling, shopping, loving, etc. Power relations are more varied and circuitous than top-down formulations of rulers and ruled allow. Because power relations are irreducibly discursive—they entail talk and representation—the purposes they serve may not be identifiable with any particular person or institution's interests. With enough infrastructure and momentum over time, a normative discourse may exert a powerful influence as if it were acting on its own accord. In criticisms of Foucault's work, this characterization of the anonymity of power has lent itself to exaggeration and ridicule that suggest he believes language to be a haunted medium animated to possess us, but his claim refers to habituation and not to metaphysics. And power always entails resistance, which follows Foucault's conviction that any idea of human agency shorn absolutely free from stricture is an unreal fantasy of liberty. In actuality, freedom may only be exercised in relation to constraint; anyone with a healthy regimen of physical exercise likely understands that strenuous repetition of bodily movement prepares for capable motion in less regimented positions. Foucault follows his declarations with instruction on how the examination of the normative influence of a discourse of power/knowledge requires a process of research and interpretation to put the discourse into evidence; to provide access to a discourse's variegated distribution, it must be reconstructed.[8]

To follow this direction, I switch influences, substituting for Foucault's terms a representation of his work that demonstrates its compatibility with a rhetorical approach to literary and cultural studies. Steven Mailloux offers the terse catalog of "tropes, arguments, and narratives" to name the types of textual evidence he usually cites and examines when composing an account of a particular discursive context that can then be identified as a historical condition of possibility for the effects of all kinds of symbolic action in that context.[9] The pedagogical value of the three keywords derives from how they prompt us to discriminate between kinds of texts and how they stand in for representation writ large. In practice, this list of terms extends to any manner of expression that has a rhetorical situation and admits a hermeneutic response. Mailloux enlivens the historical or cultural contexts he reconstructs by attending to selections of texts that address a common topic typically chosen for its social importance. He then puts into evidence the interplay between particular, even peculiar contributions and those shared ideas and expectations that give his constellation of examples sufficient coherence to be regarded as if they are an unavoidably partial but nevertheless telling record of a "cultural conversation."[10]

In sum, cultural rhetoric studies conducts historical research by reconstructing "conversations" in order to distinguish the normative presentation of dominant social values from qualitatively different examples of texts that, however unruly their engagement with expectations, can also be understood as attempts to coax discussion to recognize, affirm, and enact other values. As I proceed to arrange constellations of tropes, arguments, narratives, and images that played host to the discursive struggle to determine the Red Scare's role in the postwar politics of race, bearing in mind Warner's discrimination between publics and counterpublics will attune us to the way in which the charge of "un-American" typically connoted a marked quality of disorderly embodiment, as if sedition were corporeal. In spite of its ample physical presentation in Cold War anticommunist discourse, the American body politic, if immunized by vigilant anticommunism, was characterized as if it were a domain of abstract, universal reason undisturbed (unmarked) by "particularities of culture, race, gender, or class."[11]

Which Victory? Cold War Civil Rights' Origins

The topic of the Cold War became an unavoidable consideration for the civil rights movement from the moment that anticommunism proved a resource to divert the promises of the "Double V" campaign. Initiated in 1942 by a letter to the editor published in the *Pittsburgh Courier*,[12] publicity for a double victory responded to a popular reluctance among African Americans to serve in World War II. The "Double V" argument answered why African Americans should fight against National Socialism in Europe when the fascism of Jim Crow rule remained pervasive in the United States and the federal government showed every inclination to leave that status quo undisturbed. Following the *Pittsburgh Courier*'s lead, other African American newspapers, civil rights groups, churches, and well-known individuals promoted the idea that the expansion of Hitler's dominion would only further hurt African American prospects. Moreover, it was argued that black American contributions to the war effort would assuredly contribute to popular support and practical organization for a second victory over Jim Crow fascism to follow the defeat of the Axis powers. These claims appear to have been persuasive. Their prominent circulation in key publications and institutions helped cultivate in the black public sphere an ethos of American nationalism in which the civil rights priorities of African Americans were portrayed to be in accordance with US military objectives. "Double V" made it possible for African American participation in the war effort to be impressive even as Jim Crow restrictions continued to organize the US military until 1948, when Truman's Executive Order 9981 finally integrated the armed services.

As a consequence of the character and resolution of World War II, core promises of the Double-V campaign were realized and on a world historical scale. As Howard Winant details in *The World Is a Ghetto*, the defeat of German National Socialism delivered a rebuke to eugenic fictions of a superior race and championed universalist principles of democracy that, after the war, were codified in the establishment of international institutions dedicated to the universal preservation and flourishing of humanity.[13] A new normalcy regarding the unacceptability of racism was emergent in much of the world, a fact marked emphatically by South Africa's controversial status as the exception proving the rule when it elected to establish racial apartheid with ferocity reminiscent of the vanquished Nazis. As the title of Winant's book suggests, his outlook on race and democracy is not unreasonably optimistic; with impressive detail, he demonstrates mainly how institutional and structural racism have been perpetuated globally since the end of WWII. His interest in the persistence of racism, however, is sparked specifically by the fact that the end of the war marked the terminus of the unabashed implementation of white supremacy as the dominant principle of the world's social order. This transformation, which he refers to as "the break," was undeniably profound and salutary.[14] Yet, he finds, it also spurred the continuation and renewal of racism by subtler means.[15] As white supremacy's postwar retreat from preeminence has receded from public memory, it has become increasingly obligatory to formulate and communicate criticisms of racist practices and institutions in the face of triumphalist pronouncements that racism is no longer a significant deterrent to an individual's life prospects, at least not in the overdeveloped countries of the world. This popular attitude of post-racialism is defined, in part, by the conviction that the correlation of race and deprivation must be attributed to *those people* who suffer and not to the predictable consequences of longstanding conditions of inequality and disrepair.

In the context of the United States, the postwar break from white supremacy was made gradually, and it was negotiated through the rapid explosion of Red Scare concerns. The discourse of anticommunism became a medium in which proponents of *de jure* racial segregation and advocates for equal rights for all citizens regardless of race competed over title to American national identity. As Dudziak shows, the civil rights side of this debate won the American imprimatur when desegregation was recognized as a Cold War imperative by the US Supreme Court,[16] but that victory in 1954 came after years of segregationists stigmatizing the civil rights movement with the accusation of being a front for the CPUSA. Those aspersions did not fade away after 1954 in spite of the fact that the initial years of the postwar Red Scare had already been effective in diverting the black left into exile overseas, isolation at home, incarceration, or ceaseless court appearances. For all of the international investment in the viability of humanity as an undifferentiated constituency of concern and self-governance, in the United States it still required twenty-two years after the end of World War II before the Supreme Court's *Loving v. Virginia* decision finally disallowed states from using "miscegenation" statutes to prohibit interracial marriage. As George Frederickson explains, the "popular association of 'forced desegregation' with Communism during the heyday of McCarthyism" was a major reason for the delay.[17]

In the United States, the break from white supremacy by way of the Red Scare involved a compromise in which African Americans secured political rights at the expense of valid claims for social repair. Such compromise is why it generally requires either advanced literacy in the history of the civil rights movement or research to recollect that the demonstration gathered in 1963 for King's "I Have a Dream" speech was officially named the "March on Washington for Jobs and Freedom." National commemorations of the civil rights movement's King years too rarely acknowledge the concrete priority of jobs; nor do they usually advertise the fact that he later had the temerity to argue on national television for a federal guaranteed income policy. Photographs and film of demonstrators at the march holding posters reading "Jobs and Freedom" are an emphatic reminder that the civil rights movement was aimed at two distinct forms of redress: redistribution and recognition. A sound theory of social justice requires both; failing one, fails the other.[18] In the blurrier purview of political culture, the interdependence of political recognition and socioeconomic redistribution is also palpable, but their equal consideration at all times is harder to organize and, in some circumstances, may seem unthinkable. To put it another way, considering Cold War anticommunism's injunctions against the redress of class inequality, the mention of "jobs" in the title of the March on Washington was daring, but it could not sound as loud as "freedom." The postwar Red Scare did gradually lend strength to the civil rights movement's remarkable achievements in the area of recognition; meanwhile, redistribution initiatives were smeared as plots against the American way. As King acknowledged in public statements and showed with his itinerary in the final year of his life, only achieving socioeconomic redistribution through a fundamental transformation of the political economy of the United States would enable the majority of African Americans, indeed the majority of Americans, to experience political recognition in equal measure to its value for that minority of citizens who enjoy disproportionately "the possessive investment in whiteness."[19]

Black Radical Autobiography and the Politics of Knowledge

It is perhaps not possible to pinpoint a first instance in which the second V's imperative to terminate Jim Crow fascism was trumped by national security concern for a second victory over that other totalitarianism, Soviet Communism, but the concerted effort to break the original promise of the Double

"At first we thought the Russians had went an' dropped one on us. You can imagine how relieved we were when we found out it was only the white citizens' Council bombin' our house agin'!"

2. Political cartoon from Ollie Harrington's *Bootsie and Others* (courtesy Helma Harrington)

V campaign became apparent even before the emergence of the Cold War. Rumors circulated by HUAC Chair Martin Dies about CPUSA responsibility for starting the so-called race riots in Detroit in 1943 were an early indication that national security agencies were making ready for Red Scare racism to supersede victory over Jim Crow rule.[20] Soon after the war, abundant publicity either asserted segregation was an inviolate American tradition in a time of national defense or, more liberally, cautioned that equality for African Americans would again have to wait for the resolution of still another more critical emergency. Illustrating US racial politics in the aftermath of *Brown v. Board of Education*, in this cartoon Ollie Harrington uses realistic lines and acerbic wit to record how the Red Scare displacement of the Double V campaign's second promise continued to reverberate in the massive resistance to desegregation that accompanied every step of the civil rights movement after 1954. The single panel comic appears in *Bootsie and Others*, published in 1958 with an introduction by Langston Hughes.[21] The book collected Harrington's work that appeared previously in the *Pittsburgh Courier* and other African American weekly newspapers.

With her house shattered all around her and a young boy, probably a grandson, hugged to her side, the woman receives consolation from a minister. The caption quotes only her explanation: "At first we thought the Russians had went an' dropped one on us. You can imagine how relieved we were when we found out it was only the white citizens' Council bombin' our house agin?" Fixed on this statement of relief, the image does not give us cause to think the minister or the child are incredulous in reaction to the woman's apparently rhetorical question. To sharpen his critique of the state-sanctioned violence of the White Citizens' Councils as well as the Red Scare's diversion from fighting against racism, Harrington plays the situation straight. The woman speaks a sincere relief that the detonation was not an atomic bomb; she appreciates that the Cold War had not gone hot into an end-of-days resolution. The apocalyptic stakes of the nuclear standoff make her sense of scale not entirely irrational, but the remote hazard of total devastation is impertinent against the immediate fact that her home has been targeted for her race, with potentially lethal force, and not for the first time. Harrington's point with the ironic disjunction between her nationalist sentiment and her home's ruin is that the Cold War national security state's constant orientation to the danger of Communists provides cover for the abuse and neglect of African Americans.

This cartoon is especially suggestive for the reconstruction of the discourse of Cold War anticommunism because it puts the normative expectations of the Red Scare into evidence and subjects them to satirical critique at the same time. Harrington mocks an attitude of anxiety that all Americans, for some good reasons, were coached to experience and respect. His irony then lays bare the ways in which international concerns were being used with cynical opportunism to turn back progress on civil rights. Subtler in the illustration are hints of class and gender dynamics. The woman's hat and shoes, the minister's presence, elements of modest interior design, her caretaking of the boy, all suggest a decorum of respectability that is in keeping with the bourgeois normalcy of nuclear family values that was both a regulative ideal and a demographic reality in the 1950s for an unprecedented percentage of Americans.[22] As *A Raisin in the Sun* will show the year after the publication of *Bootsie and Others*, for African Americans in the long 1950s, lower-middle-class striving was harder and more costly even when they were spared the bombings. In Hansberry's play, recall, the happy ending sees four adults holding down jobs in order to pay the mortgage on the Youngers' new home in a majority white suburb. That house was chosen because it was affordable, unlike equivalent properties in predominantly black suburbs. Still, the woman in Harrington's picture considers national interest while surrounded by evidence of her country's disregard.

I admire the bite of Harrington's retort to anticommunism, and his biography recommends his career as a contribution to Cold War black radicalism.[23] But the texts I treat at length in this book are qualitatively different from his comics in an important regard. Across variations in genre and venue, they are autobiographical. In the first chapter, I reconstruct the influence of anticommunist discourse on racial politics by examining a John Birch Society (JBS) billboard campaign that pretended to capture King at a Communist Training School, but I turn eventually to King's well-known Riverside Address: his 1967 confession of opposition to the American War in Vietnam. Chapter 2 extends the consideration of anticommunism outside the domestic United States by discussing the Congress for Cultural Freedom's influential anthology *The God That Failed*, contrasting Richard Wright's contribution to the collection of testimonies with his unpublished personal essay "I Choose Exile." The third chapter takes up C. L. R. James's writings on American literature and popular culture, focusing primarily on *Mariners, Renegades & Castaways: The Story of Herman Melville and the World We Live In*. Written when he was detained on Ellis Island as an "alien subversive," the book concludes with a controversial memoir of his imprisonment. In chapter 4, I return to the topic of Frank Marshall Davis's alleged influence on President Obama. Entertaining Dinesh D'Souza's suggestion, in his film *2016: Obama's America*, that Davis may have tutored a teenage Obama, I examine Davis's weekly newspaper column "Frank-ly Speaking." For eight years starting in 1948, Davis employed his experience as a mainland African American in exile to teach liberals and leftists in Hawaii to recognize that the Red Scare, Jim Crow racism, and corporate attacks on unions were all of a piece with a postwar US imperialism that would ensure decolonization's tragic decline into neocolonialism. To conclude *Red Scare Racism*, I take another pass at the JBS billboard campaign in order to suggest how it set precedent for the persistent use of anticommunist discourse to sustain white privilege and to insinuate erroneously that democracy is reducible to capitalism. An all-too-typical exhibit in the archive of state-sanctioned anti-black racism in the United States, the billboard accusing King of treason is also part of the afterlife of Jim Crow segregation in which Red Scare rhetoric remains a resource for diverting attention away from the fundamental convergence of racism and class exploitation.

Although the Cold War black radicals I consider were conversant in the heritage of African American autobiographical writing and its historic resourcefulness for social protest,[24] my interest refers more specifically to the utility of life writing for their confrontations with the epistemological under-pinnings of anticommunist discourse. Autobiography is, of course, a potent means of self-assertion. For the examples of black radicalism I consider, it was more importantly a means to contend with postwar anticommunism's underlying politics of knowledge, which were complementary to the straight-forward defamation of communist ideas as well as to the Cold War reanima-tion of longstanding narratives of American exceptionalism.

In its most juridical and punishing applications, Cold War anticommu-nism in the long 1950s was a discourse of certitude. It entailed an appeal-ingly simple and popular epistemology for sorting proper Americans from un-American pretenders. Americans were presumed to maintain a plural-ity of commitments that, in a kind of constellation, would together reflect their identities in all of their rich, freedom-loving complexity. For charac-ters identified as un-American, in contrast, all interests were ulterior and relatable to a singular dedication that was, whatever their bearers' expressed intentions, integral to an existential threat to the United States. This discrimi-nation of Americans and un-Americans affiliated the former with a narra-tive of national exceptionalism that entitled the United States to the mantle of Enlightenment progress. Un-Americans were, then, not only defined as a present danger to the immediate interests of the nation-state; they were also cast in opposition to a narrative of modernity's eventual and righteous realization whenever the United States finally prevailed in the Cold War. Pre-sumed to spot Communists and fellow-travellers by telltale signs, including guilty associations, the protocols of detection voiced by anticommunism's chief investigators composed a social fiction of a creeping insurrection pro-pelled by cells of Communists that were potentially anywhere in America. That story was then treated as second nature, which is to say that apprehen-sion of an existential threat interior to the United States was intuitively cor-rect and a brute empirical reality subject to an appraisal of just the facts. In formal tribunals, it was not necessarily easy to sustain this quasi-positivist presumption that un-American character could be known in fact free from any deliberation; most famously, it required Congressmen to shout over and order the removal of unfriendly witnesses who purported to challenge the premise of "un-American" as a restriction of the right to the free expression of communism, which is a considerable idea. Anticommunist discourse represents communism as unthinkable. From its initial discrimination, the discourse of Cold War anticommunism was opposed to rhetoric; once in evidence, the fact of un-American character was indisputable.

For the Marxists I consider, turning to autobiography in defiance of positivist strictures on what counted as knowledge had a further utility. In addition to intervening against the stupefying demarcation of un-American as an ontological difference from other people, life writing was a resource to deal with the positivist problem within the Marxist tradition. The context of its emergence in nineteenth-century European intellectual history involved presumptions of scientific progress that have haunted Marxist discourse ever since with teleological guarantees that admit no doubt and pressure analyses to be selective with evidence that foretells a certain future. Kenneth Burke complained about the positivist intonations hanging over Marxism from the nineteenth century because they were a rhetorical problem with very practical consequences.[25] If it is inevitable that capitalism will be superseded by socialism, before the state then withers away entirely, giving rise to communism, then why have meetings? Burke did not believe that Marx actually proposed a teleology inviting such complacency, but his point was that Marxism's overconfident expressions of eventual victory were a diversion from the hard work of becoming political subjects collaborating to make possible a world not besieged by the barbarism of profitable exploitation or worse.

Recourse to various modes of autobiography served the Cold War black radicalism I examine to meet the presumptuous modernity of anticommunism with a Marxism renovated to avoid comparable arrogance. For Wright, James, and Davis, responding to the Cold War entailed a second round of modifications to Marxist precedent. Prior to and during World War II, they supplemented Marxism with a novel understanding of race as an autonomous category of analysis and political mobilization that was not necessarily secondary to class difference. During the Cold War, through a revisionary rhetoric of temporality that forestalls the teleology of inevitability that was pervasive in doctrinaire Communist Party literature, Wright, James, and Davis again professed that a Marxist critique of capitalism may bring together political economic insight and a regard for racism as a condition of material deprivation on par with the exploitation of class difference. Retaining the moral suasion of necessity that resonates in Marxism's teleological projections, their Cold War representations of what must be were communicated as imperatives rather than inevitabilities. As much as King's Christianity distinguishes him from secular black radicalism, late in his life he also countermanded Cold War anticommunism with an alternative sense of timing. To pronounce the "fierce urgency of now" in the imperative, he had to disrupt the apparent synchronicity between the providential temporality of Christianity and the unyielding sense of progress in narratives of American exceptionalism.

Although these men's critiques of Cold War culture aspire for the universal redress of injustices arising from the historic collusion of capitalism and racism, the texts I consider also represent their typical overvaluation of masculinity. Scholarship on each of them provides ample attention to their unexceptional lapses into sexism, and the contrary example of a contemporary such as Claudia Jones suggests that they may be held responsible for their failures to anticipate a more radical, "intersectional" attention to race, class, sex, and gender.[26] Without attempting to excuse or explain away this masculinist limitation that implicates them in the nuclear family values of Cold War America, my suggestion is that their tendency to accept masculinity as a resource can also be read to indicate their uneasy struggle to formulate and convey a version of political subjectivity in which class and race concerns are equal, inextricable priorities. Optimism about manly capacity appears to have been a means to deflect the insinuation that class and race may become rival standpoints described by tension that disfigures the coherence with which black radicalism knows racism and capitalism to be indivisible.

CHAPTER ONE

Un-American Schooling: Anticommunist Discourse and Martin Luther King Jr.

On the second day of the historic march from Selma to Montgomery, Alabama, 300 civil rights activists, including King, passed the billboard that pretends to capture him at a "Communist Training School." It had been placed directly in their path only a few hours earlier. The oversized public accusation was an insult added to injuries. The demonstrators needed three tries over two weeks to succeed in crossing Pettus Bridge on the edge of Selma, nearly fifty-four miles from their destination. In one of the most notorious episodes in the history of the struggle for civil rights, on March 7, 1965, the "possemen" and deputies of Dallas County Sheriff Jim Clark turned back the first attempt with the "Bloody Sunday" assault on the nonviolent protesters. Already sparked, in part, by the murder near Selma of unarmed activist Jimmie Lee Jackson, this first, failed march would see seventeen more people hospitalized.

Forty-eight hours later, King had arrived to lead a second effort. With many of the 2,500 demonstrators unaware of the plan, the group advanced to the bridge, knelt for prayer, and then returned to Selma to await a court's judgment on a petition for authority to conduct the march. Miscommunication and strategic differences about the decision to stop short this second try exacerbated rifts between King's Southern Christian Leadership Conference (SCLC) and the Student Non-Violent Coordinating Committee (SNCC). And, on the night of this second effort, defenders of Jim Crow segregation beat another activist to the ground, this time the white minister James Reeb who died in a hospital from his injuries two days later. With legal approval, on March 21 a group finally proceeded across the bridge and away from Selma.[1] Four days later, as many as 25,000 supporters joined the demonstration at the steps of the state capitol in Montgomery. Prior to these now legendary days of violence and public exposure, months of effort in Selma to register African Americans to vote had already been costly. Thousands of arrests and incidents of jailhouse torture had been endured by activists with only modest gains locally, but the harrowing optics of nonviolent protesters under assault by the police force and mobs of angry white citizens would prove a turning point across the United States for support of civil rights.[2]

In the context of the furious and punishing reaction against the black freedom struggle in Selma, the sudden appearance of this billboard on the morning of March 22 must have seemed to the demonstrators simultaneously predictable and surreal. Its all-too-familiar charge repeats the reactionary strategy of referring to the civil rights movement and the Communist Party as if they were one and the same in order to suggest that black American protest is actually un-American sedition and, conversely, that support for the traditions of the segregated South is an expression of American patriotism.[3] Taking its smear campaign to the streets in time to impugn federal legislation that would become the Voting Rights Act, the John Birch Society sponsored more than two hundred of the displays across the South.[4] The sign insinuates that the recent sacrifices and persistent risks suffered by the civil rights movement were unnecessary theatrics engineered by the CPUSA and its handlers in the Kremlin to stir up racial antagonisms that would undermine the stability of everyday life in the United States, opening the country to ruin or even a takeover by the USSR. Such suspicion must have seemed a fantastic alibi for the naked, visceral racism with which activists were confronted during the voter registration initiatives in Selma and surrounding areas.

Those on the march must also have regarded the sign's threatening message as tired. The photograph had already been in circulation in similar if smaller publications for eight years, and it had been even more years since the CPUSA possessed any significant political influence in the United States, especially in the states of the Solid South.[5] In countless public appearances, writings, and interviews King had rejected the charges that Communists were directing the movement for civil rights or that he espoused Communism. Less than a year earlier, he spoke in some detail on the television program *Face the Nation* about his objections to the Communist attitude on politics. He went on to criticize FBI Director J. Edgar Hoover by name for allowing his agency to "aid and abet the racists" with conjecture about un-American influence in the campaign for civil rights. A few days after completing the walk to Montgomery, he would appear on the rival show *Meet the Press* only to be obliged to answer all of the same old questions about the infiltration of Communists into his organization.[6] Nothing the ordained Christian minister said could deter opponents to civil rights who were determined to use his stature as a means to characterize the entire anti-racist political struggle in the United States as an incursion engendered by an enemy.[7] No matter its actual disposition, black political agency was painted Red by those who mistook the Cold War emergency as an opportunity to translate Southern support for segregation into a security concern the entire nation ought to share.

In this chapter, I take up the JBS billboard campaign to exemplify the discourse of anticommunism as it bears on the black freedom struggle in the United States during the early years of the Cold War. Rehearsing the history of the sign with particular attention to its intertextual composition, I provide an account of how Red Scare rhetoric was employed in support of the massive resistance to civil rights. King's numerous responses to the charge of Communist and his own appropriation of Cold War insecurities show, however, that anticommunist discourse was ultimately more compelling for the cause of desegregation than for unabashed white supremacy, a point I demonstrate with a discussion of the address King delivered over Labor Day weekend in 1957 to commemorate the twenty-fifth anniversary of the Highlander Folk School in Tennessee.[8] That celebration is the occasion the billboard alleges is a class for Communists.

Although my account of King's anticommunist rhetoric indicates he was able to exploit the same national security anxieties that animate the JBS billboard against him, I also show success harnessing anticommunism for the sake of civil rights came at a price for black freedom struggles in the United States during the long decade of the 1950s. Inviting talk of legal reforms that could encourage an international audience to affiliate the United States with the expansion of democratic franchise across racial divisions, Cold War anticommunism also removed from public culture reasonable deliberation over radical social change, especially in regard to demands justified by criticism of how disparities endemic to capitalism secure the correlation between socioeconomic stratification and racial identities. As King discovered for himself when he became an outspoken opponent of US military actions in Vietnam and went so far as to link capitalism to racism globally, Cold War anticommunism was a potent rhetorical resource for the exercise of agency on behalf of desegregation provided aspirations for equal rights did not entail an appraisal of how the official policy of anti-racism touted by the US Department of State obscured the ways postwar US imperialism was perpetuating the value of whiteness in the geopolitical order.[9] Any such rebuke to the normative stories of Cold War America was met with the immediate reprisal of association with the appealingly reductive moniker un-American, a characterization that rendered illegible the particular content and merit of the critique. For example, from within the confines of US public culture the conviction of black radicalism that the US attitude toward the Cold War would likely result in the failure of decolonization and the emergence of neocolonialism in its stead would not just go unheeded; it would remain unheard. My interest in juxtaposing King's talk at Highlander and his anti-war Riverside speech a decade later is to suggest how the early speech participates in a massive social pedagogy of Cold War anticommunism that in the long 1950s prepared public culture to accept with certainty a tendentious body of knowledge about communism, the Cold War, American national identity, the civil rights movement, and Western modernity as a history of emancipation. This popular "curriculum" of anticommunism meant the public was unready a decade later to acknowledge the merits of King's revisionist characterizations of capitalism, neocolonialism, postwar US imperialism, the black freedom struggle, and Western modernity as a history of racialization. King's delivery at Riverside was, in a word, uneasy.

An additional objective of this chapter is to elaborate on the practice of cultural rhetoric studies within my home discipline of literature. To this end, I am concerned with how a strong claim that rhetoric is epistemic informs an examination of normative discursive formations through the interpretation of particular features of language that are conventionally privileged by literary studies: figurative language and narrative. More specifically, I demonstrate how the JBS billboard campaign and related texts, including the two speeches by King, invite and reward an interpretation that negotiates between an emphasis on the rhetorical power of popular tropes and a focus on the pervasive influence of cultural narratives.[10] Reconstructing the cultural conversation of Cold War anticommunism, I suggest how the proliferation of Red Scare rhetoric in US public culture during the long 1950s was a pedagogy, in and out of schools, to make citizens expert in a social fiction of the Cold War: a narrative of sufficient normative force to train public culture to neglect, discount, or assimilate rival accounts of social reality.

Popular Tropes and Cultural Narratives: Red Scare Intertextuality

The design of the JBS billboard suggests that its photograph is definitive corroboration of well-circulated suspicions that King and the movement he represents take orders from outside America. Although his presence in the image is unmistakable, the arrow pointed at his torso emphasizes his prominent position in an iconic scene of instruction. Attentive postures and the papers on King's lap encourage this schooling inference. The all-capitals headline above the image has a matter-of-fact pretense that does not name Highlander nor acknowledge that the charge of Communist never amounted to more than a pejorative metaphor for the liberal school. Several nonverbal features of the composition carry further connotations of popular beliefs about the Communist Party. The cropping low above the heads of the assembly implies an atmosphere of secrecy, and the omission of any information indicating the time and place of the proceedings adds the impression that such training could take place nearby or as far away as Cuba, the Soviet Union, or Brooklyn. Just outside the left frame, an invisible authority figure commands attention; what un-American plans might have issued from such a source before they became famous names for social protest: the Montgomery bus boycott, the march on Washington, Freedom Summer? Counting on King's famous identity to serve as synecdoche for the whole, ongoing story of racial agitation fomented between the civil rights movement and the massive white supremacist resistance to it, the JBS display invites observers to consider how images of racial strife they were likely to have seen in newspapers and on television (if not in person) should be perceived as incidents of the Cold War. To see deeply into the conflict over racial equality, the sign suggests, is to recognize that the antagonism between black and white Americans is actually a proxy for the conflict between Red insurrectionists and free patriots marshaled in support of the American way.

The image of an illicit school to prepare the civil rights movement for Communist objectives suggests that American values are secretly anathema to King and others in the picture who must have dispersed after the gathering to infiltrate the lives of unwitting ordinary citizens. That impression cautions credulous observers to be vigilant about aliens in their midst, and the composition of the classroom with its crowded, interracial mix of men and women seated in close quarters implies that the Communists have also been recruiting. Apparently, the foreign presence is familiar enough to convert citizens to its cause. And for all the individual distinction on display in the diverse assembly, the headline emphasizes symbolically that a single, barely discernible attribute binds together everyone in the picture. I say *barely* discernible because, though being a Communist did not correspond to racial or ethnic identities that are typically associated to some extent with appearance, anticommunist propaganda from agencies such as HUAC, popular films and television, school curricula, as well as mainstream journalism in the first years of the Cold War reported on how to tell if a person is a Communist—how to read the signs. Involvement in racial causes and, more damaging, interracial personal relationships were high on the profile of characteristics inviting suspicion that a person is loyal to Communist interests and actively un-American.[11] With its strategic paucity of verbal detail, the billboard gives no indication that the only person pictured who was known to be a member of the CPUSA is Abner Berry. Seated in the left foreground with his head down over his notes, Berry covered the Highlander Folk School anniversary weekend for the *Daily Worker*. He was one of two journalists who had asked permission to be present for the event, though he did not acknowledge to Highlander's director Myles Horton that he was a party member.[12] The other journalist took the picture, but he was only pretending to be a freelance documentary filmmaker and photographer. In fact, he was working for the Georgia Commission on Education under the direction of Governor Marvin Griffin, who sought to interfere with the implementation of school desegregation by incriminating institutions and people involved in the advance of civil rights. Another telling omission in the billboard's intelligent design is any mention of Rosa Parks, who appears in the front row four seats to King's right. By 1965 her legendary reputation for refusing to surrender her seat at the end of an exhausting workday did not lend itself readily to an accusation of un-American values. Failing to indicate Parks in the crowded room, the sign does the symbolic work of distracting us from recognizing the presence of an iconic figure whose famous refusal to observe a racist law and relinquish her seat on a Montgomery bus was bound up in seemingly apolitical ideas of a respectable woman's personal frustration dignified by the fatigue of a hard day's work. Among segregationists, King's vocation as a minister afforded him no comparable respect. White supremacists in the Jim Crow South also claimed the Bible to sanctify their cause.

The visual and verbal rhetoric indicating, on the one hand, that King and other Communists are studiously un-American and, on the other, that the party holds a dangerous appeal for other Americans, follows the tendency in postwar Red Scare rhetoric to depoliticize the ideas of communism by rendering them alien and yet to task citizens with adopting an anticommunist sensibility that is ever mindful of the risk of unwittingly lapsing into un-American attitudes. The supposed reward of vigilance is to discern in the signs of communism how its desire for social control emanates not from reasoned convictions but from indeterminate, unholy compulsions. This argument against communism as a vicious, unthinking predilection was instrumental for the broader consequence of discrediting all manner of leftist and many liberal ideas for being not political thought but instead aberrant feelings, destructive impulses, or even expressions of monstrosity. Impugning even unwitting resemblance to communism as un-American, anticommunist discourse limited legitimate political ideas to the presupposed "values of the free market, private property, and the autonomous individual."[13] Christianity was also a fairly constant point of distinction from godless communism. Communist critiques of the capitalist tenets of the free market and possessive individualism only helped elevate these ideas beyond reproach, which in circular turn made any kind of complaint about them enough like communism to warrant rebuke.

Countless documents from the early years of the Cold War that advise US government agencies or the general public about the dangers of Soviet Communism in America are rife with tropes for the illicit nature of Communists' motivations. Attention to such figures has become a staple of American Studies scholarship that examines how the culture of Cold War anticommunism textualized social life in the postwar United States, giving it the impression of a secret population of foreign insurrectionists living in the guise of citizens who beneath their studiously ordinary appearances were apoplectic with un-American seething.[14] Accounts of various pejorative metaphors teach how Communists and unrepentant former Communists were made to appear substantially "other" than ordinary Americans and how the lexicon to describe their differences was also put to work as a rubric to identify Communists and fellow travelers hiding amidst unsuspecting Americans. This Cold War epistemology predicated on the simple identification of Communists and non-Communists receives its most famous, perhaps satirical depiction in the film *Invasion of the Body Snatchers*. The alien "pod people" seem identical to ordinary US citizens unless you can get them talking about the deficiencies of human emotion, the hazards of individualism, the efficiencies of parasitism, and the pleasures of monotonous, hive-minded uniformity. The acute individualism of the film's protagonist alerts him that imposters have supplanted the good people of his small town. In the actual storyworld of the Cold War United States, various volunteer, commercial, and government institutions guided US citizens to employ tropes as a measure for signs of Communist intent and the sympathy of their fellow travellers.

The allegorical rendering of the Red Scare in the popular genre of a science fiction film about alien life forms arrived to colonize Earth and take bodily possession of all its inhabitants assuredly exaggerates the plot of the Cold War to sensational effect, but the characterization of the mentality of alien enemies compulsively enacting the requirements of their form of life resonates with the hyperbole of statements on Communists by government officials and elite political pundits who were instrumental in both the domestic investigations of un-American activities and the US foreign policy of containment. The public service film *What Is Communism?* from 1963 is a typical example.[15] It asserts that Communists are a "lying, dirty, shrewd, godless, murderous, determined, international criminal conspiracy." Host Herbert Philbrick guides viewers through a succession of lessons for each of the key terms. Under "dirty," he credits Communists for a "communist-incited race riot," which is a reference to a myth, publicized by both the FBI and HUAC Chair Martin Dies, that the

Communist Party had instigated the so-called 1943 race riot in Detroit. Philbrick became a television and film personality after an FBI career in which he worked undercover as a member of the CPUSA. He reported his experiences in the best-selling memoir *I Led Three Lives* (1952), which was adapted for a television series. The show debuted in 1953 and ran for three years. Philbrick's career in law enforcement, television, and film is representative of the cooperation between government and commercial agencies to produce a popular body of knowledge about communism. In association with McCarthyism, such anticommunist initiatives are usually characterized as fearmongering; my emphasis in this section is instead on how they aimed to instill in citizens a duty and a means to become expert in the identification of this fictive, inhuman character the un-American.

Pathological tropes for the subjectivity of Communists and their sympathizers were the common property of a Cold War anticommunist consensus in the United States. Despite their protestations of difference and even animosity toward each other, conservatives and liberals collaborated in their use of a shared vocabulary to identify Communists and fellow travelers as a foreign insurgency at odds with American values. In testimony before HUAC in 1947, FBI Director J. Edgar Hoover instructed the Representatives to observe an ontological difference between a vigilant US citizenry and the Communists hidden within the nation: "Victory will be assured once communists are identified and exposed, because the public will take the first step of quarantining them so that they can do no harm. Communism, in reality, is not a political party. It is a way of life—an evil and malignant way of life. It reveals a condition akin to disease that spreads like an epidemic and like an epidemic a quarantine is necessary to keep it from infecting the Nation."[16] Hoover seasons his epidemiological figures with a hint of metaphysics. The contagion he describes is not just malignant; it is also evil. But the rhetorical power of his testimony really stems from what his maneuvers with figurative language mean for the importance and authority of his offices against the Communists and the ideas of communism. Hoover is able to delineate a manageable danger and, at the same time, describe it as unlimited. "Communist" identifies a subject of such different character from an American that he or she must be set apart as a dangerous foreign agent. For Hoover and within the discourse of Cold War anticommunism more generally, "American Communist" was an oxymoron. Yet, the appellation "un-American" hints at the closeness between Americans and Communists. With each carrier of communism standing in for a virtually limitless whole, the FBI had a perpetual excuse for the exercise of extraordinary authority. The identification of a single Communist serves in such thinking as evidence of a palpable condition that must be pursued without reserve indefinitely. The entirety of the disease cannot be arrested because each infected subject signifies a whole that can only ever be present in parts.

With each presentation of communism signaling the extension of communism elsewhere, Hoover's confident reference to a sure public victory obscures that his trope of disease secures his rationale for a permanent state of emergency. And yet, his insistence that communism is a way of life that is presumably incomparable to the common sense of the American public implies that once afflicted, the citizen-become-communist is substantively something other than what she was. Once identified in this other sense, the Communist can be contained. With magical thinking that defies the principle of non-contradiction, Hoover draws at once on these alternative valences for communism. It is a contagion that moves through a populace of unsuspecting citizens who might each become identified, in part, with the disease; each person implicated is expected to signify the danger not only of communism's nefarious designs against the United States but also of its potential appeal to unsuspecting Americans. At the same time, to name someone as a Communist is to identify her as a different kind of subject with a distinct state of being from any non-communist. The contiguity that comes from partial associations is somehow also tantamount to the wholesale substitution of character such that ordinary but vigilant, wakeful Americans will be able to identify and expose converts to un-Americanism for their incomparable difference. In *Body Snatchers*, the alien invaders take possession of people only when they sleep.

Famously regarded as a foundational document for the US foreign policy of containment, State Department official George Kennan's "Moscow Embassy Telegram #511: The Long Telegram" also manifests what Andrew Ross has called anticommunist "germaphobia."[17] In contrast to Hoover, the liberal Kennan imagines containing the risk of contagion through immunization rather than quarantine: "Much depends on health and vigor of our own society. World communism is like [a] malignant parasite which feeds only on diseased tissue. This is [the] point at which domestic and foreign policies meet. Every courageous and incisive measure to solve internal problems of our own society, to improve self-confidence, discipline, morale and community spirit of our own people, is a diplomatic victory over Moscow worth a thousand diplomatic notes & joint communiqués."[18] A number of scholars have discussed how Kennan's argument is illustrative of the strategic connection between the foreign policy of containment and a less coordinated but nonetheless robust domestic cultural program to enlist everyday habits in the Cold War.[19] Different from the volunteer commitments during World War

II such as managing petroleum rations, selling war bonds, or coordinating local air raid drills, the civic commitments of the Cold War entailed attitudes, behaviors, and moods that permitted no discrete measure other than constancy. The powerful positive thinking about local and national identity Kennan describes is implicitly more than just valuable diplomatic work. It invites consideration as a rubric for the exposure of un-American wavering on the part of those citizens whose apparent lack of spirit opens a community to the catching condition and existential threat of communism.

Whatever the personal, professional, and theatrical disagreements between leading conservatives and the most notable Cold War liberals, their common aspersions for communist subjectivity coalesced into the popular epistemology that identifies the signs of leftist convictions to be indications not of political disagreement but of pathological deficiencies. When Hoover warned the 1960 Republican National Convention that the greatest dangers confronting the United States are "Commies, Beatniks, and Eggheads,"[20] the third term of his un-American axis undoubtedly referred, among others, to Arthur Schlesinger Jr. The Pulitzer Prize–winning historian and Presidential advisor cited Hoover's and McCarthy's animus toward him as evidence of the flaw in criticisms that regard his political writings and activities in the late 1940s to have accommodated the Cold War–era assaults on civil liberties.[21] Seemingly more sympathetic than the martial Hoover, Schlesinger's work is nevertheless reflective of how Cold War anticommunism disqualified from political consideration the sundry motivations that could have propelled a US citizen to be or to have been a member of the CPUSA. Like other Cold War anticommunists across the narrowing ideological spectrum between the two main political parties in the United States, Schlesinger disregarded heedlessly how being a member of the Communist Party in the United States prior to the 1940s was often met with opposition but did not necessarily carry a criminal stigma. Diverging from Hoover and Kennan's tropes of malevolent physical disease, he identified communism in the United States as a psychological problem. In a purported exposé of "The US Communist Party" in a 1946 issue of *Life* magazine, Schlesinger debuts the character profile of the typical American Communist that he would repeat three years later in his most influential prescription for Cold War liberalism, *The Vital Center*:

> Party discipline is not, for the most part, a matter of making people do things they do not want to do. The great majority of members, for reasons best understood by psychiatrists and dictators, *want* to be disciplined. The party fills the lives of lonely and frustrated people, providing them with social, intellectual, even sexual fulfillment they cannot obtain in existing society. It gives a sense of

comradeship in a cause guaranteed by history to succor the helpless and to triumph over the wealthy and satisfied. To some it gives opportunities for personal
power not to be found elsewhere. Communists are happy to exchange their rights
as individuals for these deeper satisfactions; and absorption in the party becomes
in time the mainspring of their lives. The appeal is eventually the appeal of a religious sect—small, persecuted, stubbornly convinced that it alone knows the path
to salvation.[22]

Schlesinger presumes to expose for the readers of *Life* that Communists are
possessed of an aberrant psychology that drives them to surrender their liberty in order to be defined by a narrow set of top-down directives that restrict
their identities to their utility for the nefarious designs of the party. Although
he adopts a moderate posture in the article by faulting Representatives Martin
Dies and John Rankin for distorting the actual danger of the party through
"their wild confidence that practically everybody who opposes Franco or Jim
Crow or the un-American committee is a Red," like the anticommunists to his
right politically he denies that a US citizen could be or have been a member
of the Communist Party for good reasons.[23] In Schlesinger's America, only the
lonely become Communists or fellow travellers. The condescending tenor of
his reasoning is that in the United States the term Communist stands in for
social alienation. When he turns briefly to the topic of race, Schlesinger's economy of representation is more akin to Hoover and Kennan's concerns about
contagion. He depicts the Communists "sinking tentacles" into the NAACP;
the appendages are a metonym for the unmentioned octopus that substitutes
for the party. Schlesinger's singling out the NAACP in such a prominent
magazine no doubt contributed to the urgency with which the organization
purged leftists from its membership and distanced itself from its legendary
leftist founder, W. E. B. Du Bois, who was affiliated with groups that would be
named to the US Attorney General's List of Subversive Organizations.

In the long passage on the social frailty of American Communists, the psychological figure omits the contagious implications of Hoover's and Kennan's
diseased figures. However, in an explanation of how Schlesinger's purported
critique of the CPUSA amounts to a gendered and sexualized characterization
of any left-of-center political stance, Robert Corber observes that in *The Vital
Center* the esteemed historian resorts to homophobia to explain how the Communist Party satisfies social needs.[24] With an allusion that bespeaks his cultivated taste and elite education, Schlesinger compares illicit meetings between
Communists and their prospective members to a famous scene in Proust in
which two male characters "suddenly recognize their common corruption."[25]
Communists, he suggests, identify each other in the same way he supposes

homosexual men make contact with each other for sex: they cruise disreputable locales for those glimmers of recognition that invite illicit congress. This figure of Communist recruiting might suggest to us that Schlesinger, though spurning homosexuality, does not discern communism to be an alien, contagious threat to the existence of the United States. The confidence in the legacy of the New Deal he professes in *The Vital Center* does imply his optimism that US discipline and morality already inoculate the citizenry against it. For his original audience, however, the trope of queer cruising did indicate a health concern; in 1949 and for decades after, homosexuality was represented and policed in the United States as a danger to moral standards and public hygiene. Common fears said that homosexuality also was catching. In the context of the postwar "lavender scare,"[26] Schlesinger's psychological tropes are as illiberal as those of Hoover and Kennan. His homophobic figuration of an antisocial, queer personality also implies a dynamic in which each individual is part of the whole spreading social condition of communism.

The point of my catalog of anticommunist tropes is not that US citizens were necessarily unable or unwilling to distinguish between the literal and figurative dimensions of these common representations of communism. However, the tenor of these virulent figures is that a belief in communism, no matter the explanation an individual might offer for her commitment, was to be understood as outside all reasonable assertions of political conviction. The Cold War is often referred to as a conflict of ideologies; however, the anticommunist epistemology represented here by Hoover's, Kennan's, and Schlesinger's figurative language denies that Communists possess political reason. In unsubtle moves that invite a most basic ideology critique, anticommunist figures of disease and dysfunction obscure and mystify that un-American ideas, so called, can be a response to material conditions of political and social life rather than an expression of inhuman being. The JBS billboard accords with this obfuscation. The sign suggests anti-racism too is merely a superficial complaint voiced noisily by African Americans whose real significance is as un-American proxies for Communist agents attempting to escape notice. While singling out King personally, it nullifies his distinction by indicating that he is being rendered foreign. The incorporation of Communist training will make him like the carrier of a communicable disease: just one part of an assemblage with no determinable end.

Through its resonance with popular tropes for Communist subjectivity, which in US public culture have affixed most perniciously to subjects whose American citizenship and human ontology lack the supplement of whiteness, the JBS campaign urges the sign's sympathetic observers to see in the photograph indisputable ocular proof. For all its figurative appeal, the billboard is emphatically literal. The caption, despite its lie, reads as if it were a mere description across the top of an image that ostensibly requires no further explanation or interpretation. Cold War anticommunism's findings are self-evident. A look at King in the "Communist Training School" is sufficient to know without being told that his purpose is unmistakable and his intent obvious: the revolutionary overthrow of the United States on behalf of the USSR. Appreciating that message may require an advanced public curriculum in anticommunist doctrine, but the billboard's minimal design and multiple roadside locations also imply that such preparation is simply the cultivation of American national character for which insinuations about any Communist's moral and mental deficiencies are a matter of fact from the first determination of that un-American identity.

These features of the billboard that correspond to the anticommunist tropology that paints Communist subjectivity utterly alien and dangerously contagious are all the more effective for how the display relates them to prominent Red Scare cultural narratives. By itself, the billboard already tells a story. My description above of the appearance of an interracial classroom of adults in un-American collusion identifies an event pregnant with suggestions of what might ensue after the group adjourns. I have also suggested that the sign banks on King's iconic appearance in order to pose as a visual narrative of the civil rights movement's primal scene. The outbreak of public demonstrations of racial discontent over the preceding several years originated, the sign implies, with Communist dictation to a crowded assembly that would soon populate the public spaces, newspaper reports, and television images of the American South. In combination with the figurative characterizations of what drives Communists, the suggestion of a previously undisclosed story about the foreign origins of the civil rights movement could be taken as corroboration for cultural narratives circulating in the long 1950s about the CPUSA and the Cold War: namely, the narratives of Party secrecy, black belt insurrection, and containment.

The CPUSA's decision to go underground after the US Supreme Court in 1951 upheld the Smith Act convictions of several Party leaders added a true narrative of the organization in flight that corroborated longstanding accusations that the Party was nothing more than a vehicle for a vast, secret international criminal conspiracy directed by the Kremlin. According to the story, a favorite of Hoover's, every Communist is a spy against the United States. The prominence of just such a characterization prior to the Smith Act prosecutions helped motivate the decision of the CPUSA's Central Committee, which feared that the judgments against the defendants would spur the FBI to sweeping arrests of every Party member it could locate. Hinted at in

the secrecy of the proceedings in the photograph, the decision to go underground was, Schrecker argues, in hindsight a strategic blunder.[27] The disappearance of open Communists from public life and the ritual invocation of
the Fifth Amendment before HUAC and McCarthy's Senate committee would
lend credence to suspicions about the Party's intentions. With the CPUSA
underground, anticommunist institutions could represent more effectively
the Party's history in the United States as a legacy of sedition rather than
the complicated, uneven record of, yes, espionage, but also an impassioned
involvement in the fight against racial segregation in the 1930s and 1940s.

A second cultural narrative that had special resonance in the American South was the story that cast black Communists as "dupes" to the violent intentions of the USSR, which are suggested by the Party doctrine of
the "black belt thesis." Sanctioned as an official position of the Comintern in
1928 and only abandoned officially by the CPUSA in 1959, the thesis claims
that African Americans in the United States have two distinct classifications
based on geography. Throughout most of the United States, the argument
went, African Americans were a persecuted minority population with US
citizenship. But in those contiguous counties across the American South in
which African Americans constituted a majority population, they were not
a national minority but instead an independent nation under occupation by
a colonizing foreign power. Outside the CPUSA, this idea never met with
popular approval among Americans. The confusion surrounding the idea of
an African colony to be liberated from within the United States was useful for
anticommunists intent on characterizing black Communists as dupes to an
agenda that only the USSR could propose, and through which Stalin's regime
intended not black liberation but destructive tumult. Insofar as the JBS billboard can be read to resemble a planning session for Communist designs on
the life of African Americans in the United States, it invites a viewer who is
content more or less with how conditions are in America to imagine a violent insurrection emanating from those counties in which African Americans
outnumber the other residents.

Related to this fear that African Americans are a potential "Trojan horse"
for the interests of the USSR in the United States,[28] the most prominent cultural narrative alluded to by the JBS billboard campaign is what scholars of
US Cold War culture call the containment narrative. Defined by nationalist customs that were analogous to the US foreign policy announced by
the 1947 Truman Doctrine, containment culture encouraged attitudes of
uniform national solidarity premised on the idea that unquestioning support for traditional family values, Christian principles, and entrepreneurial
capitalism would guard the US body politic against Communist invasions or

insurrections. In *Containment Culture*, Alan Nadel is careful to distinguish his argument from an older tendency of scholarship on the Cold War that identifies the years of the Eisenhower administration with a culture of uneventful, strait-laced conformity. Nadel claims the measure of the containment narrative's importance was not the citizenry's ubiquitous assent to its premises but instead a pervasive obligation in US public culture to address the story one way or another—and with the apprehension that articulating dissent against the narrative's normative demands would entail risk. He writes, "In this regard the American cold war is a particularly useful example of the power of large cultural narratives to unify, codify, and contain—perhaps *intimidate* is the best word—the personal narratives of its population."[29] The JBS billboard is an instance of the containment narrative because as an exposé of illicit activity it affirms what containment culture ensured people in the United States learned most often about the Cold War: it is a Manichean geopolitical conflict between the capitalist West led by the United States and the communist East led by the USSR. Narratives orienting citizens to the disposition of containment typically rehearse an account of the exceptionalism of US national character while at the same time remarking on the danger represented by the surreptitious activities of Communists hiding in the midst of ordinary US citizens. We have already seen this stance in anticommunism's popular tropes. In addition to coaching anticommunist habits of exercising American national character by identifying un-American traits in others, containment narratives cast ordinary citizens as active players whose mundane behaviors play an important role in an ongoing drama for the fate of the world. The hyperbole about the imminent danger at all times from undercover agents nearby and, after 1949, atomic weaponry from afar, meant that, for example, routine attendance at church on Sundays carried national security significance. While segregationists tried to command this habit of thinking about the heightened significance of ordinary but constant support for a Cold War America, civil rights activists used similar reasoning to represent their ongoing efforts to bring about the end of Jim Crow rule as a saving grace for America in the Cold War.

Timing King's Cold War

The JBS billboard targets King with hostility, but he was also a suitable audience for some of its premises. As the sign endeavors to portray him as a traitor in the midst of America, it proposes that patriotism in the context of the Cold War requires decisive anticommunism. Over much of his career, King did more than receive that message. He enacted the idea that, in the context of the Cold War, American national identity entails concern for the potentially hazardous effects of communism on the United States and the rest of the world.[30] The billboard may deny that he personally could be a part of the Cold War efforts of the United States, but for all its resonance with massive resistance to civil rights, it does not go so far as to insist that only white Americans can pitch in against the Reds. The sign traffics in the association of blackness with being un-American, but it does not argue explicitly that race determines national identity. Such an assertion would have failed to utilize how Cold War anticommunism could facilitate racist laws and customs under the guise of ideas about national security that ostensibly enjoyed general appeal and did not deal in particular with race. Again, it was through this Red Scare diversion from racism that segregationists in the American South attempted during the early Cold War to turn the regional difference of *de jure* segregation into a worry for all Americans. Assuredly, the ideal segregationist observer of the billboard is expected to accept the conceit that interracial relations and a dedication to civil rights implies either Communist Party activities or an as yet untapped propensity for communism.[31] Yet, the sign does not preclude a partial identification that is less decisive about King but nonetheless primed to anxiety about covert foreign influences that undermine the stability of the American way of life. The basic invitation of the billboard is, then, for its viewers to strive toward American identity by adopting a properly oppositional disposition toward the USSR, its secret agents in America, and anyone with a sensibility un-American enough to disagree with the idea that democratic capitalism is at worst the least bad option for a just society. A witness to the sign in 1965 could reject the assertion that Communists trained King and still accept the following warrant for its claims: Soviet Communism is an existential threat to the United States assisted inside its borders by the activities of un-American citizens who conspire against their government. Absent the billboard's forbidding tone, King's Highlander address in 1957 includes a comparable subtext, though his apprehension about how Americans are aiding the wrong side in the Cold War refers to those who seek to conserve Jim Crow segregation and deny African American humanity. Either case is an example of the popular adjudication of civil rights in a cultural conversation about Cold War anticommunism in which influence hinges on the most effective use of the Red Scare epistemology that reduces heterogeneous political values to a blunt and certain discrimination between un-American interests and an innate appreciation for human freedom.

Delivering the keynote address for the final session of the conference to commemorate Highlander's first twenty-five years, King explains that the civil rights movement is essential to the integrity of democratic principles in the United States and to the country's standing before the world in relation to its pronouncements that Truman's containment doctrine defends human freedom against the advance of authoritarian communism. King's talk is representative of how for much of his career he invoked the Cold War to underscore the urgency of civil rights for all US citizens and to emphasize that the expansion of democratic franchise to nonwhite citizens was consistent with tenets of American exceptionalism that were thought to distinguish the United States absolutely from totalitarian regimes. The speech is also a typical example of how his sermons, speeches, and writings communicate his social vision by combining conceits of American exceptionalism with elements of classic liberalism, Christian liberation theology, a philosophy of nonviolence, the tradition of the African American sermon, and the particular history of anti-black racism in the United States. The Highlander talk recounts progress toward integration hard-won through federal legislation and judicial decisions that seem to vindicate American democracy through the expansion of franchise. Then it locates that struggle within a prophetic representation of the moral trajectory of a universal history.

Speaking just over a year after the success of the Montgomery bus boycott and three weeks before President Eisenhower will order federal troops to enforce the integration of Central High School in Little Rock, Arkansas, King introduces the topic he was asked to cover—"The Look to the Future"—with a lesson on the history of race in the United States. "Over the long sweep of race relations in America," he says, there has been an "evolutionary growth."[32] He breaks down this history into three major phases, "each representing growth over the former period." The first, the long epoch of slavery, runs from the arrival of nineteen captive Africans in Jamestown, Virginia, in 1619 until the Emancipation Proclamation in 1863. The ensuing period of segregation extends from 1863 to 1954, when began the present period of integration. Overstating the continuity of progress by glossing over the failure of Reconstruction in 1877 and the resulting regression of civic standing for African Americans, King betrays his optimism. He expresses his confidence about overcoming racism more overtly in his conclusion when he calls on his audience to "go out and work with renewed vigor to make the unfolding work of destiny a reality in our generation."[33] More precision about instances of lost progress would be out of synch with an historical overview that prepares his contention that everyday struggles toward civil rights can realize in the near future what cannot fail to take place later or sooner.

King punctuates his survey of slavery, segregation, and integration with observations about how the US Supreme Court gave legal validity to the dominant cultural tendencies in race relations for each era. Coming late in the period of slavery, the *Dred Scott* decision in 1857 ruled African Americans, free or slave, to be other than human but for electoral procedures as valuable as 3/5 of a white citizen. *Plessy v. Ferguson* in 1896 sanctioned the "separate but equal" fiction of Jim Crow segregation. The 1954 *Brown v. Board of Education* decision signifies the emergence of integration. He summarizes the three-phase history succinctly in Biblical terms: "We have broken loose from the Egypt of slavery. We have moved through the wilderness of 'separate but equal,' and now we stand on the *border* of the promised land of integration."[34] Wedding a history of struggle for African American citizenship to the Biblical narrative of Moses leading the Chosen People out of bondage, King sacralizes US history and American national identity, giving progress toward integration two orders of inevitability: the evolutionary development of human betterment and the deliverance to come from God's Providence.[35]

Having formulated the history of black and white race relations in the United States in terms of these progressive and perfect temporalities, respectively, King situates the massive resistance to civil rights in an untenable position. Fighting against civil rights impossibly, he reports, are the revitalized Ku Klux Klan and the new White Citizens' Councils. To inform his audience about the challenges before the black freedom struggle in the immediate future, King explains that these racist groups' new division of responsibilities is an advance of strategy over the defense of segregation in prior decades.[36] It may also signify white supremacists' desperation. With the working-class Klan providing direct violence against African Americans and the more affluent Councils complementing those efforts with both a gentlemanly disavowal of uncivil violence and an abusive manipulation of state governments, judiciaries, and local sites of economic influence, white supremacy in the South has the means, he explains, to delay but not to defeat the cause of integration. He cites several factors in addition to the civil rights movement itself that ensure ultimate victory over Jim Crow, including the increasing aid of white liberals and socioeconomic shifts that are industrializing the South and, as a consequence, rewarding African Americans with better employment and purchasing power. Furthermore, he notes, recent Supreme Court decisions moved the federal government finally to lend support for change against recalcitrance in the South, as Eisenhower would be compelled to do in Little Rock later that month. King also acknowledges that Christian churches in the South and North were making attempts to rectify how they had long been among the most segregated institutions in the United States. With this support for bringing an end to Jim Crow segregation, "The Old South is gone," he proclaims, "never to return again."[37]

King's Highlander address does not dwell at length on the problem of Communism in the United States, but measured references to the Cold War within the long history of American race relations acknowledge that the ultimate success of the United States hinges on the progress of desegregation. Careful not to dignify with attention the accusation that the movement for civil rights is merely a front for the CPUSA, he proposes to his audience at Highlander that nothing could be more important for the reputation of the United States in its international conflict with the USSR than the replacement of Jim Crow segregation with racial equality in all forms of public life. With characteristic facility for charitable interpretation, King's explanation of the role of the Cold War in the unfolding narrative of integration attributes to "the South . . . increasing sensitivity to the forces of world opinion."[38] In light of the massive resistance to civil rights, he represents with stubborn confidence the South's dedication to the international reputation of the United States: "Few indeed are the Southerners who relish having their status lumped in the same category with the Union of South Africa as a final refuge of segregation. It is not pleasant, either, to be shown how Southern intransigence fortifies Communist appeals to Asian and African peoples. Here is a further crippling away at old patterns."[39] In spite of the well-publicized backlash against African Americans prompted by *Brown v. Board of Education*, he invites his audience to imagine that the Klan and the Councils represent a distinct minority opinion among Southerners. "Few indeed" would unabashedly embrace being identified as racist. Most people understand, he explains, the value of keeping the United States distant from South Africa, which was notorious in the 1950s for codifying the kinds of racial hierarchies that consolidated the authority of National Socialism in Germany in the 1930s.

Although King connects the civil rights movement to the Cold War and the scandal of South Africa's apartheid regime, he does not in this speech describe the anti-racist mobilizations in the United States as a local instance of decolonization. He does not speak of US involvement with or against liberation struggles elsewhere, but instead focuses on how civil rights reforms will be an asset to the interests of the United States by redressing flaws in America's international reputation. His observation that comparisons between the persistence of Jim Crow rule in the American South and the apartheid regime in South Africa are ruinous for the identity and influence of the United States in much of the world echoes the argument that the Department of Justice presented in 1952 to the US Supreme Court in an *amicus* brief for the *Brown* case. The brief urges the Court to view the desegregation case "in the context of the present world struggle between freedom and tyranny."[40] As Dudziak notes, despite the absence of any reference to the Cold War in the decision, the justices recognized that diplomatic efforts to consolidate international affiliations within the US-led West were dependent on the coherence and plausibility of this neat dichotomy of American freedom against Soviet tyranny.[41] Outside of white supremacist circles in which "American democracy" signified the preservation of racial apartheid as a way of life, further sanction of *de jure* segregation would have rendered unsustainable the opposition of democracy versus totalitarianism. It would have lost all utility as shorthand for the simple epistemology of Cold War anticommunism.

Dudziak also recounts how news publications all over the world except those inside the Eastern Bloc greeted the *Brown v. Board Education* decision with acclaim. The Department of Justice was right to predict that a judgment against segregation would enjoy profound symbolic value internationally, and US diplomatic missions hurried to take full advantage.[42] Energized publicity campaigns outside the United States depicted achievements in integration that surpassed any reasonable estimation of actual progress in education, employment, housing, or any other institutional site in which African Americans were historically oppressed and exploited. SNCC was the subject of an admiring documentary film that US diplomats screened for foreign audiences to demonstrate the progress of race relations in America. At the same time, SNCC was being investigated by HUAC and infiltrated by the FBI.[43] Dudziak explains that *Brown v. Board of Education* was widely understood to affirm the veracity of what Gunnar Myrdal famously defined as the "American Creed," which derives from the country's foundational documents and revolutionary origins the promise of the inalienable value and liberty of all individuals regardless of particularities of race, sex, or religion.[44] The "dilemma" Myrdal and his several collaborators refer to in the title of the influential two-volume sociological study of "the Negro problem and modern democracy" in the United States is that social customs and government regulations regarding racial difference had yet to realize in practice America's bedrock principles. Identifying the United States with its promise but acknowledging that in its history the country had yet to match its ideals, Myrdal weighs in on the question of national character by endorsing the notion of American exceptionalism. He cites the persistence of pervasive racism in the United States as a failure on the part of the country to be itself. King, too, sketches a sweep of US history in which the country appears to be at last approaching the universal tenets of the Enlightenment to which the US Constitution already claimed title.

As numerous scholars have observed, *An American Dilemma* was the "foundation text of racial liberalism" that "set the terms for Cold War liberalism and discourse on race" from the time of its publication in 1944 until the mid-1960s.[45] It provided a conceptual guide and a moral vocabulary for communicating how the Cold War made it necessary to end state-sanctioned white supremacy. Bringing laws and customs into correspondence with the American Creed did not, however, entail actively rectifying the socioeconomic inequalities produced by segregation or slavery before it. When represented with a positive connotation, racial liberalism is a theory of how the modern European nation-state emerged in the eighteenth century as a democratizing institutional form grounded in Enlightenment principles of universal human worth but undermined in each case temporarily by the failure to overcome racism in its constituent populations.[46] According to this position, the persistence of racism is residual; anterior to the emergence of liberalism's state and its emphasis on individual subjects of law, racism is a primitive holdover from social tensions that precede the nation-state and which liberalism's principles inevitably will overcome. Presenting racism as a disfiguring and yet ultimately incidental feature of the United States, Myrdal uses "American Creed" to name the substantially democratic character of the country. Time and the will of the citizenry are all that inhibit resolving the discrepancy between social practices and democratic ideals.

Although published before the end of World War II, the study anticipates that race relations will be the primary impediment to the postwar aspirations of the United States to assume a leadership role in the new world order that will succeed the defeat of the fascist Axis powers.[47] Myrdal identifies Jim Crow segregation as the most significant problem for the realization of the American Creed as well as for his own hopeful aspirations for the United States to exemplify democratic values. He formulates the historical discrepancy between principles and actions according to a temporal logic that idealizes American national character. The facts of anti-black and other racisms were features of US history but were not currently representative of its national identity or what the country could symbolize to the rest of the world. Resembling theological discriminations between accidents (of racism) and substance (of American universality) or sinful acts and the redeemable being of the sinner, the disjunction Myrdal describes is reconciled as a matter of timing. His introduction explains that a remedy for racial strife has simply been delayed for now: "From the point of view of the American Creed the status accorded the Negro in America represents nothing more and nothing less than a century-long lag of public morals. In principle the Negro problem was settled long ago; in practice the solution is not effectuated. The Negro in America has not yet been given the elemental and political rights of formal democracy, including a fair opportunity to earn his living, upon which a general accord was already won when the American Creed was first taking form. And this anachronism constitutes the contemporary 'problem' both to

Negroes and to whites."[48] It is a reflection of Myrdal's confidence in the exceptional character of the United States as an example of democratic governance
and universal principles that he imagines African Americans will be granted
rights equal to those of white citizens. However, more than seventy years after
the publication of the book, we should acknowledge that African Americans
and other minority groups have been "given" nothing. They have secured
more equal rights by confronting the nation-state with unrelenting demands
for recognition, often in reference to the disparity between principles and
practices that prompts the thesis of *An American Dilemma*.

Speaking to the intricacy of Myrdal's sense of timing, Singh notes how
the American Creed appears "paradoxically already accomplished and never
quite complete."[49] This temporality accords with how narratives of American
exceptionalism do more than distinguish the country for moral superiority;
they provide a structure of disavowal in which evidence that is counterfac-
tual to virtue can be explained away as somehow not a significant indication
of national identity.[50] Without waiting on proof that it has actually done so,
Myrdal's particular formulation esteems the country in advance for overcoming the dilemma of racism. By his rendering, America is essentially bound for
perpetuity to become what it has always been. This circuitous, suspenseful
temporality that organizes Myrdal's well-intentioned scholarship in advocacy
for liberal social reform anticipates ironically how the *Brown* decision would
mar the termination of *de jure* segregation with the elasticity of the expression "by all deliberate speed," the notorious slogan from "*Brown* II" in 1955.
The familiar consequence of that qualification was to facilitate resistance to
desegregation by unceasing "gradualism."

Whatever its limitations as a spur to substantial social change to race relations in the United States, the narrative of racial liberalism exemplified by
Myrdal's text was a crucial supplement to cultural initiatives in support of
containment policy internationally. The promising story of reform addressed
the dissonance between pronouncements about American freedom and the
fact of Jim Crow segregation, which was amplified outside the Western Bloc
by Soviet propaganda and, more importantly, by the explosion of national liberation struggles that swept the colonized world over the long 1950s. Affirmed
and publicized by the passage of *Brown*, Myrdal's social scientific version of
America's true character in regard to race became a means to "manage the
racial contradictions that antiracist and anticolonial movements exposed."[51]
While *An American Dilemma* provided a timely and impressive representation of the United States as the emerging leader for a postwar order that, with
the defeat of fascism, would be defined in regard to race by the progress of
racial liberalism, it is also the kind of narrative that Homi Bhabha claims is

integral in general to the identity of nation-states in Western modernity.[52] A brief consideration of his argument will prepare us to review how King's address at Highlander elaborates on the temporality of Myrdal's thesis in order to represent the civil rights movement as an essential feature of America's long march to victory in the Cold War.

Bhabha's well-known essay "DissemiNation" discusses the narrative dimension of national identity according to successive axioms for the study of nationalism that can be inferred from his text. Narrative is an irreducible feature of nationalism as it arises in connection with the modern European nation-state. The narratives that give national identity coherence are shot through with ambivalence. The ambivalence arises from a fundamental tension in the temporal character, the "double-time," of any nation-state. "Writing the nation" through this temporal ambivalence is necessary for the generation of "the people" who belong to the nation by virtue of their appearance in and their authorship of its "foundational fictions."[53] The temporal division stems from the tension between the identification of a nation-state with reference to its origins and its association with whatever has transpired over time in the aftermath of its beginning.[54] It is a struggle, in other words, to maintain a coherent, singular national identity when qualities present at a country's beginning may be at odds with attributes accrued over time as circumstances have changed. National identity requires maintenance: reconsolidation work that reconciles discrepancies that over time may undermine the impression of continuity required to imagine the nation-state is akin to a subject who is in possession of a personal history and a willful agency. Bhabha asserts that his parallel attention to the registration of the nation at its beginning and as it has progressed involves not so much historicism regarding what has transpired but instead a discernment of the quality of temporality manifest in the narrative representations through which national cultures address their specific versions of the tension between origin and duration.[55] Working with conceits drawn from Derrida's account of reiterative signification, Bhabha recommends that we observe how national narratives involve both pedagogical and performative elements that affirm and renew citizens' passionate attachments to the national dimension of their personal identities as well as to the identity of their nation.[56]

Myrdal's treatment of the dilemma of anti-black racism in relationship to the American Creed manages the ambivalence Bhabha describes. The study provides for the continuity of national identity by representing the procession of time since the nation's founding to be marked by the struggle to get back to the original Enlightenment principles. As I have discussed, King's "The Look to the Future" also proposes a historiography of black and white race relations in America according to a double-time. His evolutionary history from slavery to segregation to integration accords with racial liberalism's account of progress; social reforms have brought laws and customs ever closer to democratic ideals that would see the United States realize its creed eventually through the elimination of racial discord, rank, and, some argue, identity.

Two features of King's speech make it importantly distinct from Myrdal's version of racial liberalism. First, he accentuates the quality of progress by rendering it in the form of the Exodus narrative. In the context of the Cold War, the metaphysical dimension of the Highlander talk resonates with the Manichean urgency of guarding freedom against the danger of totalitarianism. Almost needless to say, trepidation in the United States about the global danger of Soviet Communism often had a Christian basis; it was in 1954, after all, that the US Pledge of Allegiance was amended to add the words "under God," a revision intended to commit citizens to a religious distinction over godless communism. Children repeating the pledge to begin the school day is the kind of performative activity that Bhabha understands to reinforce pedagogies that teach citizens in the present to identify themselves as continuing the work of the nation's founders. The Pledge binds them to the origins of American national identity, but with a revisionist attribution of univocal Christian purpose to the motley collection of Christians, deists, atheists, and others who revolted against British colonialism and convened constitutional congresses.

The second distinction is that King recasts the human agency within Myrdal's version of the narrative of racial liberalism. As Melamed points out, *An American Dilemma* represents the marginalized African American populace of the United States as a cause and an opportunity for white Americans to redeem the promise of a country that could admit African Americans into full franchise if only white Americans were to invite such change. She writes: "Myrdal's compendious sociological study cedes consciousness in its narrative frame only to white Americans, while reducing African Americans to components of the race problem that usefully incite white moral conversion."[57] *An American Dilemma* expects white Americans to reconsider the morality in their hearts and to reform their sensibilities to accept all nonwhite citizens as unreservedly American. Myrdal's creed entails waiting on the conscience of white Americans to wake up to the universalist moorings of their country, but neglects the agency of nonwhite Americans. King's appeal in "The Look to the Future," as in the canonical "I Have a Dream" speech or "Letter from a Birmingham Jail," is to call on African Americans and their allies in the civil rights movement to seize the initiative to resolve the dilemma of American racism and to realize the Creed for the entire country's sake.

Myrdal's account of racial liberalism as a prospective civil religion was influential, but King's revisionary version was suited for inspiration. Adding a providential timing that exceeds ordinary history, his invocation of the Exodus narrative makes his racial liberalism prophetic. Leading into the conclusion of his Highlander talk, he assures his audience of the success of civil rights with a figure he borrows from nineteenth-century abolitionist minister Theodor Parker that became a signature of King's oratory, especially after he repeated it on the steps of the Montgomery capitol at the end of the march from Selma: "Let us realize that as we struggle for justice and freedom we have cosmic companionship. The arc of the moral universe is long and it bends toward justice."[58] With this trajectory, he attunes the history of racial liberalism in the United States to those versions of American exceptionalism that source the country's supposed moral priority not only to the absence of a feudal past or to the freedom of association in civil society but also to the pre-national Puritan errand in the wilderness to erect a shining white city on a hill. King's messianic resonance infuses his version of racial liberalism with a Christian telos of deliverance that intensifies Myrdal's sense of American progress but shares its basically paradoxical temporality. The caveat is that Myrdal's secular combination of "always and never" conveys an unacknowledged, permanent suspense while King speaks with faith in a providential theology that transcends the paradox. The urgency with which King invests his revision of the historiography of racial liberalism according to precepts of liberation theology attributes untiring resilience to the movement for civil rights while at the same time it undermines arguments for gradual change that are staked on the claim that it requires patience to resolve Myrdal's dilemma for the sake of the American Creed. Against King's vision of a messianic America that, once free of racial discrimination at home, can lead the world through the emergency of the Cold War, advocacy for gradualism on equal rights for African Americans seems an obvious, cynical strategy for permanent deferment under the insincere alibi of eventual compliance. But even with his impatience toward the abundant indications of further delay, King's talk at Highlander avails itself of the way racial liberalism promises that racist discord is incidental and not integral to the constitution of the United States.

In contrast to this vision of a modern and providential America, communism seems implicitly to be out of the natural order of things. However, unlike the Cold Warriors who used the pathological tropes for communism invoked by the JBS billboard, King did not demonize segregationists as un-Americans possessed of malevolent and aberrant drives that render them alien to ordinary US citizens. Rather than traffic in attacks that disparage the ontological character of his antagonists—that dehumanizing Red Scare maneuver so akin rhetorically to racist invective—in his Highlander address, he is able to project an image of a robust, immunized body politic because, in tune with Myrdal's discrimination between real dilemma and ideal creed, he represents un-American assistance to communism as a failing of Jim Crow segregation. With the success of the civil rights movement, any affinity for segregation will be contained within its rightful place: the past. Taking the standard vocabulary that describes Jim Crow segregation in terms of the regulation of social space and translating it into a concern for time, King appropriates the moral and patriotic authority of Cold War containment narratives to suggest that segregationists, whatever the quality of their intentions or the sources of their bigotry, stand unwittingly in opposition to the maturation of the United States and, by extension, that of the decolonizing postwar world.

King's argument does not deny proponents of segregation are culpable for their attitudes, but he neither suggests they are beyond help nor accords them importance on the topic of the national character of the United States. Devotees of Jim Crow segregation are anachronisms in but not of modern America. Pitiably obsolete, they represent social practices that fail to reflect the essential character of American nationalism that has been called into world service by the Cold War. At odds with that service and an embarrassment in both the foreign press and the meetings of the young United Nations, defenders of Jim Crow are a drag on American forward progress in a time of emergency. In this view, racism is archaic; it can be rooted out of social significance through modern statecraft inspired by the passions of liberation theology. To be un-American, then, is to be an asset to Communist propaganda by virtue of an ignorant or stubborn inability to develop with modernity. The white supremacist can integrate himself into the contemporary United States if he stops living in a past that might appear still to be in evidence but which is, according to the therapeutic communications of the American Creed, merely the insubstantial residue of a world that has already been eclipsed.

Tailored for an audience of like-minded and experienced activists, King's speech at Highlander is not a sermon. He mixes learned exposition with a field report from the front lines of the struggle for civil rights. In a celebratory weekend with many seasoned speakers—though at only age twenty-seven he was already the most renowned—there was perhaps less call than usual for him to inspire his audience. Still, with a hint of playfulness, he does conclude his remarks with an appeal for action. His conclusion amplifies the connection between (racial) liberalism and liberation theology by nominating four exemplary figures who were, in the jargon of psychology at the time, "maladjusted" in their thinking relative to commonplace, mad habits of violence and greed: the Old Testament prophet Amos, Presidents Lincoln and Jefferson, and Jesus Christ.[59] The combination joins heroic statecraft to the transmission and incarnation of God's work on Earth, appending further resonance to the temporalities of ongoing progress and ultimate deliverance. At the end of a talk that describes a prophetic sense of destiny in which the resources of American democracy can be applied to realize racial integration that is simultaneously original, under way, and inevitable, he flirts with a vocabulary that urges his audience not to be entirely at ease with the times. Like the stretch across history to join prophets to presidents, the idiosyncrasy he recommends is another instance of double time. In their protests at present, maladjusted activists signal that commercial greed and military violence must have no place in the future that King proposes to see emerging with their example. Yet, the necessity of this last move in his talk complicates his optimism with the suggestion that the prospect of the dilemma succumbing finally to the Creed is less promising than he prefers to say. It is this hint of urgent work to be taken up immediately and from the periphery of public culture that we will see elaborated in the address at Riverside. As we will see, that development of his position will require a wholesale revision of how he conceives of the Cold War.

King's sacralization of racial liberalism in "The Look to the Future" is an impassioned expression of the official anti-racism that in the discourse of anticommunism during the long 1950s won out over the ideology of Red Scare white supremacist support for segregation. Amplifying the promise of Myrdal's American Creed with a messianic resonance synchronized to the urgency of securing international confidence in the idea that the United States represents and defends an ideal of democratic freedom against the encroachment of Communist tyranny, King claims the rhetorical power of the containment narrative on behalf of the civil rights movement. Within the cultural conversation about anticommunism, he may not speak with the tautological certitude of militant red-baiters, such as Hoover, who propose to know a Communist when they see one, but his doubling of evolutionary and providential times to bind the identical fates of civil rights and Cold War America invites his audience to know the assurance of inevitability. King's Highlander speech illustrates how—in the context of international scrutiny prompted by the emergence of decolonization and the lingering moral force of anti-fascism from World War II—arguments that civil rights for all US citizens would be an asset in the Cold War were most persuasive because so necessary for foreign policy aims that could not be met if white supremacy's monopoly on state violence were not finally surrendered in the American South. Moreover, King's prophetic rendition of Myrdal's American Creed also helps to show how a narrative of racial progress that affirms the value of democracy in America lends itself to the exceptional proposition that a virtue of US nationalism is its universalism. The realization of the Creed at home, by Myrdal's and King's accounts, will be invitation enough for all the world to fall in with America as its leader and ethos.

Another Time of Necessity: King's Turn against the American War in Vietnam

Early in his public career, King's clever rendering of Jim Crow's proponents as pitiable throwbacks to a pre-modern time meant he could guide his audience to infer that segregation is an "un-American" activity, and he could do so without resorting to dehumanizing appellations. His example did not, however, discourage opponents to civil rights from persisting in tropes that attributed black political agency to the illicit and irrational work of the Communist Reds. The anticommunist epistemology encoded in the popular tropes of the Cold War anticommunist consensus also remained serviceable to those of various political orientations who accepted civil rights but remained intent on separating franchise for all citizens regardless of race from the kinds of anticapitalist interventions against social inequality that King would prioritize after passage of the Voting Rights Act and articulate so provocatively in his address at Riverside. The question I want to consider by turning to King's controversial speech of April 4, 1967, is: what was the expense of winning Cold War anticommunism to the side of civil rights within the constraints of racial liberalism? Or, what hard-to-foresee rhetorical problems for the black freedom struggle followed as a consequence of the Red Scare's instrumental role in the official victory of anti-racism over unabashed bigotry? To put it still another way, how did the success directing Cold War anticommunism to the cause of civil rights contribute to the difficulty King and others experienced attempting to impress on public culture critiques of postwar US imperialism and its relationship to the racist capitalism at home that was surviving the slow death of Jim Crow segregation?

King's Riverside Address was not his first public statement against the US conduct of war in Vietnam, but it was the first time he devoted an entire speech to the topic while linking opposition to the war to the civil rights movement. In spite of close associates counseling him to keep strictly to the topic of civil rights, King determined that with his remarks at Riverside he would fix his reputation to an argument that sees the struggle for civil rights in the United States and protests for peace overseas to be inextricable from each other.[60] To that end, in advance of his appearance he cued the press to expect a major announcement. Already persuaded of much that he would say, the group

"Clergy and Laymen Concerned about Vietnam" sponsored his appearance. King opens his remarks by acknowledging the organization's leaders and expressing his "full accord" with their recent public statement declaring that silence on the war is "betrayal."[61] Confessing that he kept silent on Vietnam too long, he argues that his opposition to the war is consistent with the belief in nonviolence he has professed from the time he began work as a pastor in Montgomery. In spite of this claim, most news reports covering his appearance indicated he had undergone a conversion. As Singh documents in the opening pages of *Black Is a Country*, the majority of public responses "pilloried" the speech. Editorials in major periodicals and even the NAACP found one way or another to refer to the talk as a betrayal.[62] When complaints did not malign King for abetting the Communist Vietcong, especially in his call for draft-eligible men in the United States to pursue conscientious-objector status, criticisms charged him with hurting the cause of civil rights by conflating domestic and foreign issues and, worse, associating the African American struggle with what was described as the shrill anti-Americanism of the youthful and unruly anti-war movement.

The Riverside Address was a scandal according to most indications of public opinion in the wake of his appearance. But in recent years the speech has been a crucial reference for scholars who describe King's development from a politics of liberal reform embedded in liberation theology to a no less spiritual, but more incisive radicalism. According to this characterization, he came to realize that no anti-racist political initiative could meet the aspiration of ending systemic racism unless it involved a critique of capitalism seeking socialist alternatives for the organization of collective life.[63] King's own words and actions encourage this period claim that divides his career between early, long-term reformer and late, short-lived radical. His support for the Memphis sanitation workers' strike, his plans for a Poor People's Campaign march on Washington, and, as I will remind us in what follows, his insistence in the Riverside Address that a complete US withdrawal from Vietnam be complemented by programmatic efforts to redistribute wealth and restructure the economy at home—all encourage the view that in the last months of his life he dedicated himself to a new view of the importance of class inequality that had not been integral to his earlier pursuit of legal standing for all citizens regardless of race. With the pressure of hindsight, King said as much, expressing regret in 1966 that the movement had made social changes that were of more value to middle-class African Americans than to the working class, poor, and indigent most in need of material assistance. Two years later he remarked that conditions for poor African Americans had actually worsened.[64]

Contrary to this now common formulation of King's career into reformist and radical phases, claims about the interdependence of racism and class difference can be found in his speeches and writings well before 1967.[65] However, he presents them in a Cold War frame to audiences schooled in anticommunism.[66] To introduce an analysis of the intersection of race and class as a necessary element of a critical response to the war, in the Riverside Address King takes aim at the Cold War subtext that insulates the anticommunist public from entertaining the idea that capitalism unchecked by other values cannot redress racism and actually exacerbates it. To register this claim, he must also challenge the dominant representation in US public culture of America's benevolent stance toward the rest of the world. Dismissing the idea that the United States intervenes militarily in other countries reluctantly and only to defend the free world against the spread of communism, he writes the United States into the history of colonialism not as the first world power to stand for anti-colonial liberation struggles but instead as a "counter-revolutionary" force exercising imperial fiat to arrest democratic processes in other countries that either did or would have elected governments unsuited for US influence. A counternarrative to the prophetic liberal historiography that animates American identity in his remarks at Highlander, the speech at Riverside communicates its optimism about American participation in righteous social change not with a paradoxical temporality of inevitability but with an emphasis on the "fierce urgency of now" that conveys a different tenor for necessity.[67] Rather than express the surety of what will happen eventually, King speaks of what must be in terms of an imperative: not what must be, but what must be done. With only the guarantee that continued barbarism is unconscionable, he insists that Americans must retrieve their nation-state from what it has become and forge a "revolution in values" that will open possibilities that have not been foretold.[68] In the process, the Cold War rivalry with the USSR will take care of itself and is, in any case, of less import than the question of whether the United States will ally itself to the revolutionary momentum of decolonization or persist in citing the Red Scare to license its involvement in the construction of an exploitative neocolonial world order for which the United States is not solely responsible but from which it is the principal beneficiary.

King's Riverside Address is organized to instruct the public in a counterintuitive explanation of the war in Vietnam that will prepare it for the more sweeping criticisms of the political culture of the United States that come in the demanding final sections of his presentation. Against the presumption that his appearance to speak out against the American war in Vietnam marks a shift in his priorities, King enumerates seven objections to the war that elaborate on how his attitude follows from his devotion to civil rights.[69] Three of his points derive from his commitment to nonviolence; he speaks for pacifism strategically and morally. War cannot spread democracy. It offends against Christian teachings of universal fraternity. And, having received a Nobel Prize, he also feels a special, public obligation to stand always for the ideal possibility of world peace. In other words, support for war must always be parochial; his anti-war view is ecumenical relative to faiths and universal in regard to humanity. In one of the most charged and memorable lines of the speech, he expresses regret that the war shows the United States to be the "greatest purveyor of violence in the world."[70] The phrase circulated in much of the press coverage. Employing anticommunism's "with us or against us" epistemology, *Life* magazine's editorial condemns King's remarks and cites the line as evidence that "much of his speech was demagogic slander that sounded like a script for Radio Hanoi."[71] In 1967 Red Scare rhetoric still served in public culture to stigmatize particular ideas as un-American. Anticommunism regards unapologetic dissent from the national state's script as simultaneously impermissible for any genuine American and unthinkable in its own terms. Whatever King actually says in opposition to US military involvement in Vietnam, the ostensible rationale for the war, fighting Communists, meant that in the Red Scare cultural conversation his objections could only express his illicit allegiance to the enemy. A common complaint was that he confused the separate causes of civil rights and peace, but in the short-form retorts of newspaper editorials and "objective" journalism this criticism appears without acknowledgment of how King's talk makes a deliberate case for the interdependent character of the fight for civil rights at home and the national liberation struggles in Europe's colonies and former colonies. In contrast to his talk at Highlander, his Riverside Address holds that decolonization is a transnational phenomenon and a concerted effort that includes the anti-racist freedom struggles in the United States.

Moral considerations inform King's other objections, but they extend more directly to political concerns. The war, he laments, has ruined the Great Society programs introduced with such promise only a few years earlier. Those initiatives of the Johnson administration should have made fundamental inroads against poverty across racial divisions, and they also could have been an intervention against how socioeconomic disparities reproduce conditions of racial inequality.[72] More immediately injurious to young black men is that they are fighting and dying in disproportionate numbers in Vietnam, and in their precarious state are tasked with killing countless other young men and women who are also people of color. He explains his tragic recognition that "[w]e were taking the black young men who had been crippled by our society and sending them eight thousand miles away to guarantee liberties in Southeast Asia which they had not found in southwest Georgia and East Harlem."[73] The point is reminiscent of Muhammad Ali's uncompromising line from the previous year: "Why should they ask me to put on a uniform and go ten thousand miles from home and drop bombs and bullets on brown people in Vietnam while so-called Negro people in Louisville are treated like dogs and denied simple human rights?"[74] The only significant distinction between King's and Ali's objections is in their choice of pronouns. King's royal "we" implicates all citizens in military actions taken in their name; Ali's "they" contests how citizens without unadulterated franchise can be conscripted into the identity of a nation-state that refuses them representation. King and Ali must have agreed that the Vietnam War was not only a serious diversion from anti-poverty programs that would have ameliorated to some extent systemic racism in the United States, but it was also responsible for exacerbating racial inequalities. King notes that those worsening conditions at home wait for those Africans Americans who will survive their integrated military service and come home to laws and customs of segregation that diminish the value of their citizenship relative to that of their military brethren who are white.

He follows his list of objections to the war with a history lesson that contradicts Cold War rationales for US military action in Vietnam. His complaint that the military draft endangers African Americans to a disproportionate degree is opposite to popular confidence that by the mid-1960s the military was the most desegregated institution in the United States, and his sketch of the recent history of Vietnam's struggle against colonialism contradicts virtually anything in periodicals in the United States outside of explicitly leftist publications such as the *Nation, Ramparts,* or the African American journal *Freedomways*, which came out against the war in 1965 and two years later reprinted King's Riverside Address. Perhaps in deference to President Johnson's support for the Civil Rights and Voting Rights Acts of 1964 and 1965, more popular African American newspapers such as the *Chicago Defender* only declared opposition to the war after he completed his term in office. Rather than accept the official line that Soviet-sponsored Communists had attempted to seize control in Vietnam as part of their expansionist effort to disrupt the way the US military presence in Southeast Asia, Western Europe, and the Middle East "encircled" the USSR, in his address King knows the Cold War to be a source of confusion that obscures how the United States had long undertaken to keep Vietnam in a state of colonial subjugation. Contrary to what an American public was accustomed to learning from television news and major newspapers, King teaches that colonialism, not Communism, has been and remains the real problem in Vietnam. He does not offer an opinion as to whether the Johnson administration and other powerful interests supporting the war use the Cold War cynically to cover for US neocolonialism or sincerely believe that Vietnam is a pawn of the USSR. He leaves open whether Johnson is unreliable in how he represents Vietnam or in how he interprets it. Either way, King insists that the United States is responsible for the antidemocratic denial of that country's right to self-determination.

King notes that under the leadership of Ho Chi Minh—whom he neither praises nor vilifies—the Vietnamese declared independence from French rule in 1945 with a document that cites the US Declaration of Independence. He then faults the United States for failing to recognize Vietnam as an autonomous nation-state and attributes the poor judgment to "support France in its reconquest of her former colony" to the "deadly Western arrogance that has poisoned the international atmosphere for so long."[75] Speaking at Highlander, he was in concert with Myrdal's regard for the American Creed as the epitome of Western modernity's promise of universal, inalienable recognition for all humanity; here, abandoning the temporality of the earlier argument, he testifies that the West has arrogated to itself universal command and set up those who suffer its paternal rule to be representative of the drive for human inclusivity that was supposed to be the mandate of the Enlightenment. King goes on to explain that when nine years of assistance to France's efforts proved futile, the 1954 Geneva Accords provided a brief interlude of democratic possibility before the United States scuttled plans for an election and in the interests of anticommunism propped up Prime Minister Ngo Dinh Diem's authoritarian rule over South Vietnam. At Highlander, he surveyed major phases in the improvement of race relations in the United States; for the congregation at Riverside, he offered instruction in how the people of Vietnam, like other countries and regions fighting their way free of colonial rule, "must see Americans as strange liberators" (235).

King engages in a thought exercise to elucidate just how strange it must be for the people of Vietnam to be expected to regard Americans as their liberators. He documents the damage to the populace and environment as he imagines it must appear to the Vietnamese, and he rehearses a series of rhetorical questions that speak to the incredulity with which they must receive pronouncements about how necessary and righteous is the US military occupation of Vietnam. Even without recourse to well-publicized atrocities such as the My Lai massacre, which would occur eleven months later, King characterizes US attacks as gratuitous in the damage they inflict on noncombatant women, children, and the aged; on infrastructures of work, travel, healthcare, and schooling; and on the natural environment (236). In the following string of questions, he wonders how, after such comprehensive destruction, Vietnam

will have sufficient means to support a state after the war: "What do the peas-
ants think as we ally ourselves with the landlords and as we refuse to put any
action in our many words concerning land reform? What do they think as we
test out our latest weapons on them, just as the Germans tested out new medi-
cine and new tortures in the concentration camps of Europe? Where are the
roots of the independent Vietnam we claim to be building? Is it among these
voiceless ones?" King observes that the victims he describes are voiceless. To
presume to speak for them hazards replicating colonial habits of paternal
condescension; he contends with that risk by speculating about their perspectives in the form of questions. Because these questions are rhetorical, they
presume knowledge. The actions of the United States described by each query
are undoubtedly inexcusable. But if the judgment against US military actions
is obvious, the question form allows King to put into evidence the knowing
subject position of the Vietnamese—the standpoint epistemology that comes
to them uniquely on the receiving end of colonial violence—without presuming arrogantly to explain precisely how they would articulate their objections
or what emotions are prompted by their sense of ruin. Including the Vietcong in the perspective he imagines for the Vietnamese, he transgresses a key
protocol of Cold War anticommunist discourse. To insist Vietnamese Communists must have a say in any treaty negotiations and in the design of the
country after the war is to disregard the Red Scare dictate that communism
is a pathological condition rather than a set of political ideas and, therefore,
Communists cannot be good faith participants in reasoned deliberation. In
spite of that expectation, King attributes to the Vietnamese heated, indignant
questions; alongside descriptions of the destruction visited on their country
by the United States, those questions must seem reasonable.

Unreasonable by all contemporary accounts in the American press are
King's five concrete recommendations for changes to US policy: end all
bombing in Vietnam; declare a unilateral cease-fire; curtail military buildup
in neighboring countries; accept the National Liberation Front (Vietcong) as
a good-faith participant in peace negotiations; and set a date for withdrawal
of all foreign troops in accordance with the 1954 Geneva Agreement (239).
Considering that the United States had rejected the treaty in Geneva and the
sum of King's list is all but an admission that the United States was responsible for perpetrating an unjust, criminal war, these proposals were a non-
starter among elected federal officials. They also convey judgments against
US actions in Vietnam that were commonplace only in the counterpublic of
the anti-war movement; in spring 1967, regular guests of television programs
such as *Face the Nation* were not addressing the suggestions on King's list to
the public at large from platforms that in the protest vernacular of the time

would be described as "establishment." Demanding that the United States take responsibility for the war in Vietnam as its mistake, King denies the United States the reputation for virtue that is a presumption of anticommunist epistemology as it is recorded in both the pejorative "un-American" and the neat, melodramatic dichotomy of totalitarianism versus democracy. King's list of recommendations was treated in mainstream reporting and federal policy debates as ludicrously impractical, and his finding the United States primarily to blame was called anti-American by countless sources. Rather than regard his demands as an index of King's idealism or naiveté, however, we should consider the value of the list to be how it confronts a misguided public culture with impossible, practically unthinkable demands in order to suggest polemically how far removed the cultural conversation is from an honest assessment of American military and commercial activities outside the United States. We might also take the list of unthinkable recommendations as an aspirational description of the common-sense imagination that King hopes to cultivate in coaching his audience to take on a dramatically different political subjectivity from what Cold War public culture has presented as necessary for the Red Scare. Using speculation to think through the ways the Vietnamese see the American presence in their country, he explains that nonviolence is a form of resistance and an attitude for learning "from the wisdom of brothers who are called the opposition" (237).

After his proposal for how the United States could take it upon itself to end the war peacefully and his plea that all draft-eligible men register as COs, King admits he is tempted to conclude his speech. His remarks to that point, he admits, have been sufficient to join the increasingly popular "crusade against the war in Vietnam"—a cause he supports unreservedly. He determines to go further, however, and explains that the war in Vietnam is merely a symptom "of a far deeper malady within the American spirit" (240). As sharp as King's rebuke of the war has been to this point, especially in his indignation at how the military conflict is creating wanton death and indigence among Vietnamese and Americans, his position still could have been interpreted in terms of the American dilemma. His government, the world's "greatest purveyor of violence," might be understood to have fallen away from the proper character of its principles. America's error in Vietnam could be thought of as a uniquely intense failure to bring actual practice in line with the principles of democracy. Instead, King drives home that the US invasion, occupation, and ongoing violence against Vietnam are representative of similarly unconscionable US military interventions elsewhere in the years since World War II. Citing an unnamed "sensitive American official overseas," King shares the opinion that a world historical revolution has been under way throughout Europe's colonies and former colonies, and the United States has been on the wrong side: responsible for counterrevolutionary violence against popular uprisings in Guatemala, Cambodia, Peru, and elsewhere. While King's reference to America's "malady" is reminiscent of Kennan's and Hoover's Red Scare representations of an American body politic grown ill with communism, the cause of the country's debility emanates not from the USSR but from its own excessive militarism in other countries. Prior to this diagnosis, there is much in King's speech that does not comport with the optimism he expressed at Highlander, yet the nation-state he describes could still be understood as tragically overzealous about fighting the Cold War in defense of democracy against totalitarianism. Noting that the Vietnam War is not an exception to US conduct or character but rather a typical entry in a list of violent state actions to repress popular social movements, King disconnects the representation of the US nation-state from the structure of disavowal afforded by American exceptionalism. Again, like Myrdal before him, in the Highlander talk he formulates exceptionalism with a rhetoric of temporality that explains the present according to the promise of the future that was pronounced by an idealized, mythic origin to which the national state is always returning. The temporal rhetoric in the speech at Riverside is contrary to such circuitous and romantic nationalism. It confronts his audience with an uneasy immediacy and without the consolation of parsing ideals and intentions from incidental bad acts.

Invoking John F. Kennedy's pithy declaration that those "who make peaceful revolution impossible will make violent revolution inevitable," King proceeds to elaborate on the comprehensive character of the violence the United States imposes on the people of other countries. His strident, anticapitalist explanation transgresses the limits of racial liberalism:

> Increasingly, by choice or by accident, this is the role our nation has taken, the role of those who make peaceful revolution impossible by refusing to give up the privileges and the pleasures that come from the immense profits of overseas investments.
>
> I am convinced that if we are to get on the right side of the world revolution, we as a nation must undergo a radical revolution of values. We must rapidly begin the shift from a thing-oriented society to a person-oriented society. When machines and computers, profit motives and property rights, are considered more important than people, the giant triplets of racism, extreme materialism, and militarism are incapable of being conquered.

Culminating in the oft-cited metaphor of "giant triplets," this famous passage from his most controversial speech expresses King's optimistic will about the potential role of his nation to contribute to an emerging anticapitalist world order. Unlike his many statements that first cite national exceptionalism as precedent for reforms that will see America recover its true identity and then underscore the urgency of that transformation with reference to the global emergency of the Cold War, here the current state of the United States is the principal source of international strife. The figure of the "triplets" means that the United States is an imperial state prosecuting violence to nullify the popular will of people in other countries in order to generate wealth through neocolonial infrastructures that exploit uneven development to secure superprofits, reserves of cheap labor, and inexpensive resources.

King's appeal for a radical change in how the United States relates to the rest of the world, especially the global South, implies that the image of the United States derived from Myrdal and disseminated by the State Department for propaganda purposes in the Cold War has been a misnomer for a foreign policy in which the Cold War national security state does the bidding of moneyed interests headquartered in the United States or its allies. His call to overcome the "giant triplets" before it is too late reverberates as King repeats three times the phrase "[a] true revolution of values will . . ." (240–41). He follows each with a description of an unprecedented structural change that aspires for a superior social life even than that promised by the American Creed. With a logic that would refute recent advocacy for faith-based, non-governmental charities to replace welfare state agencies, he describes his first example of revolution by observing the inadequacy of the Christian parable of the Good Samaritan. We must come to recognize, he insists, that personal aid to the needy is merely a first step toward recognizing that "an edifice which produces beggars needs restructuring" (241). King does not delve into explicit policy proposals, but it would follow from this first depiction of a revolution in values that dignified employment is a human right and that a guaranteed minimum income should be a feature of citizenship. Three months after the appearance at Riverside, he makes precisely that argument in a television interview.[76] His second assertion is no less sweeping in its moral claims, though its personified vision is explicitly global. The "true revolution of values will," he explains, "soon look uneasily on the glaring contrast of poverty and wealth. With righteous indignation, it will look across the seas and see individual capitalists of the West investing huge sums of money in Asia, Africa, and South America, only to take profits out with no concern for the social betterment of the countries and say, 'This is not just.'"[77] Invoking Western arrogance as the magical thinking that obscures the immorality of profiting opportunistically from uneven development in the capitalist world system, King portrays the cultivation of a cosmopolitan political conscience prepared to meet the geographic spread of multinational corporations that organize social life economically without yet having to answer to a commensurately transnational and powerful political order. The third feature of a "true revolution of values" concerns war, which King insists cannot be abided as a means of "settling differences." These seemingly impossible expectations for an anticapitalist, cosmopolitan, and pacifist disposition are, he claims, viable in America because of the privileges that follow from the country's wealth, influence, and might. And what's more, to generalize these revolutionary values into a gracious common sense would turn the Cold War rivalry with the USSR into a genuine contest of ideology and then win it for the United States with a "positive thrust for democracy" rather than a "negative anticommunism" (242).

King describes an anticapitalist, global, and pacifist attitude that defies both *realpolitik* admonitions about what is practical in international relations and social Darwinist assertions that zero-sum competition over profit is the innate core of the human species. He preaches with the aspiration of engendering a normative subjectivity that was still unrecognizable within the cultural conversation of Cold War anticommunism at the time. However, he coordinates his terms to undermine the epistemological moorings that demonize critiques of capitalism and, from behind Red Scare hyperbole, obscure how the United States actively contributed to the transformation of decolonization's liberation struggles into a neocolonial world order that has been punishing for what we now call the global South (and can locate virtually anywhere precariousness is more common than privilege). Outside of its favorable reception by groups and individuals who already opposed the war (such as the clergy and laity in attendance at the Riverside Church that night), the speech was predictably vilified as un-American propaganda cooked up for the international criminal conspiracy of communism.

We can complicate the dichotomy of early and late King, reformer and radical, by acknowledging the extent to which he worried about class inequality throughout his career and, on occasion before 1967, spoke openly about the role of colonialism in the perpetuation of racism in Western modernity. However, the quality of those concerns does change when his Riverside Address revises the normative story of the Cold War in order to recast the United States as a colonial and imperial power and, by extension, to suggest that the temporality bestowed on American nationalism by racial liberalism was out of synch with the true character of American activities at home and abroad since the end of World War II. The significance of the difference in the temporality of the two talks I have examined includes not only the shift from the certain necessity of inevitability to the uneasy necessity of the imperative but also a reassessment of the relationship between the national state and racism. According to Myrdal's American Creed and the early King's prophetic rendition of it, racism is a tragic accident of history but not in principle a definitive feature of the state. In the Riverside Address, in contrast, racism at home and abroad is both constitutive of and constituted by the national state.

But this is not to say he holds that racism is an unavoidable fate in the United States. King's litany of revolutionary values is full of promise, and he cites the late-eighteenth-century American and French revolutions against monarchical rule as precedent for the transnational struggles that caught fire against white supremacy after 1945. He also notes the tragic irony that the states born of those revolutions have squandered their legacy and become the "arch anti-revolutionaries" (242). Near the conclusion of his address, King again employs successive rhetorical questions to pose a challenge to be met, at once, in communication with those outside America who presently suffer the imperialism of the Cold War national security state: "Shall we say the odds are too great? Shall we tell them the struggle is too hard? Will our message be that the forces of American life militate against their arrival as full men, and we send our deepest regrets? Or will there be another message—of longing, of hope, of solidarity with their yearnings, of commitment to their cause, whatever the cost. The choice is ours, and though we might prefer it otherwise, we must choose in this crucial moment of human history" (243). Immediately after this demanding passage, he brings his talk to an end with a verse by James Russell Lowell that speaks of an instant of decision between good and evil (243–44). His questions and the citation conclude his address with an affirmative representation of temporality. The ending is momentous. The choice poised before us that can wait no longer delineates between a retreat into nationalist resignation or the more difficult aspiration for universalism. And while this opposition participates in the rousing idealism of human rights and Christian fraternity, it also conveys a further reorientation of the place of the United States in King's imagination.

I have emphasized the rhetoric of temporality in both talks; at Riverside, the imperative supplants the sense of inevitability he imparts at Highlander. He abandons the consoling fiction of national identity's double-time of continuity and progress. In the succession of questions that confronts Americans with how to account for ourselves to those outside the United States who suffer from the sovereign exceptionalism it exercises in our name outside its borders, King's perspective does not map onto the imaginary geography of the Cold War that divides the world into blocs of West, East, and as yet unaffiliated. Unlike the Highlander address and many of his other early invocations of American dreams that on the other side of the dilemma of racism will possess universal value, here speculation about the situation of others in the world outside the United States is the means by which Americans can recognize a different dilemma: national interests defined by militant "forces of American life" are irreconcilable to global concerns predicated on the conviction that humanity is a viable constituency of political aspiration. Although King assuredly would never have chosen the word, his closing argument suggests that, in the midst of the American war in Vietnam during a longer era of postwar US imperialism, the only stance from which to think and act for a just social order must be, quite literally, "un-American." The "malady" of "racism, extreme materialism, and militarism" has meant that, for people caught up in new colonial relations with the United States under the auspices of the Cold War, the connotations of "American" do not ring true with the meaning of democracy. Facing up to the American war in Vietnam, King sees and says that the extension of American nationalism as if it were in itself universal in fact serves particular interests and then hides that partiality with occupying violence undertaken with the presumption of service to the world.

CHAPTER TWO

Essaying to Be an Exile: Richard Wright Following *The God That Failed*

For if I am to be taken seriously as saying that secular criticism deals with local and worldly situations, and that it is constitutively opposed to the production of massive, hermetic systems, then it must follow that the essay—a comparatively short, investigative, radically skeptical form—is the principal way in which to write criticism.

—Edward Said, *The World, The Text, and the Critic*[1]

By Said's account, doubt is essential to the viability of the essay as a form of critique. His reference to skepticism recalls Montaigne's long-standing reputation in literary studies for introducing the genre of the essay. The personal, introspective, relatively short but highly variable form of written reflection on all manner of topics was suited to Montaigne's habit of questioning both the social mores of his day and the sources of his own misgivings. A long history of the form has followed his example. Said, however, does not invoke the legacy of the essay; his observation does not concern tradition. He identifies doubt as a property of the essay form. Like Theodor Adorno's discussion in "The Essay as Form" of how the provisional, speculative qualities of the genre contradict positivism's fixation on empirically verifiable certainty as the only basis for really knowing,[2] Said's remark pits the essay in necessary opposition to the "production of massive, hermetic systems." His mention of "local and worldly situations" may seem to indicate a range of topics, but familiarity with what he characterizes elsewhere as his contrapuntal approach encourages us to imagine the pairing in a relationship of restless dialectical mobility.[3]

A proper essayist in Said's sense negotiates between these poles of the local and the worldly to arrive at the sort of incisive knowledge that has explanatory power in a particular situation possessed of general importance. This incessant interest in what is at hand and what is global characterizes Said's secular injunctions against the invocation of transcendental explanations and the production of insular, perfect systems of thought that forestall suspicion and resist the unpredicted contingencies of history. He represents skepticism as the impetus and manner of the essay, which for him refers as much to a practice of thought as a category of textual form.

Said's emphasis on mobility is especially resonant with a common observation about a challenge integral to any personal essay in which the author endeavors to account for herself. Such essays are most meaningful when the writer's character and situation stand alone while still inviting us to identify with her. The problem is that to be singular may communicate idiosyncrasies of circumstance and identity that can be admired but which deny us strong connections; at the same time, to be representative of others is to risk effacing the qualities of experience and occasion that prompt the essay. When restless skepticism animates the tensions between these particular and general tendencies, an essay has an economy of expression that moves back and forth between the self-reflective admissions of partiality and speculative indications of general significance. In this balance, the essay insinuates that incontrovertible proof is not the only warrant for truth.

For the project of *The God That Failed*, the skepticism of the essay was a problem to be solved: an impediment to sure convictions and not, as Said advises, an exercise to prize. I refer to this influential anthology as a "project" because soon after its publication it became an initiative of the Congress for Cultural Freedom (CCF), which promoted the volume at events throughout Western Europe and contributed to its commercial distribution internationally. Founded in Berlin in 1950 by a conference of intellectuals and artists who dedicated the ostensibly volunteer organization to advocacy for democratic ideals and public opposition to totalitarianism, the CCF was secretly created, funded, supervised, and to an extent directed by the US Central Intelligence Agency. The anthology had obvious appeal for the CCF. Each of the six contributors recounts how he became a member or supporter of the Communist Party in Germany, Italy, France, England, or the United States, only to determine after years of activity that he had been duped and that the party was a mere auxiliary to the authoritarian interests of Stalin's regime. Taken together without attention to the details that distinguish them, the essays can be said to document how the Cold War is a Manichean conflict in which it is incumbent on all the world either to affiliate with the democratic West led by the United States or to become subject to the totalitarian USSR. With this imperative to choose the West, *The God That Failed* recruited its original readers to identify themselves as part of a transnational coalition rooted in anticommunist convictions and sensibilities. To this end and in tension with the skeptical inclinations of the essay form, the collection endeavored to be firm about the validity of envisioning the postwar geopolitical order as a sheer division between Western and Eastern blocs, with the further understanding that unaffiliated regions and countries must inevitably be tied to one side or the other. In concert with this global vision, the anthology's introduction proposes that the testimonial essays show how the personal experiences of the authors make them unimpeachable witnesses to the perfidy of the Communist Party and to the emergency situation of the Cold War that organizes and threatens everyday life throughout the world.[4]

While editor Richard Crossman and lead essayist Arthur Koestler were the prime movers behind the volume, for the CCF's objectives Richard Wright's participation was most important. Pointing to the hypocrisy of postwar American claims to lead the "free world" while state-sanctioned racial segregation and routine incidents of lynching defined life for African Americans in the Jim Crow South, internationally disseminated Soviet propaganda charged the United States with intending to carry on in the tradition of the racist imperialism that spawned colonialism and the slave trade. That message was most damaging to the reputation of the United States among Africans and Asians inspired by the prospect of decolonization, but it was also important to Western European audiences intent on making sense of the relationship between the principles, policies, and actions of the most formidable military and economic state power still on its feet at the end of World War II. Arguably the most prominent black novelist in the world at the time the anthology was released, Wright represented individual achievement and African American progress that were unimaginable according to the portrait of the United States presented by the USSR. The mere inclusion of Wright's "I Tried to Be a Communist" alongside the work of a prominent literary figure such as Nobel laureate André Gide seemed to contradict Soviet aspersions. The content of his essay goes further by putting his reputation and racial identity behind the idea that the CPUSA's involvement with "the Negro problem" in America was mainly a ploy to foment unrest in the service of a party agenda that was not genuinely invested in black freedom.

If Wright's contribution provided the anthology with a direct connection to the narrative of racial liberalism that the US State Department circulated internationally in the long 1950s as if it were a doctrine of American nationalism, the immediate influence and lasting reputation of the volume have also been instrumental in shaping how the author's career has been understood in literary studies. As Bill Mullen demonstrates, Wright's public disavowal of his party membership endorsed the emerging cultural narrative that portrayed the CPUSA's retreat from desegregation during World War II as evidence that the party's involvement with the black freedom struggle in the United States had always been characterized by "dictatorial and brutalizing tendencies of the white

Left—particularly the Communist Party" that denied voice to black American activists.[5] Criticizing this narrative as the "long shadow" cast by Wright's essay and reputation over the history of black cultural politics in Chicago, Mullen argues that during the late 1930s and early 1940s relations between black and white artists, intellectuals, and activists on the left were in fact vital, mutually supportive, and more persistently radical than "I Tried to Be a Communist" acknowledged when it first appeared in two consecutive issues of the *Atlantic* in 1944. However, with the postwar Red Scare in full swing five years later, the reprinting of the essay in *The God That Failed* amplified Wright's complaints about the CPUSA, ensuring that his account would long dominate how "black and Red" relations in Chicago were remembered and would even overshadow his own criticisms of Cold War culture in the United States.

Wright's cooperation with *The God That Failed* was facilitated by a combination of his genuine aggravation with the CPUSA, late editing under duress, a convoluted publication history, and bad moral luck. The differences in the various editions of the essay reveal how Wright's storied break with the CPUSA was remade for the Cold War by the considerable efforts of the CCF. The result is that the Wright of "I Tried to Be a Communist" has overshadowed the Wright who essayed in the 1950s to demonstrate that normative accounts of the Cold War circulating in American public culture were expressive of an irresponsible, uncritical attitude toward the dominion of the United States in a world on the cusp of a profound and potentially anticapitalist transformation resulting from decolonization.

Wright's reception might have been very different if *Ebony* had published his first essay that is explicitly and adamantly opposed to the programs and discourse of Cold War anticommunism, the as yet unpublished "I Choose Exile." The decision of publisher John H. Johnson to reject and suppress the piece is an example of how the discourse of Cold War anticommunism facilitated unofficial, uncoordinated, but nevertheless effective cooperation between seemingly unrelated institutions. The discourse of Cold War anticommunism rendered "unsayable" the black radical characterization of historical capitalism as inextricable from the history of anti-black racism. Government, civic, and commercial institutions, as well as individuals, also enacted those normative constraints by obscuring any grievance that dispelled confidence in the progress of race relations, intimated that the free trade of private property is an insufficient basis for ethical and flourishing social relations, or identified the interdependence of race and class to suggest the black freedom struggle must be anticapitalist. The CCF and *Ebony* shared a narrative of racial progress that the publication of "I Choose Exile" would have distressed impermissibly. Had the essay appeared in 1952 as Wright anticipated, it would have

borne witness to his difference from the anticommunist attitude that all contributors to *The God That Failed* were said to exemplify.

Bad Transnationalism: The Congress for Cultural Freedom

In the final chapter of *Representations of the Intellectual*, his 1993 paean to
intellectual independence and activist writing, Said cites *The God That Failed*
as a near-perfect bad example. He objects to the six contributors ever having
relied on otherworldly, trans-historical explanations for social reality, but he
finds the stance they adopt toward their Communist pasts especially aggra-
vating. Defined by what he calls the "aesthetics of conversion and recantation,"
the anthology invests the Manichean division of democracy and totalitarianism with metaphysical significance.[6] The ineluctable choice between the
virtue of the democratic West and the vice of the communist East omits any
hint of the aspirations for autonomy that at the time were inspiring national
liberation struggles in dozens of Europe's colonies and former colonies across
Asia and Africa. Writing with the presumption that they have liberated themselves from any dogma, the essayists of *The God That Failed*, according to
Said, actually endorse a geopolitical vision that is shot through with religiosity. He reads their recantations as ritualistic pledges of fealty to a West that
would seem to be only all that the totalitarian East is not.

Said takes personally the collection's designs on the public cultures of the
United States and its Western European allies because he remembers too
well immigrating to the United States as a young boy when "McCarthyism
was in full course."[7] Public confessions such as those in *The God That Failed*
helped induce "mass hysteria" and shape "a bloody-minded intelligentsia, to
this day hung up on a wildly exaggerated internal and external menace."[8] In
what follows, I discuss how Said overstates the contents of the volume, but he
is right to identify the book as integral to the participation of intellectuals in
the efforts of the US federal government and select allies to instruct people
everywhere in how best to understand the Cold War. Dedicated to persuad-
ing the people and states of Western Europe to reject the USSR, the CCF's
programs of cultural exchange and artistic expression promoted the notion
that the West, led by the United States, represented freedom's ultimate stand
against the spread of totalitarianism. It was easy for the CCF to adopt *The
God That Failed* as its own initiative. Koestler was a key leader in both efforts.
The manifesto he drafted for ratification at the inaugural CCF conference
accords with the arguments Crossman and he make in their contributions
to the anthology.[9] CCF support enabled *The God That Failed* to sell 160,000

copies in English by 1954 and to be translated into sixteen other languages.[10] Other than Gide, who died before the book was published, each contributor participated to some extent in CCF events during the 1950s.

With very few exceptions, the initial book reviews represent the collection to express a consensus on the Cold War that coincides with the perspective of Crossman, Koestler, and the CCF.[11] Arthur Schlesinger Jr.'s review for the *Saturday Review of Literature* is an especially telling and influential single example. He corroborates the anthology's sense of a geopolitical emergency by referring to the rise of Communism—always capitalized by Schlesinger— as the "great issue of our time" and characterizing it as a "tragic deception" worse than fascism.[12] His review concentrates on rehearsing how contributors Ignazio Silone, Koestler, and Wright converted to the Communist Party and then became disillusioned. While identifying the particular details of dates and locations (e.g., Italy, Germany, and the United States, respectively), his synopses say little that differentiates any contributor from the others. Only Crossman is set apart because his introduction has an air "of the slight superiority of a Socialist who never fell for the Communist nonsense." Schlesinger's pronouncement that Communism is more pernicious than fascism signals his agreement that the Cold War confronts the world with an imperative to side actively with the anticommunist West led by the United States or to surrender all liberty. Any such suggestion in 1950 recalls that it was the entry of the United States into the European theater of World War II that enabled the defeat of the fascist states of Italy and Germany. That recollection interpolates the majority European essayists of the anthology into a North Atlantic cultural alliance that implies their participation in the American Century.

Schlesinger's explanation of how Communism is worse than fascism refers not to the relative strength of the Soviet Union nor to the supposed momentum of Communism's spread to China; instead, he refers to a difference in how each ideology preys on the psychology of prospective converts. He describes fascism with tropes he had previously used in *The Vital Center* to denigrate Communism. Fascism, he declares in the review, "took in only the desperate and depraved." Communism, in contrast, is a "corruption" that makes "an insidious and powerful appeal to men of good will." Fortunately, as evidenced by the anthology's six contributors, such "men" are likely to "rediscover through bitter experience that sense of the preciousness of the human personality which Communism excludes." Schlesinger concludes his review with the pronouncement that the anthology ought to be required reading for "American doughfaces." Soft on Communism, these liberals, he insists in a dramatic last line, find "virtue in despotism and brotherhood in slavery." Following his explanation of how "men of good will" inevitably must see through the Communist deception, his closing insinuates that liberals who dissent from the anticommunist consensus may lack the individual character traits that facilitated the ex-Communist essayists' returns to a proper regard for "freedom and decency." The review affords him a chance to reiterate an idea that he insinuates throughout *The Vital Center*: political attitudes to the left of his brand of centrism correspond to a deficient masculinity that cannot muster the resolve necessary to contend with communism.

Unnoticed in any early publication about *The God That Failed* and unacknowledged by its sponsors was the CIA's involvement in creating, funding, and directing the CCF's activities. Referred to in the CCF Manifesto as "an inalienable right of man," intellectual liberty was afforded the appearance of free reign by secret designs that exempted the CCF from the standards of transparency that were purportedly central to the organization's mandate. For Said, the covert affiliation between the CCF and the CIA means that the essayists of *The God That Failed* were propagandists for state interests who betrayed what he contends is an intellectual's obligation to be open, skeptical, and critical in her relationship to institutions of power. He insists that the "intellectual, properly speaking, is not a functionary or an employee completely given up to the goals of government or a large corporation, or even a guild of like-minded professionals."[13] Allied with narratives of American exceptionalism reignited for the Cold War, *The God That Failed* represents for Said the kind of doctrinal nationalism that is as much the impetus for his critical secularism as is religion:[14] a responsible intellectual must be worldly yet in exile from particular affiliations of identity that inhibit ruthless scrutiny and a universal horizon of expectations.

A striking feature of Said's synopsis of *The God That Failed* is, however, its inaccuracy. Acknowledging that more than four decades after its initial appearance the volume is remembered best for the "religious cast" of its title, he explains that the book's contents "do deserve brief summary."[15] The overview he then provides is, for him, uncharacteristically mistaken. Although each essay in the anthology does relate how its author converted to Communism only to later make an unequivocal break with the party, Said's account of this common path elides significant differences among the pieces, and, more importantly, confines all six to a uniform endorsement of the idea that the Cold War imposes on states and people the world over an unavoidable "choice" between liberty or enslavement. The development of each essay's narrative from the author's zealous immersion in the teachings and practices of the Communist Party to a disillusionment that compels public denunciation of the "irreducible evil" of communism, Said observes, replaces the "vital interchange" of politics with "religious enthusiasm."[16] The book represents the

Cold War as a "morality play." As a record of blind faith, the episodes of Communist involvement establish an opposition of moral absolutes; the "recantation" of each essay, Said contends, inverts the author's loyalty without relaxing the thoughtless dichotomy. Having been the enemy of the Communist dupe, democratic capitalism becomes for the penitent the redemptive pole in a metaphysical geopolitics of us against them. And in that context the ex-Communist is supposed to know best how to discern the danger Communists and communism represent for the West.

Contrary to Said's summary, however, the recantations of Communist involvement in the six essays do not each resolve in the author's renewed commitment to American-style democratic capitalism, or even to capitalism at all. Ignazio Silone, for example, in spite of his profound disappointment with the Comintern's betrayal of the aspirations for justice that first drew him to the party in Italy, ends his essay with a profession of continued faith in socialism. Respect for human dignity requires anticapitalist values and, he writes, "[s]ocialist values are permanent." They could be the basis, he explains, for "a culture, a civilization, a new way of living together among men."[17] The resolution of Gide's essay makes clear that he attacks the political practices of the Soviet Union not because they are communist but because they are actually capitalist. The last lines of his essay read: "The same old capitalist society has been re-established, a new and terrible despotism crushing and exploiting man, with all the abject and servile mentality of serfdom. Russia, like Demophoön, has failed to become a God and she will never now rise from the fires of the Soviet ordeal."[18] In contrast to Gide's mythic figuration of avarice, Stephen Spender's recantation describes party membership as Freudian self-mutilation: "The Communist, having joined the Party, has to castrate himself of the reasons which have made him one."[19] Although this characterization of the dysfunctional subjectivity of a Communist lends itself to the absolutist dichotomy Said finds objectionable, Spender's essay does not declare a political loyalty. Instead, he proposes that "[n]either side, in the present alignment of the world, represents what I believe to be the only solution of the world's problems." A solution will only come when "the millions of people who care more for bread than for freedom" can finally afford to care for the quality of their liberty.[20] To call for moderating the interests of the few to serve the material needs of the many is hardly a typically capitalist attitude. Louis Fischer, too, ultimately promotes an internationalism that is not beholden to the US version of capitalism. Wright is the only essayist to address the CPUSA and the internal political culture of the United States. Said makes no particular mention of Wright's essay but, as we will see, it too is only partially compatible with Said's account of the "aesthetics of conversion and recantation."

Describing the contributors as apologists for an unreflective vision of the Cold War West, Said misrepresents most of the content of the anthology while nevertheless getting right how the collection has typically been received since it was first published. Especially if we consider them in light of the esteem with which he regards the essay form, his uncharacteristic oversights should be understood as evidence of how forcefully the significance of *The God That Failed* has been informed by the discourse of Cold War anticommunism. The anthology has never been taken to mean what it says. The framework provided by Crossman's introduction, the example set by Koestler's lead essay, the institutional support provided by the CCF, and the initial reviews, especially well-placed reviews in the United States by prominent intellectuals, together communicate that the ex-Communists and former sympathizers tell tales that reveal the Cold War to be a pitched battle between the United States and the USSR that represents the interests of human freedom against the machinations of a state that is indifferent to suffering. The inaccuracy of that overview of the anthology's substance did not deter it from acquiring social significance. Irrespective of inconsistencies and differences of opinion between the essays, the book stood for a series of warnings with a common ultimatum: Cold War neutrality, "third way" alternatives, political dissent from the left, and vocal "exile" from the United States would all be assets to the Soviet Union's interests in the Cold War. To the exclusion of much else that the book says, Said's summary shows that he gets that message; the polemic he attributes to the volume must have recommended it to the CIA. His misreading forty years after the original publication is, then, an appropriate indication of how the book has been received. And considering how the collection's reputation seems to have distracted Said from noticing those features of the essays that are in accord with his admiration for the genre, the question raised by his misreading is how the discourse of Cold War anticommunism enjoyed sufficient rhetorical power to facilitate a public reputation for the anthology that corresponds to a partial view of its contents. Regarding Wright, the circulation of this selective misrepresentation of the volume was instrumental in the public failure to acknowledge his discrimination between anti-Communism and anticommunism.

It is worth noting that Crossman and Koestler's commitment to a Manichean vision of the Cold War is not the only influence for Said's selective reading of their anthology. A further source for his perspective is the story that *Ramparts* magazine was the first to corroborate in detail about the CCF in March 1967. Prior to that time it was widely rumored that the CIA was involved with and perhaps responsible for the organization; by 1960 Wright was convinced such rumors were true.[21] In the face of a CIA smear campaign in the periodicals *Human Events, News-Weekly*, and *Washington Star* as well as attempts to subvert the operations of the magazine by blackmailing staff members, *Ramparts* ran an exposé on how the CIA founded, funded, and directed the CCF.[22] Appearing within a few months of articles in the *New York Times* that disclosed the CIA's participation in illicit military interventions and assassination attempts on political leaders who were not amenable to US foreign policy interests, the articles on the secret origins of the CCF added to the CIA's reputation for nefarious influence over any institution that could be used to consolidate US hegemony over its sphere of influence and to bolster America's advantage in its rivalry with the Soviet Union.[23] That storied history evidenced little acknowledgment of other nation-states' right to self-determination and no compunction about staging demonstrations of "free thinking" in events planned and paid for secretly by government officials. The revelations destroyed the influence of the CCF. A name change would not be enough to preserve its relevance, and it would cease to exist in 1978.[24] Surviving it would be the cultural narrative of CIA deceptions that helps script Said's errant but telling representation of *The God That Failed*.

Said's account of the CCF's purpose in Western Europe and its use of *The God That Failed* contributes to a literature that associates the CIA's handling of the cultural Cold War in Europe with the increasingly imperialist underpinnings of US foreign policy from the end of World War II. From this perspective, the containment strategy imagined in Kennan's "Sources of Soviet Conduct" and announced as the Truman Doctrine in 1947 served during the Cold War both to describe the hostile but mutual standoff between the United States and the USSR and to excuse US military interventions that violated democratic principle and the right of self-determination in a number of what in the 1950s would come to be called "third world" countries. In a long essay for the *Nation* in 1968, Christopher Lasch argues that liberal anticommunist organizations such as the CCF, its US affiliate the ACCF, and the Americans for Democratic Action were in synch with the Cold War national security state.[25] Intellectuals affiliated with domestic and international liberal anticommunist institutions contributed to the cause of American militarism by defending the view that the United States either lacked or had abandoned a history of imperialism.

With the benefit of extensive archival materials more available in the 1990s than in the late 1960s, Frances Stonor Saunders prepared what amounts to an encyclopedic elaboration of Lasch's thesis. Characterizing her book as a "disenchantment" of official fictions, Saunders inquires into how self-described liberal, independent intellectuals could knowingly (or naively, for those

unaware of CIA involvement) volunteer their talents under the same anticommunist banner that the CIA used to justify the overthrow of democratically
elected Premier Mossadegh of Iran in 1953 and the democratic administration of President Arbenz in Guatemala in 1954.[26] Careful to emphasize that a
critique of US Cold War policy and its CIA propaganda programs in Western
Europe should in no way be construed as acceptance of the Stalinist Soviet
Union's incomparably worse gulag state, Saunders nevertheless challenges the
CIA's assumption that "principles of western democracy couldn't be revived
in postwar Europe" without undemocratic, secret initiatives involving soft
displays of cultural superiority designed both to reinforce Western Europe's
(already manifest) commitment to independence from the USSR and to help
justify US military interventions in Asia, Africa, and Latin America.

Recent efforts to rehabilitate the reputation of Cold War liberalism and
to promote among liberals in the United States a renewed commitment to
Schlesinger's notion of "the vital center" have been keen to explain how the
furor over the CIA's involvement with the CCF was more a function of the
timing of the revelations than of the substance of the discoveries. Disclosed
at the height of the Vietnam War by a magazine with open ties to the New
Left and the peace movement, the connection between the CCF and the CIA
was made public at a time when mention of the intelligence agency con-
jured images of state-sponsored coups and politically motivated assassination attempts. Defenders of the CCF claim that this heightened context led
to an anachronistic distortion of the organization's purpose and activities.[27]
Forgotten were both the "fighting faith" values of Cold War liberalism in the
1950s and the belated attempts of its leaders to counsel against militarism in
Vietnam. Kevin Mattson's *When America Was Great* targets Saunders's book
specifically for projecting Vietnam-era turmoil back onto the early years of
the cultural Cold War.[28] Like Peter Beinart's call for Democrats after 2003 to
join in the conflict against "totalitarian Islam" by repairing to the attitude of
Cold War liberalism, or Richard Rorty's earlier appeal to cultural leftists to
engage "real politics" by embracing the romance of American nationalism,
Mattson's book regards the leading figures of groups such as the CCF and
the ADA as heroic.[29] They took seriously, he claims, the international threat
of Communist totalitarianism, fought the Communist conspiracy at home,
and insisted on their differences from McCarthyism. For proponents of the
CCF and Cold War liberalism as usable pasts, it is necessary to represent the
American war in Vietnam as an anomaly in the US foreign policy. Said, in
contrast, reports in *Culture and Imperialism* that the United States intervened
militarily somewhere in the Third World annually from 1945 to 1967, when his
source, Richard Barnet, stopped counting.[30]

If the question of the CCF's character functions as a neat litmus test to determine whether a scholar of Cold War cultural studies avows or denies that the United States became (or remained) an imperial state following World War II, the history of contentious reception of the organization also suggests it has been practically obligatory to spar over who has a superior command of the plans of the group's chief personnel and their relative awareness of the CIA's involvement. Across their opposite appraisals of the CCF's significance, Saunders and Mattson share a focus on questions of intention. Debate over the character of the organization's key personalities threatens to devolve into an infinite regress of alternating claims about whose evidence enjoys more authority. Where she discerns implications of collusion with the illegitimate exercise of state violence, he identifies well-meaning efforts to instruct that same state in the legitimate limits of its authority. Neither characterization is without warrant. Saunders sees the CCF as an exemplary agent of cultural imperialism. By her account, the CIA's covert authority over the CCF points to how the arts and culture programs that were propaganda for the soft conflict between the United States and the USSR in Western Europe were of a piece with the misinformation campaigns and violence the CIA undertook in the Cold War's hot zones such as Iran, Guatemala, and Southeast Asia. Mattson, in contrast, emphasizes that the CCF should not be seen as a supplement to either the secret militancy of CIA-directed coups in sovereign states or the anticommunist histrionics of McCarthyism in the United States. Instead, the CCF should be lauded for having been an alternative means to preserve national interests through cultural exchanges and diplomacy that bolstered the appeal of containment as a durable, patient approach to contest the international influence of the Communist Party.

For Saunders and Mattson, then, questions about the quality of the leadership's intentions are bound up in determining how precisely the CCF relates to the interests of the US nation-state. The CCF did sponsor programs devoted explicitly to the promotion of an ideal of America. Careful to avoid unwelcome attention from other domestic agencies that shared in anticommunism's nativist tendencies, the US State Department organized international tours of jazz performers and traveling exhibitions of abstract expressionist paintings. Jazz and abstract expressionism share a reputation for originating in America. The signature stylistic features of improvisation and nonrepresentational form, respectively, were each cited as examples of free expression. Audiences were encouraged to associate that liberty of form with American democracy on offer to the so-called free world.[31]

However, emphasis on those features of the CCF that were in direct if unacknowledged service to the US national security state still obscures how the particular initiative of *The God That Failed* was a distinct undertaking. The anthology was not designed simply to inspire international allegiance to the United States in its power struggle with the USSR. Rather, it served to promote an idea of "the West" as a transnational, North Atlantic cultural identity defined by common history and principles that include an absolute objection to the values of communism. On behalf of this identity, and despite instances of dissent within particular essays, the volume on the whole seeks to compel its readers in this West to engage in a metaphysical conflict to which the essayists of *The God That Failed* and other ex-communists are said to bear extraordinary witness.

In the final line of his introduction, Crossman boasts that "[t]he devil once lived in Heaven and those who have not met him are unlikely to recognize an angel when they see one."[32] Said cites this line as evidence of the text's unsubtle implication that the conversion narratives to follow will corroborate how the standard story of the Cold War ought to be characterized as a Christian allegory. Ex-communists, by Crossman's logic, are equipped to guide popular opinion. His religious metaphors convey that those who have trafficked with the devil of Communism in the past are mostly likely to identify and value the difference between democracy and tyranny. Moreover, to see the signs of Communism is to discern how its desire for social control emanates not from reasoned convictions but from indeterminate, unholy compulsions. Communicated through images and narratives of monstrosity, this kind of argument was instrumental for the broader consequence of discrediting all manner of leftist thought.

Koestler's lead essay is most responsible for the anthology's inventive depiction of anticommunism as a positive disposition—an attitude of thought and feeling in contrast to which Communists and their like appear unholy, inhumane, and thoughtless. In the context of the anthology's composition, promotion, and initial reception, the other contributions are affiliated with this stance by virtue of their representations of Communist subjectivity in depoliticizing tropes. Whatever their differences in regard to Cold War geopolitics, the "narratives of conversion and recantation" invite us to retrace the production of autobiographical subjects who, though once duped, finally enjoy a principled and visceral objection to the Communist Party. In Koestler's case, the world-historical urgency of consolidating anticommunist solidarity is especially pronounced; he seeks to revitalize the West for the emergency of the Cold War. To that end, his essay's autobiographical narrative mobilizes several tropes to identify the errant Communist ontology of his youth. Including "Asiatic" along with blind faith, stupid mechanism, and drug addiction, he gives the Cold War a racial subtext that implies it is, essentially, a conflict between incomparable and incompatible civilizations. Early in his essay, he introduces his Orientalist view of the character of Russian Communists: "The Russians, as semi-orientals, are congenitally unpunctual; and as, consciously or unconsciously, every Party bureaucrat tried to live up to the Russian style, the habit gradually filtered down from the top Comintern bureaucracy into every national CP in Europe."[33] Later remarks on his travels in the Soviet Union return to the Asian subtext of Communism: "I could not help noticing the Asiatic backwardness of life; the apathy of crowds in the streets, tramways, and railway stations; the incredible housing conditions which make all industrial towns appear one vast slum."[34]

Timothy Brennan has noted that the "oddity of the terms 'East' and 'West' is that they allude both to the Cold War and to an imperial divide of race and civilizational conquest."[35] Rendering the Cold War antagonism between capitalism and communism indiscernible from the older division between East and West imagined by Orientalism, Koestler insinuates that the root difference in the Cold War is racial rather than ideological. The further aspersion of "backwardness" invokes the old canard that the timing of Western modernity is set to the European nation-states while colonial spaces and elsewhere lag behind, primitively unpunctual. Fixing the emergent bipolar division of the Cold War to a Eurocentric deep-time perspective, Koestler intimates that an obligatory expression of Western identity is strident anticommunism that claims for the "Occident" exclusive title to freedom.[36] By casting the Cold War as a civilizational conflict rooted in quasi-racial identities, Koestler denies to each side any share in the other's most definitive properties. For example, his essay makes no explicit mention of capitalism. This key criterion of the Cold War West remains unmarked and, it follows, any anticapitalist sentiments had to be marked by their exclusive affiliation with the monolithic East.

As it appears in *The God That Failed*, Wright's essay is comparable to Koestler's because of its reductive portrait of the mental habits entailed by Communist Party membership. His essay is most complementary to the CCF's objectives with the volume because of his ultimate concern for what African American political liberty could mean for US national identity. Wright's essay supports the anthology's vision of transnational anticommunism to the extent that his struggle with the party in the United States appears to be only a part of the cosmopolitical conflict Koestler puts into evidence. This limitation of Wright's essay, its emphasis on national well-being, is complementary to the anthology on the whole because it constrains the American case to a single chapter and staves off the suggestion that the transnational cultural identity of anticommunism articulated by *The God That Failed* is merely an alibi for an alliance manipulated to back the United States. The local demeanor of

Wright's essay encourages readers of the collection to infer that the United States is just another part of the whole of transnational anticommunism. The American contribution may involve more military readiness outside its borders, but its anticommunist character enjoys no privilege over other sites that in Koestler and the CCF's version of Western modernity might also stand for the freedom of democracy in opposition to totalitarian communism.

Complementary to the CCF: Wright's American Exceptionalism

When first prepared for the *Atlantic Monthly* in 1944, Wright's "I Tried to Be a Communist" was an excerpt rather than an essay. Taken from the final section of an autobiography that was scheduled to be published as *American Hunger*, the excerpt covers Wright's life from the time he arrives in Chicago, through his involvement with the John Reed Club and the CPUSA, until his rapport with the Communists in Chicago dissolves into open animosity and a physical assault against him. After a delay, the autobiography was published in truncated form with the title *Black Boy: A Record of Childhood and Youth*; the passages appearing in the *Atlantic* were not included. Dissimilar to those of Wright's texts from both before and after 1944 that are more conventional examples of the essay genre, "I Tried to Be a Communist" does not address his subject position or his relationship to his audience. In direct contrast to the retrospective stance of Koestler's essay, Wright recreates how he experienced and evaluated events in Chicago as they took place. The *Atlantic* initially promoted the excerpt as an advance look at Wright's forthcoming autobiography from Harper's. The last-hour involvement of the Book of the Month Club resulted in a dramatic change of plans for publication. As club director Dorothy Canfield Fisher communicated to Wright and his agent Paul Reynolds, the club was keen to make his memoir a selection but only on the condition that he remove the second part of the narrative, which included the pages of "I Tried to Be a Communist." The club wanted the book to recount Wright's experiences as a child in Jim Crow Mississippi up to the point in the narrative in which he arrives in Memphis as a young man en route to a future in Chicago free from *de jure* racial segregation. Having been a club selection for *Native Son* in 1940, Wright understood well the unrivaled ability of the organization to generate book sales, critical interest, and, as a consequence, favorable contracts for future books. His decision to comply with the request for drastic revisions meant the *Atlantic* had to print an apology for the inadvertent error in the advertisement that boasted "I Tried to Be a Communist" was an excerpt from Harper's forthcoming *Black Boy*.[37] Wright's text would remain an independent "essay" until it appeared in 1977 as part of the posthumous *American Hunger*, which included just the long section of the original autobiography refused in 1945 by the Book of the Month Club. In 1991 the publication of *Black Boy (American Hunger)* finally made available a restored text that is faithful to the manuscript Wright completed for Harper's before the well-intentioned offices of the Book of the Month Club initiated the book's convoluted publication history.

As an excerpt of the complete *Black Boy (American Hunger)*, the episodes from Wright's time as a Communist attribute the dysfunctions of the party to a combination of rigid doctrine, dogmatic leadership, and anti-black racism that is endemic to the United States. He even sets the racial problems of Chicago and the party in uncanny parallel to the abusive milieu of the American South detailed in those sections of the manuscript preferred by the Book of the Month Club. In its isolated appearance in the *Atlantic*, "I Tried to Be a Communist" seems to take singular aim at the CPUSA. His former associates in the party certainly regarded the essay as a bad-faith direct attack; fellow South Side Writing Group member Frank Marshall Davis was particularly aggrieved, noting years later that he had not forgiven Wright's betrayal.[38] Aside from the omission of a title, Wright's contribution to *The God That Failed* reprints verbatim "I Tried to Be a Communist." Without any mention of its relationship to *Black Boy* or its prior appearance in the *Atlantic*, however, it reads as if it were written for the occasion of the Cold War. In this context, without any mention of strong authorial claims regarding what Communist means for geopolitics at the time of the anthology's release, the framework of Crossman's introduction and the example of Koestler's lead essay implicate Wright's piece in a more resolute and urgent didacticism than is apparent in his essay's first appearance five years earlier.

Angered by the party's retreat from race when it endorsed calls for African American men to enlist in the segregated US military to fight the Axis Powers in Europe and Asia,[39] Wright's portrait of the party in the United States is willfully reductive. The picture of his treatment at the hands of the party in Chicago insinuates that the CPUSA made cynical use of anti-black racism to advance an agenda of Stalinist social control. By implying that African Americans had been tools for a party that was not genuinely invested in racial equality, he affirms the cultural narrative that says black Communists were pawns and dupes of the party's nefarious designs for the overthrow of the United States. With the disclosure of the Venona files and the opening of archives in the former Soviet Union in the 1990s, it is now indisputable that the USSR operated an extensive espionage ring in the United States throughout the 1930s and 1940s. And the agents and propaganda of the Soviet Union did call on nonwhite people in the United States and elsewhere to rally against the hypocrisy with which the United States proclaimed itself the leader of the free world in spite of the endurance of state-sanctioned apartheid throughout the American South. However, by playing exclusively into narratives about the CPUSA's exploitation of racial tensions, Wright's essay neglects the perplexing complexity of the party's identity during the decades prior to World War II. Even as the party was the institutional basis in the United States for a criminal network of spies, outside of the major civil rights organizations it was the only formidable advocacy group on the left for issues of racial justice.[40] As Michael Denning, Glenda Gilmore, Robin G. Kelley, Allan Wald, and others have demonstrated, local chapters and individual members of the CPUSA often acted independently from the mandates of international Communism that issued from the Soviet Union.[41] Wright, however justified his indignation at the party's retreat from race, had to realize that his personal narrative of frustration and conflict would elide the inconsistency between the party's historic record on race in the United States and its disappointing acceptance of a segregated military as a means to victory over Germany in World War II.

Episodes in which the John Reed Club and the party's South Side Chicago organization conduct internal investigations are a second feature of the essay that resonates especially well with the anthology's other characterizations of the authoritarian demeanor of the party. Wright represents the phenomenon of the "show trial" to illustrate the ease with which actions of the party and the subjectivity of its members can be defined by dysfunctional pathologies rather than political belief. A key episode early in the essay involves the brief but sensational career of a new member of Wright's John Reed Club, "Comrade Young of Detroit." Having been elected executive secretary of the club as a result of a power struggle within the membership between non-communist writers and Communist painters—the writers endorsed Wright's candidacy expecting that the painters would be compelled to support a black American in order to show their communist universalism—Wright is responsible for receiving Young and vetting his request to join the group. He also provides the penniless man a temporary place to stay in the club offices, which allows the charismatic newcomer to ingratiate himself to other members. At a meeting of the club, the suddenly influential Young denounces a popular, longtime member, Swann, accusing him of being a "traitor to the workers, an opportunist, a collaborator with the police, and an adherent of Trotsky."[42] Wright describes how the conflict that ensues divides and disorients the members; as the lead officer, it falls to him to confront Young about his motivations. The man tells him that he has been tasked with ridding the club of traitors to Communism; with "bulging eyes" and a "face quivering with passion," he declares to Wright that they must have a "purge" (124). Before his accusations can be investigated and the conflict resolved, Young disappears. A search of his things reveals an address in Detroit. Wright mails an inquiry and receives this response: "Dear Sir: In reply to your letter, we beg to inform you that Mr. Young who was a patient in our institution and who escaped from our custody a few months ago, has been apprehended and returned to this institution for mental treatment" (125). The realization that neither the club nor the party had detected Young's mental instability and that the man had met with approval from many for his revolutionary fervor provokes a crisis in Wright's confidence. "Thunderstruck," he asks, "what kind of club did we run that a lunatic could step into it and help run it? Were we all so mad that we could not detect a madman when we saw one?" The experience, he explains, made him a "sobered and chastened Communist" (126).

While the crisis Young provokes ends abruptly with his capture and return to the mental institution, the episode prepares us for Wright's later narrative of how Ross, another black Communist, was subjected to a bona fide show trial. Despite having announced his resignation from the party, Wright was urged to attend Ross's trial so that he might "learn what happened to 'enemies of the working class'" (153). Curious but wary that he might be the real target of the inquiry, Wright attends. The lesson he takes from what he witnesses is that there is no reason to doubt the most damning reports about the notorious Moscow trials of 1936. Having interviewed Ross at length for a planned series of member biographies, Wright knows the various charges of disloyalty to be fabrications, and he recognizes Ross's dismay when the most harmful testimony comes from the man's closest friends. But what is most telling about the proceedings is that Ross, with no apparent regard for his innocence, responds to all charges by confessing his guilt. "The vision of a communal world" in which he is "one with all the members" is more important to Ross than any other concern; his admission of guilt, promise to reform, and plea for forgiveness compose a ritual to unify the party membership through his abjection. Attesting to the veracity of negative accounts of the Moscow show trials and suggesting that his former Chicago comrades would be no less murderous if they were to possess the power of the state, Wright levels polemical, unambiguous complaints at the CPUSA.

Wright's essay is most complementary to the project of *The God That Failed* when he represents quitting the party in Chicago as a breach of faith necessitated by his disenchantment. His religious terminology affirms the anthology's title and looks back on his service as an expression of misplaced devotion. His essay concludes with the story of how two white communists from the South Side section of the party forcibly expel him from the May Day parade. They objected to his standing in the ranks of the party members. In the weeks following his attempt to resign from the party, he had been branded a Trotskyite and traitor. Encouraged by a black Communist to join him in the parade, Wright mistakenly presumed that the working-class solidarity of May Day would override the animosity party leaders were directing toward him. With the sound of the *Internationale* being sung in the street, the bruised Wright sits alone on a bench in Grant Park to reflect on how he was beaten by two white communists as an interracial crowd of other members watched. He determines that he can never again commit his literary talents to the cause of communism: "I remembered the stories I had written, the stories in which I had assigned a role of honor and glory to the Communist Party, and I was glad that they were down in black and white, were finished. For I knew in my heart that I would never be able to write that way again, would never be able to feel with that simple sharpness about life, would never again express such passionate hope, would never again make so total a commitment of faith" (162). In his introduction, Crossman cites the final sentence of this passage to emphasize how Communism is "a gospel of liberation among the Colored peoples" that may be accepted unreservedly by those nonwhites who, in contrast to Wright, have not also been exposed to the countervailing principles of Western democracy.[43] Appearing just three paragraphs from the end of Wright's chapter in *The God That Failed*, the passage corroborates the collection's general representation of the party as a religious institution that requires absolutist faith from its members. However, an examination of how this incident of religious recantation appears differently in other versions of the text suggests that Wright's compatibility with the mission of the CCF has been overstated. Editorial demands imposed by others, institutional support for the CCF, the volume's timing, Wright's exile from US public culture, and additional happenstance conspired to elide what he regarded a significant difference between, on the one hand, opposition to the CPUSA and Stalin's regime (anti-Communism) and, on the other, sweeping, depoliticizing, punishing injunctions against all manner of anticapitalist thought (anticommunism).

Anti-Communism becomes Anticommunism

Coming at the end of an essay that records how his relationship with the party was constantly embattled, especially over questions about the place of literary artistry within proletarian politics, Wright's concluding reference to a "total commitment of faith" should be unexpected. Nowhere previously does the essay describe the kind of conversion experience that could be the basis for such a fervent recantation. Like Koestler's essay, early in his text Wright accounts for how he comes to the ideas of communism through an intense reading experience. But where Koestler depicts reading Marx as an epiphany,[44] Wright recalls how, as impressed as he was with the prospect of international working-class solidarity, he saw deficiencies in the texts of the Communists and was confident he could aid the cause with improved writing: "The Communists, I felt, had oversimplified the experience of those whom they sought to lead. . . . I would try to put some of that meaning back. I would tell Communists how common people felt."[45] While Wright did in fact prepare dozens of articles for the *Daily Worker*, his essay describes how his writerly ambitions were thwarted by party dictates and mocked by other members as the bourgeois habits of an intellectual. When the CPUSA convened the American Writers' Conference in New York in 1935, Wright spoke in opposition to the elimination of the John Reed Clubs. Although he knew that his stand "would be interpreted as one of opposition to the Communist Party," he cast a dissenting vote in favor of the clubs. With the clubs dissolved, Wright resolves that his "relationship with the Party was about over."[46] His fight for the survival of the clubs, like his ongoing pursuit of a place for literary expression in a revolutionary political organization, indicates that his disposition within the party had always been contentious.

Wright's omission of nuance and complication regarding the semi-autonomy of the party was unfair to its history of anti-racist activism prior to the entry of the United States into World War II. To critique the CPUSA at the time of its wartime neglect of race was an altogether different proposition from repeating that identical critique in 1949, when the Soviet Union was entrenched in US public culture as an enemy and the popular misuse of the concept of totalitarianism conflated all positions on the left, equating them to National Socialism. In other words, "I Tried to Be a Communist" combines principled and polemical objections to the Communist Party at a time in which anticommunism had new appeal for many African Americans. The verbatim account in *The God That Failed* in 1949 did not appear in the context of African American disapproval of the party's retreat during World War II from "The Negro Question." Instead, it resonated with the postwar anticommunist discourse that painted political dissent as heresy and leftist precepts as diseased. And while that discourse was made to support the official anti-racism of federal policy after *Brown v. Board of Education*, in 1949 it remained impressively useful for white supremacist antagonism toward civil rights for African Americans.

Had the original publication of "I Tried to Be a Communist" in the *Atlantic* been followed by the republication of those pages in the complete edition that after 1991 we know as *Black Boy (American Hunger)*, its differences from the normative story of the Cold War promulgated by *The God That Failed* would have been more pronounced. Perhaps Wright would not have been such an attractive candidate for inclusion? Consider again how Wright's essay handles its most damaging evidence against the CPUSA, the show trial against Ross. At the height of this sharp rebuke, Wright alludes to race relations in the United States as a condition of possibility for the trial, which he calls a "spectacle of horror." Of his former comrades, he writes: "The blindness of their limited lives—lives truncated and impoverished by the oppression they had suffered long before they had ever heard of Communism—made them think I was with their enemies. American life had so corrupted their consciousness that they were unable to recognize their friends when they saw them."[47] In the context of *The God That Failed*, this passage is in keeping with the conviction that Communism preys on social distress to its advantage, but returned to *Black Boy (American Hunger)* the more likely inference is that problems within the party are not independent from social disrepair located squarely in the racial state of the United States.

In the text of *Black Boy (American Hunger)*, Wright's final reference to Communist faith (lost) is out of synch with his consistent skepticism about any manner of religion. Living at age twelve in the home of his grandmother, a devout Seventh Day Adventist, Wright is confronted with the collaboration between his family and his classmates to see him "saved" before the end of a summer of religious revivals. In dialogue with a boy his age who pleads with him to pray for salvation, Wright replies that he "simply can't feel religion," and informs us in an aside that this explanation is "in lieu of telling him that I did not think I had the kind of soul he thought I had."[48] Near the end of the exchange in which his shocked friend leaves in tears over Wright's dismissive attitude toward the obligations of faith, we come to a rare passage in which the narrative voice hints at the consistency between Wright's youthful rejection of religion and the author's secular attitude at the time of his writing:

> It would have been impossible for me to have told him how I felt about religion. . . . Embedded in me was a notion of the suffering in life, but none of it seemed like the consequences of original sin to me; I simply could not feel weak and lost in a cosmic manner. Before I had been made to go to church, I had given God's existence a sort of tacit assent, but after having seen His creatures serve Him at first hand, I had had my doubts. My faith, such as it was, was welded to the common realities of life, anchored in the sensations of my body and in what

my mind could grasp, and nothing could ever shake this faith, and surely not my fear of an invisible power.[49]

Black Boy (American Hunger) is an "open" autobiography, in which the life recorded is still in progress and the author typically "refrains from shaping his life neatly in a teleological plot."[50] But in this passage, the statement "nothing could ever shake this faith" conveys the certainty of hindsight. Wright records the permanence of his youthful refusal of Christianity or any metaphysical doctrine that proposes to animate reality with an otherworldly agency. The complete autobiography represents Wright as a secularist from start to finish with the isolated exception of the single, belated mention of a "total commitment of faith" in Communism. That instance cannot be read without ambivalence; in the context of the complete autobiographical novel, Wright's reference to faith does not dissuade us from the impression that while he was *in* the Communist Party, he was never entirely *of* it. He represents his own involvement in the party as a practice of political activism that abides too patiently and for too long structural limitations and interpersonal conflicts that derive from the confluence of foreign dictates for Party discipline and home-grown racism.

In *The God That Failed*, Wright's profession of broken faith is followed almost immediately by his reflection on his sense of isolation and a final, stirring pledge to confront the alienating facts of human existence by hurling "words into this darkness . . . to tell, to march, to fight, to create a sense of the hunger for life that gnaws in us all, to keep alive in our hearts a sense of the inexpressibly human."[51] For an attentive reader of Wright's works at the time of *The God That Failed*, the conclusion to his essay must have read like a reprise of the conclusion to the original 1945 edition of *Black Boy*. Each text speaks of his devotion to the written word and points toward a struggle for human recognition that must inevitably be won. As Janice Thaddeus and Jeff Karem have documented, the last ten paragraphs of the 1945 edition of *Black Boy* were added by Wright in response to the requests and suggestions of Fischer for the Book of the Month Club. Her concern had been that the ending was too bleak and that Wright should be more forthcoming about how the promise of independence in the American North is expressive of the trajectory of US national history and an inspiration for him personally. The Book of the Month Club requirements transformed a comprehensive narrative critique of the racial formation of the United States, South and North, into an uplift narrative that traces how Wright fled from Jim Crow oppression toward the supposed freedom from racial discrimination in the North.[52] Echoing those nineteenth-century fugitive slave narratives that acknowledge how among slaves the North served as an imaginary geography in which the ideal of inalienable self-possession might be realized for all people, the amended *Black Boy* concludes before actual experiences in the North could complicate and undermine that promise. As a result, *Black Boy* affirms the normative story of racial liberalism that distinguishes North from South according to a temporal schema in which the decrepit land of Jim Crow rule is a feudal anachronism that the modern America being realized in the North will inevitably overcome. By characterizing Jim Crow segregation as the residue of an uncivilized social order that was anomalous to American national character and certain to give way to progress, racial liberalism explained away the contradiction between postwar claims for the United States' leadership of the free world and the persistence of state-sponsored racial discrimination and terrorism. Interestingly, Koestler's Orientalist characterization of communism as a retrograde culture appeals to the same temporality of modernity.

As I have said, the simple fact of Wright's inclusion in *The God That Failed* was expected to corroborate the racial liberalism narrative of the unyielding progress in the United States from a racist past and toward the inevitable end of discrimination that in the contemporary American Century was somehow already secure despite not yet being manifest. But with the loss of Communist faith followed in short order by an impassioned commitment to writing, Wright's essay does more to corroborate the racial liberalism narrative than represent a black American author welcome in the company of white intellectuals and artists of international renown. Where *Black Boy (American Hunger)* makes explicit the parallels between the South and the North, the excerpt appearing in *The God That Failed* invites us to regard the CPUSA as the chief impediment to liberal democracy's overcoming racism. The essay provides an un-American origin for his negative experiences in Chicago, as if the optimism with which the 1945 *Black Boy* ends were disappointed exclusively by the Communists rather than by the *de facto* hold of racial segregation on the urban North. Insulating Chicago from culpability in the reiteration of experiences of discrimination and violence that dominated Wright's life in the Jim Crow South, the essay implicitly endorses the narrative of racial liberalism encoded in *Black Boy* retroactively by its final ten paragraphs. When the essay reappears five years after *Black Boy*, the context of the Cold War means that a narrative of America's racial liberalism was readily available to virtually anyone interested enough to pick up *The God That Failed*, especially if the copy in hand had been distributed by the CCF at the time the group was working so assiduously to circulate the image of Wright and other African American artists and intellectuals as proof positive that in the United States the redress of racial segregation was under way with no further delay.

In *Black Boy (American Hunger)*, nearly two pages intervene between Wright's profession of broken faith and the commitment to writing he makes in his final paragraph. In that interval he revisits the major phases of his life. His conclusions fail to recommend anywhere he has lived: "Well, what had I got out of living in the city? What had I got out of living in the South? What had I got out of living in America? I paced the floor, knowing that all I possessed were words and dim knowledge that my country had shown me no examples of how to live a human life."[53] This reflection may come in the wake of his final confrontation with the party, but it omits any particular reference to Communists. Instead, Wright sources the adversities that define his life to the urban North, the rural South, and their synthesis in the nation. Unlike the hopeful final paragraphs of the 1945 *Black Boy*, America appears here as no exception to the rule of systemic racism. Contrary to the conclusion of "I Tried to Be a Communist" in either of its appearances, the failures of the CPUSA in regard to race are as much an expression of its American setting and membership as any edict issuing from the Soviet Union.

By contrasting Wright's essay for *The God That Failed* with the significance of its initial appearance in the *Atlantic* and its markedly different arrangement in *Black Boy (American Hunger)*, I am arguing for a distinction between his rejection of the Communist Party and his stance toward the discourse of Cold War anticommunism. The reductive either/or epistemology to which *The God That Failed* contributed disallowed the modest complexity of a position that rejects the party while identifying the general anticommunist assault on the left as an affront to democratic principle and an impediment to the anticapitalist dimensions of the black freedom movement. And while Wright's portrait of the party, as I have indicated, is a sweeping indictment, at the moment in the essay in which he recognizes his mistake in joining the party he does not pronounce himself devoted to the cause of fighting Communism. Instead, he thinks to himself, "I'll be for them, even though they are not for me."[54] This gesture of rapport may not have tempered Communists' denunciations of the essay in 1944, but it separates his characterization of Communist convictions from the anticommunist epistemology that informs Koestler's vision of the West and that provided a crucial rhetorical bulwark for official efforts to identify communism as a mode of criminality and communists as ontologically distinct from people of virtually any other political disposition. In all three appearances of his essay, his statement signals that Wright does not embrace the either/or epistemology that the CCF project of *The God That Failed* uses to impress on readers that a commitment to the West against the communist East is imperative.

Certainly, nothing in the anthology or its reception in the United States hints at how Wright went on record in France in 1948 with the position that Western Europe ought to maintain its independence from the United States and the USSR. Nor does the collection acknowledge his belief that as an American intellectual in exile he was obliged to be critical of both sides in the Cold War. A remark in 1950 to the Brazilian periodical *Revista Branca* expresses his view in an emphatic contradiction of the normative story of the Cold War represented by *The God That Failed*: "Russian Communism and Americanism, as they now appear, are not two forces one of which is good and the other evil. They are two evils confronting each other, and in my opinion the errors of both should be exposed."[55] In the initial, extended months of success for *The God That Failed*, the absence of such remarks from Wright in publications based in the United States meant that even as he lived in exile his voice and reputation were retained at home for the sake of Cold War anticommunism. The fact of his residency in Paris may have been well publicized, but his convictions about the critical responsibility of life in exile went mostly unrecorded in America and were strategically neglected by the CCF. A telling exception was a document available at the time only to officials of the Federal Bureau of Investigation. He was frequently a subject of surveillance by both the CIA and the FBI, and at some point between March 1952 and July 1953 an unidentified agent of the latter filed a report that evaluates Wright's attitude about the Cold War: "He has maintained a position, so far as the East-West conflict is concerned, tantamount to 'a plague on both your houses.'"[56] This cliché incorrectly assigns Wright a viewpoint that sees any differences between the United States and the USSR as incidental. Later in the same Brazilian interview in which he refers to the Cold War as a confrontation of evils, he clarifies that the two superpowers are not exactly moral equivalents. Were a direct war to break out between the two countries, Wright pledges that he would unequivocally support the United States, which is not just his homeland but also a state in which the tenuous but persistent relevance of democratic legitimacy affords him some hope for its future political culture. The USSR, in contrast, is a lost cause; no "individual political freedom" exists there.[57] Although the FBI report errs in the false equivalency it attributes to Wright, it does at least identify him with a position outside the epistemological bind of Cold War anticommunism. The project of *The God That Failed* endeavored to render any such stance incoherent. In Wright's particular case, fitting his essay into the neat opposition of West against East provided a counterpoint to Communist propaganda about the inescapable conditions of oppression for African Americans in the United States. That effort in regard to Wright would be aided in the United States by *Ebony* magazine of Johnson Publishing, a corporation that has long embodied the conviction that capitalism is the way forward for African Americans and not, as the black radical tradition teaches, an impediment that reproduces unceasingly those social conditions that invented and facilitated anti-black racism as it has been known in the long run of Western modernity.

Essaying to be an Exile

Invited by *Ebony*'s managing editor Ben Burns to report on "what happens when a Negro goes overseas and suddenly finds the freedom he has long been seeking,"[58] in December 1951 Wright submitted an essay that extols the racial climate in France for African Americans but extends criticisms of US public culture that range beyond the topic of race. Had he merely elaborated on his experiences as an ex-pat writer living at a remove from the anti-black racism in America that would deny him liberties, resources, and opportunities his literary achievements and reputation afforded him overseas, his piece could have fit neatly into the magazine's pattern of showcasing promising true stories of successful African Americans. Founded in 1945, *Ebony* was addressed to a growing black middle-class readership. From the beginning, cover photographs have featured African American celebrities, and lead stories routinely applaud examples of successful black entrepreneurship.[59] Also a popular source of information about the struggle for civil rights in the United States and the global fight against colonialism, in its reporting and editorials the magazine reiterated the American narrative of racial liberalism: the struggle to end discrimination is ongoing and overdue but has no better hope than the promising, even inevitable expansion of democratic franchise in the United States. Progress on Myrdal's American dilemma, in other words, was well under way and bound to succeed. With the popularity and sales of *Ebony* and *Jet*, Johnson Publishing was emblematic of the argument on behalf of African American progress.

As a best-selling, critically acclaimed novelist, Wright was an obvious interest for *Ebony*, but it was an inauspicious venue for his criticisms of the racial formation of the United States. Had it appeared in print, "I Choose Exile" would have been a nearly unprecedented departure from the magazine's optimistic portrayal of progress on race. It might also have brought Johnson Publishing unwelcome attention from tribunals and police operations seeking to identify un-American activities. With a brash and disparaging response to such labeling, "I Choose Exile" coordinates three critiques of the public culture of the postwar United States to indicate Wright's sense that, with the Cold

War's emergence, anticommunism, capitalism, and the possessive investment in whiteness constitute an invigorated network of social interests poised to sustain racial inequality at home and abroad even if Jim Crow rule in the American South were somehow brought to an end. Although the essay makes no explicit reference to *The God That Failed*, Wright's recommendation of exile is a rejection of the anticommunist imperative to choose liberty in the West or servitude in the East. His romantic portrait of France at a remove from the conflict challenges the Cold War geopolitical imaginary that maps all the world into two spheres of influence plus those regions and countries that have yet to align themselves with one bloc or the other. His essay also faults the exceptional affluence of the United States, implying that the values of capitalist advancement are noxious in an ever-smaller world order. The mutual support between legal and voluntary protections for the socioeconomic value of whiteness, the Red Scare, and postwar American affluence, he concludes, are also likely to mean that his criticisms can make no impression on a body politic insulated by a nationalist ethos primed to dismiss criticism as a mere symptom of communism. Unlike *Ebony*'s support for State Department and White House efforts to project an international image of the United States defined by the federal government's official antiracism, "I Choose Exile" personifies America as a consciousness too oblivious to recognize how the United States relates to the rest of the world. *Ebony* urged the federal government to expand programs to educate people in other countries about the United States. In November 1951, the issue preceding the appearance of "The Shame of Chicago," the magazine printed an editorial on "How to Stop the Russians" that acknowledges the greatest liability to the international reputation of the United States is the persistence of state-sanctioned racism. In addition to continued progress against racial discrimination at home, the magazine recommends that representative African Americans be sent abroad as emissaries to instruct people "about the amazing advances we have made to show them that Willie McGee and Cicero are the exception rather than the rule. The abysmal ignorance of most Europeans about the life of the average Negro in America is appalling. Little do they know that most US Negroes enjoy a higher standard of living than most Russian commissars."[60]

Against the emerging optimism that the Cold War would compel the US federal government to enact antiracist policies, Wright suggests that anticommunism exacerbates racism. For him, the rejection of his essay by *Ebony* (and later the *Atlantic*) was evidence of its thesis. On January 23, 1952, he contacted Burns to share his impression that *Ebony* must think the essay is "too strong" in its complaints to be printed in the magazine. His letter acknowledges that the most volatile works are sometimes more appropriate for mainstream venues that do not suffer the scrutiny and vulnerability of African American publications: "let white periodicals carry the moral burden of printing articles that might harm Negro publications in the eyes of Government," he writes.[61] The *Atlantic* had contacted Wright with an invitation much like *Ebony*'s; the magazine wanted a piece on Wright's experience as an African American in France. It would take Wright several more months to reclaim from Johnson title to the essay. In the meantime, the *Atlantic* reviewed the piece and rejected it, prompting Wright to observe to his agent, Paul Reynolds: "I was a little surprised at The Atlantic's reaction, but it simply means that the fear has reached even to Boston."[62]

As Wright's biographers note, *Ebony*'s founding publisher John H. Johnson retained his right to the piece for more than two years just to ensure it remained unpublished and unknown. Johnson sent a telegram to Wright in 1953 acknowledging he would release "I Choose Exile" for Wright to sell to another publisher. His message suggests disingenuously that only "further editing" would have been required for the piece to appear in *Ebony*, and insists that in exchange for the return of the essay he expects Wright to allow his family to be photographed in their Paris home for a future *Ebony* photo-essay on their lives in France.[63] The exhibition of cosmopolitan and affluent lifestyle enjoyed by an African American celebrity, presented without his withering critique of the persistence of racist capitalism in the United States, illustrates how the stance of Johnson Publishing was to promote racial equality through an editorial commitment to American capitalism as a first principle for human freedom rather than a surety for the conditions of exploitation that black radicalism understands to be a necessary factor in the reproduction of anti-black racism. The relationship between Johnson Publishing and the author had been uneasy before the rejection of "I Choose Exile." The essay was to be the second of four Wright contracted to provide *Ebony* over twelve months starting in November 1949, but he only managed to deliver his first contribution, "The Shame of Chicago," in August 1951. Over several months following the start of the contract period, Burns sent letters entreating Wright to deliver new writing. A letter of December 7, 1949, opens: "Dear Dick, Don't you love us anymore?" In May 1950 he writes, "We are still anxiously awaiting your first piece for *Ebony*." A September 1950 letter ends, "When are you going to get around to collecting all that nice money we offered you?"[64]

"The Shame of Chicago" appeared as a cover story in December 1951, the same month that Burns and Johnson received Wright's draft of "I Choose Exile." Objecting to the bleak assessment of the racial stratification of Chicago, Johnson permitted "The Shame of Chicago" to appear only on the condition that an unsigned editorial be included in the same issue to rebut Wright's claims. Burns was charged with writing the piece, entitled "Return of the Native Son." He never acknowledged his authorship, and as late as 1953 Wright was still complaining in letters to Burns that he had never received promised copies of the issue.[65] Access to the magazine's rebuke of this first article might have helped Wright anticipate that his even harsher criticisms of American public culture in "I Choose Exile" would never receive Johnson's approval.

"The Shame of Chicago" recounts how the city proved a difficult place to shoot the film adaptation of Wright's novel *Native Son*. He describes how the presence of African American production staff and performers provoked suspicion and resistance. Police scrutiny of their location shoots obliged Wright to arrange regular bribes to ensure the production's permits would be honored. Prohibitions at downtown hotels forced him to enlist white associates to trick and cajole managers into providing accommodations for African Americans working on the film.[66] None of Wright's anecdotes about his struggles with the film production are of concern in Burns's unsigned response. Writing for the editorial board, he objects instead to how Wright's reflections on returning to Chicago after a twelve-year absence characterize the city as stricken with vast inequalities of wealth that result in especially dirty and impoverished conditions for its predominantly African American South Side.

Burns opens with the puzzling admission that the magazine's board found itself in the unusual position of "agreeing with every word of Wright's" while considering his report "distorted and one-sided . . . a warped, often-naïve, and incomplete study."[67] The illogic of this opening judgment implies that *Ebony* was keen to represent the great literary figure in its pages but not his ideas. The editorial attempts to make sense of its initial contradiction by dismissing Wright's observations as too partial to bear on the true standing of African Americans in Chicago. Conceding that conditions of profound and racialized impoverishment do persist, Burns insists that Wright's vision of such conditions is informed to a fault by his portrait of Depression-era Chicago in *Native Son*. Wright's new observations in 1949 are oblivious to the evident change in status of African Americans during his absence from the city. "However, when it came to the better side of Negro life in Chicago," Burns asserts, "Wright was wearing blinders." Printed opposite a full-page photograph of a palatial home owned by the publisher of the *Chicago Defender*, John Sengstacke, the editorial criticizes Wright for failing to recognize that since the end of the Depression the living standards of African Americans in Chicago were superior to those found among all citizens of France: "Go right down the line of what most people in the world consider the measure of better living—food, clothing, shelter, job security—the Chicago Negro is better off than most Frenchmen." Preparing his editorial before receiving the typescript of "I Choose Exile," Burns could not have known how his sweeping, unlikely claim would conflict neatly with Wright's polemical assertion that there is more freedom to be found "in one square block of Paris than there is in the entire United States."[68]

Omitted from Burns's summary of "The Shame of Chicago" is sufficient recognition of how Wright complicates his criticisms of persistent racism in Chicago with his recognition that a burgeoning black middle class is enjoying the rewards of America's postwar affluence. In Wright's view, change in the living standards of African Americans has not disrupted the constancy of white resistance to integration:

> The situation among the white citizens of Chicago is *bad*, but it contains an element of hope; but the situation among the Negroes of the South Side is not *too* bad, but it is distinctly hopeless. Meaning this: Chicago whites still grudgingly withhold from the Negro the right to living space, full citizenship, job opportunities; but the Negro, within these hopeless limits, is making progress in his material standards of living, in education, in business, in culture and in health.[69]

Contrary to Johnson Publishing's optimism about the progress of race relations, in this passage Wright sees that the African American acquisition of economic and social capital has no bearing on what, in a rejection of popular refrains about the Negro problem, he elsewhere calls the white problem.[70] Improved finances among African Americans have not, he observes, resulted in true franchise as citizens or equal access to opportunities. Wright's separate consideration of race and class is a reminder of his break with the Communist Party, which in its orthodox economic determinism insisted that race is secondary to class. While he calls "hopeless" the prospects of black progress against the advantages reserved for (some) whites, in "I Choose Exile" his judgments are more discouraging.

Wright opens the essay with a double gesture that underscores how his choice of exile situates him at once outside and in a relationship to the United States. On the one hand, he writes, "I live in voluntary exile in France, and I like it. There is nothing in America—its drugstores, skyscrapers, television, movies, baseball, Dick Tracy, Black Belt, Jew Town, Irish Section, Bohunks, Wetbacks, dust storms, floods—that I miss or yearn for."[71] On the other hand, despite his intention to remain away from the United States, he pledges in the essay's introduction to remain an American citizen, pay his taxes, retain his passport, support and receive Social Security, and refuse to aid his country's enemies. The subject position he describes rejects what he regards as materialistic and racist cultural norms in the United States, but he embraces the signs and obligations of his American civic identity. Voluntary exile does not mean he has abandoned his homeland; on the contrary, he relocates to pursue values over which American nationalism has typically claimed unique title. In a political and racial climate that he sees worsening as a result of the social values promoted by postwar consumerism and Cold War anticommunism, Wright determines that his claims for American identity, democratic principles, and personal liberty can only be pursued outside the United States.

When he proceeds to define five properties he expects of freedom, he intervenes directly against the familiar semantics of anticommunism. He appropriates "un-American" to characterize the values he holds dear:

> My Un-Americanism, then, consists of the fact that I want the right to hold, without fear of punitive measure, an opinion with which my neighbor does not agree; the right to travel wherever and whenever I please even though my ideas might not coincide with those of whatever Federal Administration might be in power in Washington; the right to express publicly my distrust of the "collective wisdom" of the people; the right to exercise my conscience and intelligence to the extent of refusing to "inform" and "spy" on my neighbor because he holds political convictions differing from mine; the right to express, without fear of reprisal, my rejection of religion.[72]

With Senator McCarthy's notorious denunciations of a dubious list of Communists in the State Department still very much alive in public culture, Wright volunteers for the assignation "un-American" but insinuates in his redefinition of the term that those who wield it pejoratively are the opponents of freedoms of expression, thought, movement, and religion. Pleading guilty to being un-American in this sense, he also insists "that I'm not Anti-American, which, to me, is the important thing."[73] Wright's criteria for freedom mean, he claims, that his politics are chiefly democratic but "mob violence," including "anonymous blacklisting," has made him skeptical about the viability of democracy in America.[74] He refuses calls such as Hoover's 1947 assertion before HUAC that patriotic citizens must be vigilant in surveying their everyday environment for evidence of the contagion of communism. The expectation that civic identity entails voluntary surveillance against one's neighbors is creating, Wright suggests, a tyrannical majority rule that extends beyond electoral politics into ordinary social life. Wright's FBI file is an example of such civil vigilance; it includes letters by a number of private citizens complaining to the agency about the publication and influence of the disloyal, un-American *Black Boy*.

Despite his feelings of alienation from his country, Wright claims to know Americans so well that he can predict the standard response to his choice of exile. People will say, he explains, that he has fled to France solely to escape Jim Crow racial segregation.[75] He refuses this anticipated reduction of his motives because racism, he insists, is not the only consideration in his decision. Other commonalities of postwar America culture persuade him to remain away. Curiously, Wright immediately follows his claim about how factors other than racism compel his choice of exile by recounting an experience of racial discrimination. The pertinence of his anecdote for his broader argument emerges when it becomes clear that the discrimination he suffers involves none of the Jim Crow iconography or obviousness implied by his imagined auditors' predictable reference to segregation. Instead, his story takes place in rural New England, and it involves the understated regulation of residential space according to racist protocols that are less visceral than signs for "whites only" but nonetheless pernicious in the way they sustain racial inequality.

Frustrated with living in the city, in the spring of 1946 Wright determines to move with his family to the country. Choosing a place in the country, he reminds the would-be readers of *Ebony*, is a precarious undertaking for an African American. The history and persistence of lynchings rob outdoor settings of their Arcadian innocence.[76] Careful reflection about the potential hazards of living in the countryside leads Wright to optimistic thoughts of the Northeast. Hawthorne, the transcendentalists Emerson and Thoreau, and the abolitionists were all from New England; surely, it would be different from the precarious rural locations of every other region of the country. Resolved to make a home in New England, Wright stayed for several days in Hanover, New Hampshire, with friends who offered to assist his search for a property. As Wright recounts the story of how he found but failed to buy the perfect house in Connecticut, he shows that his all-too-familiar experience of anti-black racism was an embarrassing revelation to his well-intentioned white friends. His being denied the right to buy a house exposed that white and black Americans can be in the same place while inhabiting strikingly different realities.[77]

After two days of searching, Wright found a house he wanted to buy. A half-mile from the nearest neighbor, it would have afforded him and his family the quiet remove from the city he desired. And the $6,000 asking price was no deterrent to this writer of international reputation and impressive sales. He offered to make complete payment on the spot, but the real estate broker responsible for the property insisted they wait for confirmation from the seller before proceeding. The required delay was Wright's first inkling that more than money would apply to any transaction over the house. Promised a response to his offer within two days, he describes waiting four before asking one of his friends to make inquiries. His friend returns from the real estate office with the news that the house's owner refuses to allow an African American to buy the property. Calling their conversation a scene with a legacy of hundreds of years in America, Wright describes his conscientious white friend's difficulty trying to protect Wright's feelings while telling him the shameful truth that the house's owner preferred losing the sale to receiving immediately the full value of the house from someone black. And Wright describes trying, in turn, to protect his friend from feeling responsible for the painful, unconscionable fact of racism; he reassured him that what happened was no surprise. On the contrary, for African Americans it was an ordinary experience. Whatever assurances he offered his friend were finally insufficient for Wright himself, who decided after the experience to leave the United States. Why, he asks, "continue this pointless grappling with racial muck?"[78]

Wright's story serves as a corrective to the mistaken attitude that the American North is substantially better than the South regarding race—a view, recall, supported tacitly by the ending of the Book of the Month Club version of *Black Boy*. Locating a tale of discrimination in the region that gave rise to abolitionism and which is presumed to be removed from Jim Crow rule, he forecasts how, even if *de jure* segregation were ended, anti-black racism would be sustained institutionally through the regulation of residential property. His emphasis on real estate is prescient. Before, during, and after the two decades of the civil rights movement's most visible achievements in legal recognition for African Americans, extraordinary efforts to reject the integration of residential communities were made by white citizens, commercial institutions, as well as local, state, and federal government agencies.[79] Lipsitz recounts how realtors in the United States between 1924 and 1950 adhered to a code that in its discrimination against blacks and other people of color effectively awarded whites an unearned asset. Social capital from being identified as white routinely translated into a cash advantage. The code reads: "a realtor should never be instrumental in introducing into a neighborhood a character of property or occupancy, members of any race or nationality, or any individual whose presence will clearly be detrimental to property values."[80] Lipsitz's research into revisions of property law as well as standard real estate practices demonstrates that this stipulation remained in effect in most of the United States for more than two decades after the Supreme Court's decision in *Shelly v. Kramer* determined in 1948 that the imposition of such standards by government or a professional association was unconstitutional.

In "I Choose Exile," Wright does not surmise whether the homeowner or the real estate broker are motivated by a concern for declining property values should he and his interracial family move into the area. Nor does he dwell, as Lipsitz later does, on the limits of the *Shelley v. Kramer* decision. Preventing state and local authorities from imposing racial prejudice on individuals consenting to a financial transaction but leaving open the possibility of individual bigotry, the decision would have made no difference for Wright even if he had been attempting to buy a home after 1948. A modest improvement in the standing of African Americans as citizens and consumers, the decision would still have been no impediment to the homeowner's decision to refuse to sell to Wright. Had the owner and Wright agreed to a sale, the ruling would have merely prevented the state of Connecticut from refusing the white owner the right to sell his house across racial differences. The case, like other judicial and legislative decisions to follow over the next two decades, provides some progress for the civil rights of nonwhite citizens while at the same time it affords prerogatives to whites who, through their own bigotry or even their own unhappy compliance with social pressure, would be expected to do their part to hem African Americans into urban spaces or the rare suburb known for its majority of black residents. The means by which *de facto* racial segregation has survived the outlawing of racial discrimination has been and remains chiefly location. Discerning that his personal experience in New England is demonstrative of a massive, unacknowledged infrastructure that will be unmoved by the passing away of Jim Crow, Wright is compelled to find a place outside the United States from which he can exercise principles and habits that anticommunist discourse deemed un-American.

He corroborates his tale of systemic racism in northern real estate with an account of how difficult it proved to move his family from the United States. Despite the intercession of prominent friends such as Gertrude Stein and Marc Chagall who arranged for French officials, namely Claude Lévi-Strauss, to invite the Wright family to be guests of the French state, he was unable to obtain a passport from the US State Department. Nor were the grounds for delay and refusal disclosed to him. He finally secured a passport only when his increasingly desperate entreaties led him to Evelyn Walsh McLean, a reputed fascist sympathizer, who agreed to introduce Wright to an influential associate of his in Washington. After consorting with a reactionary, the ex-Communist but still leftist Wright secured a passport within an hour of meeting with McLean's contact. The precise details of McLean and his friend's intercession are unavailable, but Wright's difficulty anticipates how within a few years both W. E. B. Du Bois and Paul Robeson would have their passports rescinded by the State Department, which acted to keep the celebrated intellectual and performing artist from airing their complaints about racial inequality and class exploitation before audiences outside the United States.[81]

If the anecdote about being denied a place to live in New England instructs us in how unofficial, seemingly personal racism retained its institutional basis through the regulation of private space, the story about the difficulty acquiring a passport hints at the ease with which the State Department could confine him without acknowledging its involvement in adjudicating how the United States will be represented abroad. "I Choose Exile" explains how Wright became certain that racial strife in the context of the Cold War was the reason for his difficulty obtaining permission to leave the country. At a party a few days after his arrival in France, a "strange white American," he presumes an official of the US Embassy, took him aside to whisper in his ear: "Listen, for God's sake, don't let these foreigners make you into a brick to hurl at our window!"[82] The admonition alerts Wright that, according to state authorities, "a bare recital, when uttered in an alien atmosphere, of the facts of the Negro's life in America constitutes a kind of anti-American propaganda. America must needs be jealous of her Negro problem."[83] He explains that when confronted by reporters at his hotel, he was intent on disappointing both the US Embassy official who hinted he should dissemble and the French Communist Party journalists who expected him to offer apologetics and lies about race relations in America.

Following the chronology of Wright's relocation to Paris in 1946, the second half of "I Choose Exile" focuses on his experiences in France. Contrasting his reception in France leads him to draw the conclusion that white Americans' militant racism is barbarous. His essay and his communications with *Ebony* suggest he either was not familiar with or simply chose to disregard the magazine's stance as venue for middle-class, capitalist aspirations. However, "The Shame of Chicago" and "I Choose Exile" do demonstrate cognizance of the magazine's predominantly African American readership. An audience all too familiar in the 1940s with the frequent reports in the African American press of the lynching culture that greeted black military servicemen upon their return to the United States would have been impressed by the final anecdote in "I Choose Exile." Wright explains that one day he was driving by himself back to Paris from Switzerland and became lost. Pulling into a roadside café to ask directions, he was met with excited shouting from two young women and their mother. As Wright soon learned, the girls' father, the woman's husband, was an African American who came to France during World War II but after Germany's defeat remained in France rather than return to segregation in the United States. The owner of the café and of an auto repair garage next door, the ex-soldier is a picture of middle-class stability.[84]

Wright's pronouncements about the virtual absence of anti-black racism in France are altogether too romantic; he completes "I Choose Exile" around the time that Fanon's early work is explaining the masking Francophone blacks from Africa and the West Indies undertake when they travel to metropolitan France or encounter its white representatives in a colonial setting. Wright does pause in his appraisal of France at one point to acknowledge that the country is not without problems; he does not see it as a utopia, he claims. But like many other American ex-pats living and writing in France during the 1950s, he does not risk his welcome in the country by writing vociferously about the wrongs of French colonialism and how justice demands not a battle for Algiers but a surrender of colonial authority. Instead, in "I Choose Exile" Wright thickens his description of how the public culture of France values intellectuals by explaining that the existentialists he has befriended are inspired and able to speak out against their country's policies without repercussions. In its McCarthyist phase, the postwar Red Scare in the United States permitted no such liberty, especially not for black Americans. Whatever imprecision attends Wright's account of how leftist French intellectuals fared in their relations with the French state in the late 1940s and first several months of the 1950s, the point he argues clearly is that the liberty he attributes to them and which is unavailable to him in the United States is not too much to expect in a democracy. It should not be necessary to go into exile in order to level criticisms at, for example, the thoughtlessness of those who would block government programs to improve water resources because in the hyperbolic ethos of anticommunism such plans by the state are too easily denigrated as un-American socialism.[85] To make such a complaint while in the United States would have volunteered his name to the blacklists and won him an audience with HUAC. Wright was careful not to return to the United States after the emergence of McCarthy, though he was confronted in his Paris home one afternoon by David Schine, who traveled with Roy Cohn to purge un-American writings by Wright, Langston Hughes, and several others from United States Information Agency libraries.[86] With Wright in exile and out of reach of HUAC, *Ebony* did its part to censor his essay even without his having been made to appear suspicious, defensive, defiant, or even compliant before the US Congress.

Although Wright describes how residing in France alleviates his defensive double consciousness for the first time in his life and concludes that anti-black racism in the United States remains barbaric, he does not regard race relations as the primary difference between the two countries. More significant is what he sees as the difference in how the public culture of each country treats the topic of poverty and people who are relatively poor. In a surprising reversal of a conceit of American exceptionalism, Wright cites Europe's feudal history favorably. He views it as a source not of class strife but of an attention to other sources of personal value than wealth. He faults US initiatives to promote Americanism around the world because of their tendency to suggest that the affluence of the United States derives from the merits of American national character. Consequently, the poverty that defines life for great swathes of the human population worldwide is made to appear as if it were not a legacy of colonialism, a consequence of uneven development, and a result of international agreements that rewarded the North Atlantic countries disproportionately. Instead, impoverishment outside the United States is represented with ontological connotations about the vast populations who suffer from it. Wright follows these observations with a polemical, rhetorical question suggesting that it ought to be a crime to conflate poverty with criminality.[87]

In texts that examine or promote the doctrine of American exceptionalism, the observation that the United States was not burdened by a feudal heritage that produced a social infrastructure of class division and its attendant resentments is typically invoked either as evidence that the United States lacks the requisite conditions for a socialist revolution or as the reason that rugged individualism could enable an American to advance socially across distinctions of wealth that in Europe would have corresponded to fixed and unsurpassable divisions. Wright reverses this second evaluation, claiming that the promise of upward mobility in the United States has endorsed a mercenary sensibility that races to the top all the while cultivating the attitude that those left behind are to be blamed for their disrepair. Exile did not afford Wright a complete escape from pronouncements about the social mores of the United States. He complains that Voice of America radio programs broadcast to the world that poverty is the fault of the poor.

Arturo Escobar has demonstrated how development theory after World War II resulted in the global North's use of economic pressures to divert the national liberation initiatives of decolonization. The discourse of development facilitated for many states a transition from colonialism to neocolonialism with a minimum of national self-determination. Critical to this result was international agreement among the major postindustrial Western powers on the topic of poverty, which they defined as a social problem of global proportion that called for intervention from the most developed and resourceful states and institutions. Turning the poor "into objects of knowledge and management," the World Bank in 1948 defined countries as poor if they had an annual per capita income below $100.[88] The result was that two-thirds of the world became poor in the eyes of the most powerful international organizations and states. To receive the financial aid that they were bound to need as a result of the advantages international monetary policy bestowed on the North, the former colonies had to agree to compromise their hard-won autonomy and to concede to foreign authority over national economic policy. The postwar "discovery of poverty," Escobar explains, was a chief means for modernization programs authored in the North and imposed on the global South that denied the indebted former colonies full autonomy by regulating their industries.[89] Wright's reference in "I Choose Exile" to approximately two billion global poor may seem to resonate with the premises about poverty with which development theorists and policymakers justified arrangements that we now call neocolonial. But the valence of his statement moves in the opposite direction from the projection that poverty is a problem of and by the global South. Suggesting that to stigmatize poverty as criminal ought to be considered a criminal offense in its own right, Wright makes plain that, however the United States might respond to global economic disparity, answers will not come from common-sense Horatio Alger attitudes about uplift. International institutions overseen by the West should not appropriate the agency of those it deems in need. As Wright acknowledges, his argument is unsuited to be persuasive before an audience schooled in the Cold War to understand international US military interventions as reluctant but necessary actions to defend the interest of human freedom against totalitarianism.

In his final paragraph, Wright returns to the idea that the remove of exile does not free him from responsibility for his country. On the contrary, he feels an obligation to communicate the "gloomy insights" that come from an outside, worldly perspective on what the United States represents elsewhere. He wonders if he could "somehow warn Americans against a too self-righteous display of wealth in face of a naked and shivering world; if I could in some way inject into the American consciousness a consciousness of <u>their</u> consciousness. . . ."[90] Reflecting Wright's participation in the midcentury French revival of interest in Hegel, the repetition of "consciousness" in this statement personifies a uniform American character that fails to reflect on itself. Absent self-consciousness, this national subject is unaware of how its affluence is an affront to much of the rest of the world and no doubt oblivious to how its enrichment has been facilitated, in part, by underdevelopment elsewhere. Wright determines, however, that no such message can be received. He concludes by assuming his argument's ultimate failure. Were he to urge the United States to identify its responsibility for deterring the emerging neocolonialism that would reformulate but nevertheless extend the inequities of the colonial order, his advice would "sound suspiciously like communist propaganda." He speculates:

> Would it [his advice] not seem to place a morally objectionable question mark after our fondest convictions of the invulnerability of material might? An offer

of help of that sort might well merit a militant attack on the part of those determined, in their shortsightedness, to defend at any cost their American purity. . . .
So I watch my country from afar, but with no sense of glee, no smug self-satisfac-
tion; rather it is with a strange perturbation of heart.[91]

Situating himself as an "un-American" spectator perturbed with the hopeless-
ness of any intervention, Wright characterizes the Cold War United States as
insulated from criticism by an unrelenting righteousness that obscures the
connection between affluence and indigence in the world-system.

Unable to publish the essay, he never tests whether his final tactic of indirect
complaint about an audience incapable of hearing him would have protected
him from the militant reaction he expects for any overt recommendation that
the United States cease mistaking its superior resources as a sign of its des-
serts. In a typical instance of the cultural Cold War in America, independent
institutions guarded against Wright's heretical essay reaching the public. As
if in anticipation of that response, Wright's final paragraph forecasts that the
message he would like to deliver to the American citizenry would only be
heard as advocacy for the side commonly regarded in the West as against
freedom. We may imagine that, had this unpublished essay appeared in a
popular magazine such *Ebony* or the *Atlantic*, his contrarian invocation of
"Un-American," his embarrassing anecdote about the State Department, and
his rejection of the presumption that capitalism is a viable social ethic would
have circulated to disrupt and complicate the reception history that had
already gathered around him as a consequence of the Cold War reiteration
of "I Tried to Be a Communist" in *The God That Failed*. Rather than serving
as the exemplary figure for African American political disappointment with
the party's cynical retreat from race, Wright's period of transition from the
United States to exile could have been characterized more readily as a rejection of the normative stories told about the Cold War on either side. And the
polemical force of the critique of greed that comes near the end of "I Choose
Exile" would have impressed on Wright's readers that his break with Communism did not signal a retreat from his black radical conviction that in the
history of Western modernity the punishing impositions of white supremacy
and capitalist exploitation have always entailed each other.

CHAPTER THREE

Writing Congress: The Appeal of C. L. R. James's American Studies

I take no issue with those who would praise the contributions which have been made to our society by people of many races, of varied creeds and colors. America is indeed a joining together of many streams which go to form a mighty river which we call the American way. However, we have in the United States today hard-core, indigestible blocs which have not become integrated into the American way of life, but which, on the contrary are its deadly enemies.
—**Senator Pat McCarran,** March 2, 1953[1]

I know of few more thrilling moments in literature for a modern reader, one of us, than when Melville says that the crew is composed of renegades from all over the world.
—**C. L. R. James to Jay Leyda,** March 7, 1953[2]

Soon after his friend Richard Wright chose exile in France, C. L. R. James applied to become a US citizen. He first arrived in the United States in late 1938 for a speaking tour sponsored by the Socialist Workers Party (SWP). Even after adding a visit to Mexico City at Trotsky's invitation to confer in person on the "Negro question,"[3] his itinerary should have returned him to England after only a few months, in time to report on the opening of the next professional cricket season. Instead, after a bus trip from Mexico to New York City through the American South exposed him for the first time to that region's particular iteration of Jim Crow segregation, he abandoned his plans. And when a visa extension expired in late 1940, he remained in the United States without permission for thirteen more years, writing under various pseudonyms for leftist periodicals such as the *New International* and working as an activist in a succession of Marxist organizations but never the CPUSA. From the time he first read Marx as an émigré to England from Trinidad in the early 1930s, he determined that under Stalin the USSR was a perversion of the anticapitalist and radical democratic tenets he knew to be the core of Marx's writings. James tried but failed to make his anti-Stalinism meaningful to the US Cold War authorities who ultimately deemed him unfit for citizenship and compelled his exile from America in 1953.

James married an American citizen, Constance Webb, in 1946. Her memoir describes how agents of the Immigration and Naturalization Service (INS) and the FBI routinely showed up at their New York apartments to question them about their relationship, their political loyalties, and the activities of their friends, especially African American literary celebrities such as Wright, Chester Himes, and Ralph Ellison.[4] In 1949 she gave birth to their child. James dedicated his Melville book to him with this inscription: "For my son, Nob, who will be 21 years old in 1970 by which time I hope he and his generation will have left behind them forever all the problems of nationality."[5] This wish for the hazards of nationalism to be overcome in less than two decades hints at James's optimistic vision of a cosmopolitan "new society" to succeed the world system of global capitalism and its complementary infrastructure of inviolate sovereignty reserved for a powerful few nation-states.[6] An inauspicious quality for a prospective US citizen during the early years of the Cold War, his devotion to radical change proved decisive for federal officials tasked with judging his ability to become a citizen. In the decision against him, his political convictions trumped his family ties. The birth of his child may have made becoming a US citizen a priority for James personally, but the political culture of anticommunism meant his timing was unfortunate. Federal legislation spurred by the postwar Red Scare ordered the INS to crack down on undocumented immigrants, especially the kind of political subversives Senator McCarran deemed insoluble obstacles to the healthy progress of the American way of life. Having a family with roots in America was not enough to make James's black radicalism palatable to representatives of the Cold War national security state. After more than five years of contending against the threat of deportation, including several months of detention on Ellis Island, he repaired to England before US authorities could expel him. His voluntary departure was a strategy to salvage the possibility of returning to the United States should the political climate ever become less forbidding.

Detained on Ellis Island in 1952 by the INS pending the outcome of an appeal, James prepared an unlikely last-ditch petition for citizenship: a book-length essay of literary criticism on Herman Melville entitled *Mariners, Renegades and Castaways: The Story of Herman Melville and the World We Live In*. The book is a demonstration of James's appreciation for American literary culture and, at the same time, an interpretation of Melville's work that argues for its special pertinence after 1945. James concentrates on how the novel *Moby-Dick* communicates an uncanny forewarning about the danger of the postwar Red Scare. In James's account, Captain Ahab's monomaniacal quest for vengeance against a whale that he imagines to be possessed of a malevolent intelligence prefigures by a century the US national security state's unconscionable drive to deny civil liberties and constrain democratic social movements in the name of anticommunism. James insists that his detention is a symptom of that mad Cold War condition. Writing criticism in the bur-geoning field of American literature provided him a means to contend against Red Scare legislation and the normative discourse of anticommunism while forestalling the easy dismissal of his discontent as supposed proof of his un-American character. Who but a person of intellect, industry, and morality would undertake to elucidate the oeuvre of Melville, who was reputed to rep-resent how US literary culture, with the American Renaissance of the 1850s, finally matured to rival the masterpieces of Europe?

James's colleagues in the Johnson-Forest Tendency sponsored the book's publication. On the back cover of the original edition, a picture of James includes a caption in which he explains the book "is a claim before the Ameri-can people, the best claim I can put forward, that my desire to be a citizen is not a selfish nor a frivolous one." In a more direct appeal to the federal author-ities responsible for the laws that identified him as a "subversive alien," cop-ies were distributed directly to people and institutions with public influence, including the elected representatives of the US Congress. In a long letter to George Padmore, James explains: "We circulated 5000 copies with material to correspond. Every member of Congress got one, Governors, mayors of large cities, the Supreme Court, every important official, editor, lawyer, journal-ist, broadcaster, labor leader, etc."[7] His erudition in American literature went unacknowledged by the Congressional legislators who sanctioned the laws that criminalized his ideas. While *Mariners* enjoyed no positive influence on the legal procedures that denied him a place in America, the 1950 judgment against him cites several of James's earlier titles of Marxist historiography to indicate that the West Indian immigrant was un-American and an intolerable presence in the United States.[8]

By all accounts, his years in America were essential and transformative for the development of his singular contribution to the black radical tradition. In addition to acquiring a wide-ranging cultural literacy about the United States, he dedicated himself in the 1940s to a reconsideration of Marxism. In his dialogue with Trotsky in 1939, he established his attitude about the rela-tive autonomy of race as a site for the mobilization of political activism that need not heed Marxist expectations for a final analysis that hinges on class differences. Trotsky and he agreed that, in their struggles against anti-black racism, African Americans across the United States should be regarded as a potentially revolutionary force that could be complementary to anticapitalist objectives with or without affiliations to Marxist organizations. James's "The Revolutionary Answer to the Negro Problem in the USA" challenges "directly any attempt to subordinate or to push to the rear the social and political significance of the independent Negro struggle for democratic rights," which should be understood as a "constituent part of the struggle for socialism."⁹

While James appreciated Trotsky's responsiveness to his counsel on race, he was uneasy about his attitude on two other topics that became the basis for his Johnson-Forest Tendency's split from the Socialist Workers Party in 1950: the nature of the USSR and the role of party leadership in revolutionary politics. From early in the 1940s, James and Raya Dunayevskaya—"Johnson" and "Forest"—agreed that Trotsky was wrong to characterize the USSR as a workers' state in decay temporarily as a consequence of Stalin's iron rule; they contended, on the contrary, that the USSR's centralized control of the national economy was organized by the systemic exploitation of the workers by those agencies that controlled the means of production. In other words, the USSR under Stalin was an instance of state capitalism, a thesis James, Dunayevskaya, and Grace Lee elaborated in *State Capitalism and World Revolution* in 1950. More important for James's legacy as a theorist of revolutionary politics, the Johnson-Forest Tendency also disavowed Trotsky's adherence to a Leninist (but not Lenin's) conception of the necessity of a vanguard party. Balking at the idea that the leadership of the party vanguard can facilitate the transformation of workers into the political subjects of the proletariat, James insisted that a revolutionary political mentality emerges only from the spontaneous actions of the masses. With increasing intensity through his American years, his self-styled black Marxism threw off the Cold War presumption on both sides that capitalism and communism differ primarily on whether property should be private or public. He focused instead on the conviction that institutions involved in the reproduction of social life should be owned and directed by their workers.¹⁰ Confident in the spontaneity and creativity of ordinary people bound together by the exploitation of their labor or their oppression on the basis of race, the political philosophy he crafts while in America presumes that any organization can be made more just through the democratization of its power structure. Inclined to think genuine populism lends itself to leftist political attitudes, James trusted that radical democracy entails anticapitalist social values and institutions. Such confidence in the vitality of laborers animates his interpretation of *Moby-Dick*.

Scholars and activists from an impressive cross-section of academic disciplines and political organizations have agreed that James's extended period in America was instrumental for the development of his political philosophy. And even a cursory review of scholarship on his work published since his death in 1989 shows how routinely he is characterized as "second only to W. E. B. Du Bois in the twentieth century of black thinkers."[11] However, his writings from his time in the United States that concentrate on American history and literary culture have been received less easily. His optimism about the United States as a promising site for social change has caused some consternation. Endeavoring to cast Marxist precepts in an American context with a vernacular that would resonate with working-class readers who had no formal training in philosophies of historical materialism, on occasion James wrote with an enthusiasm that seems to resonate with the excited circulation of public pronouncements that explained American exceptionalism was the source and warrant for the relative affluence of the postwar United States.

The reception of *Mariners* has been specifically contentious. Debate concentrates mainly on the character of the book's final chapter, which appends James's autobiographical reflection on his experience in detention on Ellis Island. Incensed that he was classified and housed with detainees who were card-carrying Communists, James objects to how the discourse of anticommunism collapses all manner of leftist opposition to capitalism into the single category of un-American. Insisting in polemical fashion on his difference from the CPUSA, he incorporates into his personal narrative an at times scathing portrait of the inmate M, his pseudonym for the Communist leader who served as a spokesperson for the cellblock that James lived in during his detention. Some responses to *Mariners* suggest that James's derogatory characterization of the CPUSA traffics in red-baiting and fault him for effectively endorsing the monolithic accounts of communism put forward by the FBI, HUAC, the US Senate, and other organizations intent throughout the long 1950s on stamping out any vestige of anticapitalist thought from US public culture's lexicon of legitimate political speech.[12] A remark by Darrell Levi is typical: "*Mariners* suffered from James's immediate crisis. His denunciations of communism and communists—intended to persuade McCarthy Era immigration authorities of his political respectability—were too categorical and unfair." A competing tendency in the reception history of *Mariners* rejects this suggestion that, in the emergency situation of Ellis Island, James capitulated to anticommunism in an effort to win the favor of federal authorities. Instead, affirmative readings recall how his objections to the Communists on Ellis Island are consistent with the anti-Stalinist convictions he had published since first coming to Marxism.[13] While the former interpretation treats *Mariners* as an exception to James's body of work, the latter insists the book is as "Jamesian" as his others. The dispute over the quality of the autobiographical turn to conclude *Mariners* has been pointed in the academic discipline of American Studies because James is often recommended as a

precedent for the field's transition in recent years to a transnational orientation that involves both critiques of the political culture of US imperialism and
attention to the ways in which cultural geographies that are not exclusively
nationalist instruct and shape subjectivity.[14] If negative appraisals are correct
that James's study of canonical American literature concludes by indulging in
the kind of red-baiting that was an asset to US imperialism and a reactionary mode of American nationalism, the most distinct and charismatic book
among his American writings would be an uneasy precursor for American
Studies at present.

   Taking up this topic of James's curricular value, I contribute in this chapter
to the debate over the conclusion of *Mariners* by examining how the account
of *Moby-Dick* he writes while imprisoned on Ellis Island contrasts with his
discussion of Melville three years earlier in the manuscript "Notes on American Civilization," which was posthumously published as *American Civilization*.
Commentary on the relationship between these texts characterizes the earlier
document as a preparation for the book he writes in detention. For example,
Robert Hill, James's literary executor, describes *American Civilization* as "foreshadowing" the prison writings on Melville, while Anna Grimshaw and Keith
Hart write that *Mariners* is a "distillation" of his earlier ideas. Contrary to the
priority assigned to the later text, I argue that *Mariners* marks a retreat from
the representation of Melville in the chapter in *American Civilization* on nineteenth-century intellectuals. James's refraining in *Mariners* from reiterating
American Civilization's most challenging observations about the confluence of
race and class in the history and unyielding aftermath of slavery in America is
a sign that he struggles with the exigencies of his situation in detention. As an
alternative to disputing whether or not *Mariners*' final chapter has an anticommunist subtext, reading James's "American" books in tandem provides instruction in how the normative story of the Cold War interfered with aspirations
for black liberation by denying the accordance between recognition claims
and demands for redistribution. James's discussion in *American Civilization*
of abolitionism teaches that for African Americans redistribution initiatives
may be responsive to particular moral claims for reparations. Such attention
to political economy and still unpaid slave labor is not absent entirely from
Mariners, but relative to *American Civilization* it is understated. The argument
of his prison writing concentrates instead on how James's exclusion from the
US body politic is facilitated by federal authorities exercising exceptional sovereignty under Red Scare emergency provisions that had become routine. The
lesson I recommend with the juxtaposition of James's distinct treatments of
Melville is that the discourse of Cold War anticommunism cost US public
culture serious consideration of reparations for slavery. This deficiency that I

mark as legible in the difference between James's representations of Melville in *Mariners* and *American Civilization* transpired at a time in which the spreading liberation struggles of decolonization as well as the emergence of international institutions in observance of universal human rights should have enabled a public reckoning about America's active participation in overt and tacit modes of white supremacy.

The publication histories of the two texts complicate their assessment. In addition to *Mariners* being composed mainly during his confinement on Ellis Island and then circulated to publicize James's case, subsequent editions published in 1977 and 1985 have contributed to the dispute about the final chapter. Encouraging suspicions that James's portrayal of Communists was a lapse of conscience that implicated him in anticommunist efforts to censor leftist ideas and later embarrassed his Marxist colleagues, these editions omitted all or part of the final chapter. Donald Pease's introduction to the restored version of *Mariners* he edited in 2001 insists that budgetary concerns were the only reasons for those omissions, but speculation about other motives remains an important feature of the book's reception history. In contrast to *Mariners'* overtly public address, *American Civilization* was an unfinished manuscript circulated privately to a select number of James's close associates, primarily other members of the Johnson-Forest Tendency with whom he had recently engaged in a lengthy correspondence about the importance of Hegel's *Science of Logic* for understanding the writings of Marx and Lenin. Those exchanges culminated in 1948 in the preparation of James's manuscript *Notes on Dialectics: Hegel, Marx, Lenin*, which was first published for sale in 1980. The group was also responsible in 1947 for publishing the first English translations of key chapters from Marx's *Economic and Philosophic Manuscripts of 1844*, which was discovered in German only in 1927. Writing in a style that resembles the direct address of his letters, in *American Civilization* James assumes his reader is conversant in the particular articulation of Marxism that informed the Johnson-Forest Tendency's decision to become independent from other political organizations. A prefatory note admonishes recipients to protect his "Notes" as a private communication: "This document is absolutely confidential. This means that it should not be talked about to anyone, should not be seen by anyone. Any exception made to this will be looked upon as a breach of trust."[15] James's purpose in writing "Notes on American Civilization" further qualifies the status of the manuscript. He composed it as a prospectus for a primer on the history of American public culture that would be written for ordinary citizens.

With James in exile from America, the popular book described in *American Civilization* was never written. Despite these qualifications, *American*

Civilization should still be read as a unique curriculum in American literary culture and political history. James's two "American" books are, respectively, an appeal for citizenship addressed to an American public for which anticommunism had become common sense and a curriculum proposal conveyed to a counterpublic of like-minded Marxist intellectuals who were devoted to the proposition that the United States could be a site for radical social changes that upset global capitalism. The pairing represents James's commitment as a black radical intellectual: to recognize and sustain links between efforts against racism and struggles against capitalism. Together, those efforts and struggles compose for James the project to bring a belated termination to that singular modernity of global capitalism that, through European colonialism and the enslavement of Africans, conceived of white supremacy while decorously calling itself Western civilization. Negotiating his way through the literary writings of the American Renaissance and the protest literature of the abolitionists, James sought to demonstrate that such an audacious, reaching objection to the so-called "American Way" could be located in the best, even exceptional traditions of American culture.

American Totalitarianism: The Monomania of McCarranism

In the floor speech to the US Senate cited in the first epigraph for this chapter, McCarran employs a rhetorical gambit characteristic of officials who distinguished themselves within the anticommunist consensus for identifying a persistent internal threat to the existence of the United States. Depicting the body politic as a great waterway that has a sensitive constitution and no tolerance for inassimilable foreign entities, he implies the immigrant who fails to Americanize is indigestible and even lethal, a metaphor that represents a public health hazard as palpable as Kennan and Hoover's descriptions of communism as malignant diseases. Blending tropes for political subversives with nativist terms that traditionally depict the undocumented immigrant as a foreign presence that feeds parasitically on the domestic economy, McCarran's version of anticommunist discourse is predicated on the racist premise that the surest immunity against communism is Anglo-American whiteness. The stakes he associates with inoculation against foreign interference are even higher than the well-being of the nation. He precedes his discrimination between hygienic and toxic immigrants with an apocalyptic profession of faith: "I believe that this nation is the last hope of Western civilization and if this oasis of the world shall be overrun, perverted, contaminated, or destroyed, then the last flickering light of humanity will be extinguished."[16] This remarkable statement is an example of the kind of magical thinking that Étienne Balibar cites to demonstrate that, contrary to its usual association with particular identities, racism, when formulated as a kind of exceptionalism, facilitates "a 'specific universalization' and therefore an idealization of nationalism."[17]

While McCarthy and Hoover remain more storied in the history of anticommunism in America, "McCarran" has equal warrant as a personal name to characterize the tenor and reach of the postwar Red Scare. He codified his zeal for saving Western civilization from un-American incursions in two laws that expanded and shaped the edifice of federal and state institutions dedicated to the investigation and censure of political dissent. Passed in each case over President Truman's veto, the Internal Security Act of 1950 and the Immigration and Nationality Act of 1952 were commonly known as the McCarran and the McCarran-Walter Acts, respectively. The earlier law required Communist organizations and those deemed Communist "action groups" and fronts to register with the federal government, abide constant surveillance, and adhere to various stipulations for their group's activities. For example, publications sent through the mail by a registered group were required to be labeled: "Disseminated by (group's name), a Communist organization."[18] To ensure that suspect organizations did not evade registration, the McCarran Act established the federal Subversive Activities Control Board (SACB) to conduct formal reviews and hearings to determine if a group should be identified as Communist. With the Communist Control Act of 1954, the SACB's powers were expanded to allow it to identify an organization as merely "communist-infiltrated," which proved an especially useful tool for discrediting unions and denying them recognition from the National Labor Relations Board.

The McCarran Act also established the Senate Internal Security Subcommittee, the Senate's equivalent of the better-known HUAC. In recognition of its first chair, SISS was commonly referred to as the McCarran Committee. Succeeding McCarran as chair were Richard Jenner of Indiana and then James Eastland of Mississippi, who would oversee the subcommittee from 1955 until it was abolished in 1977. In the months preceding his appointment as chair, Eastland became the most vociferous and well-known federal official opposing the Supreme Court's decision in *Brown v. Board of Education*. In a 1955 floor speech to the Senate, he challenged the legitimacy of any ruling based on the findings of researchers he named Communists: Kenneth Clark, Du Bois, Frazier, and Myrdal, all figures cited in the footnotes to the *Brown* decision.[19] In the position invented by McCarran, Eastland was unrelenting and prominent in his insistence that civil rights were a Communist plot.

Linking the danger of communism to undocumented immigrants and, it alleges, lax border controls, the McCarran-Walter Act was unsubtle in its

insinuation that people of color entering the United States were a more significant security risk than white immigrants. As Rachel Buff explains, the act
was characterized by contradictions regarding race. Imposing restrictions on
immigration, it did not interfere with the Bracero Program, which is to say
that it did not deter the exploitation of "Third World," non-citizen labor within
the United States that after World War II often served to suppress wages and
undermine the efforts of citizens' labor unions.[20] Although the McCarran-
Walter Act abolished prohibitions against the immigration of any person on
the basis of race (e.g., exclusions of Asians), by retaining the quota stipulations of the Johnson-Reed Act of 1924 it effectively sustained preferences for
white immigrants. More pertinent to the geopolitics of the Cold War, the act's
distinction between political and economic immigrants created a racialized
division between people fleeing the political conditions of Eastern Europe
and those immigrants from nonwhite regions of the world who were drawn to
the United States because of supposedly non-political economic conditions.[21]
While the latter constituencies were characterized as needy masses compelled
to seek haven in affluent America because of the traditional disrepair of their
backward homelands, the former were presumed to be discerning, rational
subjects in flight from the insupportable, autocratic conditions imposed by
an expansive Iron Curtain. As we have already observed at various points
in this book, the discourse of Cold War anticommunism facilitated systemic
racism by social regulations that ostensibly had no direct connection to race.
As a document and, in its implementation, an institution of Cold War anticommunism, the McCarran-Walter Act was an unusually explicit indication
of how the postwar Red Scare was a racial project that, in spite of its ultimate
denial of any doctrine of racial supremacy, provided formidable support for
the understated but palpable fact that whiteness was a property of American
citizenship. The franchise available to those without it was at best a semblance
of uncompromised belonging.

In *Mariners*, James cites McCarran's signature legislative achievements as
proof of an argument he had introduced in a 1945 essay on "The New Germany" and then advanced throughout *American Civilization*, in which he
writes: "I find the American pattern to be the dominant social pattern of our
time and in this conviction I give a fairly detailed treatment of totalitarianism in the world at large and totalitarian tendencies in the United States."[22]
McCarran's success pushing the anticommunist bills into law over Truman's
vetoes provided James corroboration and a proper name to substantiate
his claim that the codification of the postwar Red Scare into police actions
against political dissent steered the United States in the direction of totalitarianism. The spread of McCarran's influence over anticommunism after

1950 allows James to be more precise in *Mariners* about the ways in which American nativism, with its potent fiction of an indigenous Anglo-American citizenship, was a strong impetus among others for elements of totalitarianism to emerge in the United States.

James also had a personal grievance with the McCarran acts because each was applied to his case inappropriately. Needless to say, his application to begin the naturalization process was hampered by his lengthy illegal residency in the United States, but the administrative and judicial reviews of his case were complete before the Internal Security Act of 1950 was passed into law. It was applied to him nonetheless. Then, in the midst of appeals to the judgment against him, he was incarcerated at Ellis Island under the provisions of the second law.[23] While James and his attorney maintained that the retroactive application of these laws to his case was improper, in *Mariners* he makes the further claim that the capricious exercise of state authority was integral to McCarran's approach to anticommunism. The federal government's handling of James may have seemed unusual, but he discerned that an anti-democratic sovereign exceptionalism was scripted into the laws. As he explains in the lengthy letter to Padmore about *Mariners*, he regarded his personal situation as a political case because it could "bring the whole anti-civil liberties, anti-alien persecution in the United States before the public."[24]

Including a reflection on totalitarianism in his appeal for citizenship, James presents his Melville criticism in a vocabulary that helps define his implied Cold War reader. His terms were also familiar to the actual audience of public figures who received the original copies of *Mariners*. Rehearsing the conviction that totalitarianism was the gravest danger for the United States and the world, James seems to join the anticommunist chorus that posed a characterization of totalitarianism against an image of sheer American liberty. Turning the concept of totalitarianism inward to an examination of US federal efforts to police political dissent was a more difficult maneuver, but not unprecedented. Even President Truman described the first McCarran Act as an attack on freedom of "opinion and belief," warning in his veto message on the bill that it was "a long step toward totalitarianism."[25]

Totalitarianism, however, has never been a promising concept for a Marxist critique of the role of states in socioeconomic exploitation and racial oppression. The most cynical response to the term's utility, voiced by Slavoj Žižek in *Did Somebody Say Totalitarianism?*, is that it was never a concept so much as a mere trope, a figurative stopgap, of Western propaganda during the Cold War that dictated how popular opinion in the United States and among its allies must, without irony, assume actually existing communism in the USSR and capitalism in the United States to embody the difference between slavery and liberty. To employ the idea of totalitarianism is to fall irremediably into an apology for capitalism, argues Žižek, because "throughout its entire career, 'totalitarianism' was an ideological notion that sustained the complex operation ... of guaranteeing the liberal-democratic hegemony, dismissing the Leftist critique of liberal democracy as the obverse, the 'twin', of the Rightist Fascist dictatorship.... [T]he moment one accepts the notion of 'totalitarianism', one is firmly located within the liberal-democratic horizon."[26] As I noted in the introduction, the interests of both anti-black racism and anticommunism were served in the United States after World War II by the hurried translation of public animus from Germany to "Russia." And a review of the statements and writings of major figures of the postwar new liberalism including Truman, Niebuhr, Schlesinger, Lillian Smith, and others would confirm Žižek's premise that the concept did serve arguments designed to characterize, really caricature, leftist political convictions as finally indistinct from the far-right attitudes of fascism.

Melville's *Moby-Dick* provided James with a narrative and a vocabulary of character types to appropriate anticommunist discourse's typical account of totalitarianism. He communicates leftist grievances against the disposition of the US national security state in its imperialist, anti-democratic activities at home and around the globe. His critique of the totalitarian tendencies of Cold War America does not concede to postwar centrist liberalism's presupposition that reality permits no better social order than democratic capitalism. However, in the autobiographical turn to conclude *Mariners* he does acknowledge the value of liberalism's historic and principled regard for political recognition. Invoking Melville's humble figure of "Mariners, renegades and castaways" and the novelist's further, recurring allusion to an "Anacharsis Clootz deputation," James represents the symbolic act of claiming political recognition as a potent means by which the excluded and dispossessed can achieve rights and, as importantly, impose substantive social changes.[27]

Melville's Nationalist Revivals

Considering that the nativist anticommunism of "McCarranism" was responsible for James's detention, the literary fiction of Melville was an ironic topic for his final appeal to remain in America. Practically lost to literary history at the end of the nineteenth century, Melville's writings only began to reclaim literary esteem on the centennial of his birth in 1919. Necessary to the success of this first "Melville Revival," argues Paul Lauter, was the appeal of his early novels to the interests of a reading public in the United States that had grown increasingly anxious after World War I about the influx of immigrants to the United States from southern and eastern Europe.[28] Melville's seafaring adventure novels prior to and including *Moby-Dick* in 1851 were read as representations of a multiethnic world order in which diversity flourished but rugged white American men traversed seas and oceans demonstrating their superior character. Or, as Lauter explains, Melville's novels "could be appropriated to the needs of America's cultural elite to model a correct relationship to 'primitiveness.'"[29] Around the time of Melville's revival, this sense of white superiority and even the salience of fictional racial identities such as "Nordic" were codified into a succession of restrictive federal laws culminating in the 1924 Immigration Act, which established annual quotas for legal immigrants correlated to census data from 1790 when the demography of the young United States was biased heavily toward white citizens of Western European descent.

In contending against the characterization of James as a troublesome foreigner, his lawyer invoked the 1917 Immigration Act that required legal immigrants meet standards of decency, literacy, and health. Citing James's identity as a husband and father who wrote books, articles, and lectures to provide for his family, he proposed that his client would be a productive citizen and that his deportation would create undue hardship for his wife and child, both US citizens who depended on his support.[30] In contrast, *Mariners* resists the presupposition that the well-assimilated national subject possesses superior morality. The book advocates instead for a cosmopolitan global citizenship that values differences without hierarchical biases. To populate his vision of a transnational model of solidarity and cooperation, James observes in Melville's characterization of non-American subjects a worldly intelligence that was ignored by those nativist readings of the novels that took foreign subjects to be mere foils to affirm the superiority of white American national character.

By World War II, rationales other than reactionary nativism had emerged to single out *Moby-Dick* as Melville's finest work, a great American novel rival in quality to the literary masterpieces of Europe, and narrative proof of the doctrine of American exceptionalism. In English studies, the formal complexity and difficulty of Melville's prose style meant practitioners of the New Criticism favored his work.[31] More pertinent to James's reading, the interdisciplinary field of American Studies embraced *Moby-Dick* as an allegorical treatment of the opposition that the discourse of anticommunism identified as the dominant fact of geopolitical reality: the world is described by the ideological conflict between democracy in America and totalitarianism in the Soviet Union. This common understanding of the novel as an allegory of anticommunism was based on F. O. Matthiessen's earlier reading of the text as an essential precursor to anti-fascism. As Pease demonstrates in "*Moby-Dick* and the Cold War," Matthiessen's *American Renaissance* made a successful case for the novel's figuration of Ahab's monomania as an uncanny foretelling of European fascism in the twentieth century. His monumental treatment of the great literary achievements of Emerson, Whitman, Poe, Melville, and Thoreau between 1850 and 1855 was arguably the most significant piece of scholarship for setting curricula in American literary studies in departments of English and for programs in American Studies. Published in 1940, its motivating conviction was that US isolation as the Axis powers imposed fascism on much of Europe and Asia was unconscionably at odds with a chief tenet of American exceptionalism: an unyielding dedication to human liberty.

According to Matthiessen and the other critics who followed the lead of what Pease calls the "canonical thesis," opposite Ahab's peerless despotism stands the narrator we call Ishmael.[32] A humble member of the crew who poses no challenge to Ahab's iron rule during the fateful voyage, in retrospect he is the only individual who lives to tell the tale of the *Pequod*'s destruction. His survival and the agency of his narration ostensibly make him emblematic of democratic freedom. His perspective affords us critical purchase to admire Ahab's charismatic hold over his command and, at the same time, to recognize that his centralized planning dooms the cult of sailors he has gathered to his cause and personality. The agency of Ishmael's voice as storyteller marks his ultimate independence from Ahab, claims the thesis. Alive in the end, he is the exception on the manifest of the *Pequod*, and his example satisfied postwar American Studies' insistence on the compatibility of the story of the nation's exceptionalism and the significance of its representative literature.

By the end of the 1940s, the popularization of the concept of totalitarianism to identify Hitler's Germany and Stalin's Soviet Union as iterations of a single category facilitated the appropriation of Matthiessen's thesis for the Cold War. According to Jonathan Arac, American Studies scholars who became prominent in the field just after World War II were responsible for a nationalistic co-option of Matthiessen's work that ran "contrary to his intentions."[33] The standardization of the canonical thesis in the early Cold War years was also facilitated by the increased professionalization of the field of American literature and the discipline of American Studies as represented by the founding of the Melville Society in 1945 and the American Studies Association in 1950. The year following the start of the ASA, at least four conferences were held in the United States to recognize the centenary of the publication of *Moby-Dick*. Communicating the professional industry around Melville to a general public, between 1949 and 1952 leading "Melvillean" Howard Vincent published reviews in the *New York Times* of Richard Chase's *Herman Melville: A Critical Study*, William Gilman's *Melville's Early Life and Redburn*, Leon Howard's *Herman*

Melville: A Biography, Jay Leyda's *The Melville Log,* Geoffrey Stone's *Melville,* and Lawrence Thompson's *Melville's Quarrel with God.*[34] The conversation around the author and his most celebrated novel were an inviting medium for presenting against the grain a popular, accessible, and Americanized version of those ostensibly un-American, "Bolshevik" convictions that James maintained had been enacted time and time again by spontaneous, popular interventions that make up the insurrectionist history of the United States.

Reading James Reading Melville in *Mariners*

James shares with the canonical thesis the observation that *Moby-Dick* reads more powerfully after the origin of the totalitarian state in the twentieth century. He too accords Melville prescience about the catastrophic developments in technology and government that materialized in the hundred years after he composed his most famous work. In his single-page introduction, James affiliates his book with this standard reading of Melville and with the Cold War anticommunist conceit that identifies Nazi Germany and the Communist USSR as comparable variants of totalitarianism:

> THE MIRACLE of Herman Melville is this: that a hundred years ago in two novels, <u>Moby-Dick</u> and <u>Pierre,</u> and two or three stories, he painted a picture of the world in which we live, which is to this day unsurpassed.
>
> The totalitarian madness which swept the world as first Nazism and now as Soviet Communism; the great mass labor movements and colonial revolts; intellectuals drowning in the incestuous dreams of psychoanalysis—this is the world the masses of men strive to make sense of. This is what Melville coordinates—but not as industry, science, politics, economics or psychology, but as a world of human personalities, living as the vast majority of human beings live, not by ideas, but by their emotions, seeking to avoid pain and misery and struggling for happiness....[35]

In the earlier *American Civilization,* James concludes his introductory chapter with a disclaimer that the "common name" of totalitarianism does not mean that Hitler's and Stalin's regimes are identical. The characterization, he explains, "has been made merely to emphasize the ultimate social consequences of any kind of regime which does not develop along cooperative creative lines, developing the creative spirit of the mass. Politically speaking the differences between Stalinism and Fascism, particularly on a world scale, are of immense, in fact of decisive importance."[36] Absent this earlier priority of a nuanced discrimination between the regimes of Hitler and Stalin, the opening of *Mariners* is inviting to readers who by 1953 were accustomed to popular opinion that elided differences between Hitler's Germany and Stalin's USSR and maintained that they were equally and absolutely devoid of the human liberty presumed to characterize democracy in America. To win legitimacy for his appeal from the beginning, James indicates he is conversant in the topics of American literature and the Cold War.

Presenting himself like any other American with a common-sense appreciation of the hazard the Cold War represents, James guides us initially to understand that he believes the USSR to represent the chief danger in the world for the prosperity of the United States and the prospects of human life everywhere. The absence in the passage of any specific mention of US involvement in the Cold War allows his reader in the early 1950s to presuppose at the outset of the book that James accepts that the role of the United States in global politics is to contain the threat of expansive Stalinism. Explicit in his indictment of the USSR, he provides barely a hint that his values are not strictly in accord with anticommunist sensibilities. He withholds for the moment his contention that fascism in Germany; Stalinism in the USSR; and the reactionary, anticommunist defense of democratic capitalism in the postwar United States are all expressions of inherent faults in Western civilization. Between references to totalitarianism and the perversity of intellectuals, he does mention "the great mass of labor movements and colonial revolts," but the pairing appears without a judgment.[37] For a reader from James's inner circle, the wildcat strikes across American industries in the 1940s and the national liberation struggles against European colonialism that followed World War II would be connected intuitively as two features of popular resistance to the capitalist imperialism of the powerful nation-states of the West. But a reader more innocent of James's political philosophy might pass over this initial juxtaposition without notice or alarm, regarding it as simply a description of recent events that coincide with the emergence of totalitarianism. Discussing Melville's characterization of the crew of the *Pequod* later in the text, James is more forthcoming about how the novel's anti-imperialist subtext resonates with his contemporary perspective that advocacy for labor in the United States and revolutionary direct actions against European colonialism all over the world are features of a common project that aspires to make socialism possible.

James's introduction offers the further qualification that *Mariners* is a popular book that requires the reader possess no special knowledge: "the book has been written in such a way that a reader can read it from beginning to end and understand it without having read a single page of Melville's books."[38] The omission of references to Melville scholarship reflects his consideration for a non-specialist audience rather than a lack of familiarity or preparation with research by academic professionals. His extensive attention to the writings of "Melvilleans" is on display in the letter he wrote in March 1953 to Jay Leyda, Melville expert and author of one of the books reviewed by Vincent in the *New York Times*.[39] In the letter, James singles out Henry Murray's, at that time influential, argument comparing Ahab to Satan. He faults the analysis for its metaphysics, explaining that Murray "shows to perfection the method I am challenging."[40] Reflecting his insistence that literary interpretation address texts in relationship to pressing social circumstances at the time of their composition, James argues that Ahab is not a transhistorical representative of "universal human nature."[41] He is, instead, a figure that conveys Melville's critical reflection on a mid-nineteenth-century historical context in which the strident individualism applauded by American exceptionalism is not a viable way to understand nor to conduct social life. To "relate [literary] structure to the age," scholarship must "begin with the social ideas," James insists, adding the slogan: "The literary leads to the social, the social back to the literary."[42] This edict for reading also describes how he understood the dynamic appeal of discussing Melville in public.

In *Mariners* his confidence that readers need no particular expertise to recognize the significance of Melville's narratives, as he recounts them, comes from his experience giving talks "in many parts of the United States."[43] James claims to have learned through these exchanges that Melville's characters are recognizable to contemporary audiences simply as a result of their experiences living in the world over the previous two decades, "particularly the last ten" years. Warner's "Publics and Counterpublics," recall, argues that the "principal act" of public deliberation "is that of projecting the field of argument itself."[44] James prepares the reader of *Mariners* to understand that disputation over the global state of affairs dominated in the popular imagination by the normative stories of the Cold War can be resolved, which is to say revised, satisfactorily by following Melville's insights. And he promises in this brief introduction that cognizance of the emergence of totalitarianism and other transformative world historical events of the 1940s will be sufficient for his reader to follow his regard for the prescience of Melville's narratives. *Mariners* is not, then, a typical secondary text. Written through an engagement with Melville, it is an original presentation in the "spirit of what Melville had to say."[45] With Melville's aid, it is James who "coordinates" the popular struggle for happiness at a time of difficulty for "masses of men" to make sense of the world.

He makes good on his assurance that no knowledge of Melville is necessary to read *Mariners* when he opens his discussion of *Moby-Dick* in his first chapter with a narrative retelling of a key episode from the novel:

> One evening over a hundred years ago, an American whaling-vessel is out at sea on its way to the whaling grounds, when suddenly its one-legged captain, Ahab, asks Starbuck, the first mate, to send everybody aft. There he tells the crew that the real purpose of the voyage is to hunt down a White Whale well-known among whaling men for its peculiar color, its size, and its ferocity. This is the whale, he says, which took off his leg and he will chase it round perdition's fires. His passion and his tactical skills win them to excited agreement.[46]

Writing as if the events occurred in history rather than in the storyworld of Melville's novel, James notes that a century earlier Ahab rallied his crew to his cause. His use of present tense involves us further in what happens. He proceeds to bring textual evidence from Melville's novel directly into his opening scene with a citation from Starbuck's shocked response to Ahab's plot: "for the jaws of Death too, Captain Ahab, if it fairly comes in the way of business we follow; but I came here to hunt whales, not my commander's vengeance. How many barrels will thy vengeance yield thee even if thou gettest it, Captain Ahab? It will not fetch thee much in our Nantucket markets."[47] Incited by Starbuck's prudent analysis of expenses and benefits, Ahab spurns market value. No measure of money can match the return on conquering the White Whale—a point Ahab drives home by striking his own chest saying, "my vengeance will fetch a great premium *here!*"[48] With Ahab's charismatic purpose and Starbuck's ineffectual dissent in evidence, James ventures a comment about Melville's text. He observes that Ahab defies the customs of free enterprise, the "unchallenged foundation of American civilization in 1851."[49] Moreover, in Cold War America, Ahab's defiance of the reasonable expectation that he must secure a reliable profit rather than plunge into unaccountable risk in pursuit of an ineffable return would, James quips, prompt an FBI investigation into the captain's loyalties and result in his being blacklisted from "any kind of job by every employer in the country."[50] By identifying Ahab's un-American avocation, James reinforces that he is a legitimate reader of the novel in the context of the Cold War and, furthermore, that the reader of *Mariners* only needs to be an ordinary citizen attuned to the concerns of anticommunism in order to follow James's explication of Melville's discerning personification of totalitarianism in the characterization of Ahab. James boasts that "after our experiences of the last twenty years" we can "understand him far better than the people for whom the book was written."[51]

Typical of how *Mariners'* critique works through extended rehearsals of episodes from Melville's texts and lengthy direct citations followed by analysis, the retelling of Ahab's exchange with Starbuck from chapter 36 of the novel, "The Quarterdeck," seems to support William Cain's suggestion that James's treatment of *Moby-Dick* is a "vivid reimagination" of the novel rather than a disciplined amendment to Melville scholarship.[52] However, we should note the significance of James's electing to retell the story starting with this particular chapter. Skipping over the many episodes that precede Ishmael's first stepping foot on board the *Pequod* as a member of the crew, James introduces the novel's story by zeroing in on an episode that was crucial for Matthiessen's examination of Melville in *American Renaissance* and the further Cold War canonization of his thesis. Ahab's rebuke of Starbuck is at once crucial and troubling for Matthiessen's argument. The difficulty stems from the ways in which Ahab's response to Starbuck can be read to exemplify abusive authority and to extol the virtues of rugged individualism that refuses to conform to the mundane dictates of standard business practices.

In his demonstration of how Matthiessen's reading was persuasive for American Studies during the early years of the Cold War because the discipline's scholars were overly invested in claiming the novel exemplifies American exceptionalism, Pease observes that "The Quarterdeck" is inauspicious textual evidence for an argument that sees in Ahab the personification of totalitarianism in advance of its time.[53] As Matthiessen pursues his vision of the novel as a prescient narrative argument in defense of American liberty against a "monomaniacal" iron rule that portends fascism in the twentieth century, he must contend with Ahab's defiant speech against Starbuck's resistance to his rash aspirations. The exchange between the captain and his first officer is problematic for *American Renaissance* and might have been an obstacle to the Cold War appropriation of Matthiessen's thesis on *Moby-Dick*. Matthiessen and, by implication, the Cold War scholars who followed him claim Ahab's rebuke of Starbuck is proof of his authoritarian and coercive social control that anticipates the reigns of Hitler and Stalin, respectively. To advance that view, Pease reveals, Matthiessen must elide the plausible claim that Ahab's rebuke of Starbuck and pledge to his crew are also indicative of the kind of self-reliance ordinarily affiliated not with communism's personality cults but with nonconformity. Ahab's presentation of his singular aspiration to pursue the White Whale is, then, the kind of rebellion that readers of the novel could identify as domineering and still associate it with the core convictions of American cultural nationalism in its most prominent formulations in either the 1850s or the long 1950s. His unmitigated attachment to individualism may be a source for the narrative's tragic resolution and a vehicle for

Melville to critique that popular conceit of American nationalism, but it does not comport with readings that for the sake of the Cold War expected to see Ahab's authority as an abuse of human liberty that is antithetical to American exceptionalism.

Matthiessen's impressive but strained reading of "The Quarterdeck" struggles to differentiate Ahab's anti-democratic authoritarianism from a strident individualism in the tradition of Emersonian self-reliance. Neglecting how tendentious is Matthiessen's uneasy reconciliation of a contradiction internal to the characterization of Ahab, the discipline of American Studies formed a chorus to name the *Pequod*'s captain un-American. *Mariners* acknowledges Ahab's hyperbolic individualism but proposes that in Cold War America the captain's nonconformity would see him blacklisted from employment and investigated by the FBI. However, after establishing his credentials as a sincere, learned opponent of totalitarianism, James proceeds to argue that Ahab's authoritarian personality is also a figure that connects the European fascism that precipitated World War II, Stalinism in the USSR, and the industrial capitalism of a Cold War America turned aggressively against the creativity and rights of laborers outside and inside its borders. Including the United States in this lineage, James supplements the concept of totalitarianism so that it represents sheer authoritarian dominance of a body politic as a social order that seems to be self-perpetuating but only because it is, in reality, the ultimate instantiation of industrial capitalism's drive toward the maximally efficient exploitation of labor. Individualism is not, then, for James, necessarily a value to be set neatly opposite fascist or Stalinist collectivism. A more meaningful actualization of democratic principles in social relations than individual liberty would be the democratization of creative control over state, civil, and commercial institutions involved in the production of social life.

Affiliating his text at the outset with the struggle of democracy against totalitarianism, James does not wait long before representing anticommunist epistemology with an incisive twist that concentrates his critique of totalitarianism on the US Cold War national security state. He makes this shift in three deft moves. While admitting the differences between Hitler's and Stalin's regimes, he insists that, like the United States and the rest of Europe, these states were "born and nourished in the very deepest soil of Western Civilization."[54] Then he observes that from the late eighteenth century on, especially in the nineteenth-century context to which *Moby-Dick* responds, Western civilization was linked inextricably to nationalism. And with nationalism, James explains, a dimension of racism is irreducible. This series of the West, nationalism, and racism then propels him to turn his defense of democracy against a totalitarian tendency in the United States that is manifest in the anticommunist regulations and customs that license his incarceration and demean his political ideals:

> The political organization of Modern Europe has been based upon the creation and consolidation of national races. And the national state, every single national state, had and still has a racial doctrine. This doctrine is that the national race, the national stock, the national blood, is superior to all other national races, national stocks, and national bloods. This doctrine was sometimes stated, often hidden, but it was and is there, and over the last twenty years has grown stronger in every country in the world. Who doubts this has only to read the McCarran Immigration Bill of 1952, which is permeated with the doctrine of racial superiority.[55]

Nazi Germany and Communist "Russia," as James, in American idiom, refers to the USSR, are examples of how totalitarian tendencies can flourish into the form of an absolutist state. Ahab personifies that degree of social control, which James emphasizes is a production of a mad ideology heightened by modern technology and the know-how of the undervalued workers. It is important to note that James does not object to technological progress, and his criticisms of Ahab's totalitarian ends are complicated by a curious admiration for this "extraordinary character."[56] In concert with most variants of Marxism, James's attitude toward modernity is ambivalent. Across different phases of his writing over several decades, he identifies "modernity" alternately with the narrative of political modernity that is marked by the late-eighteenth-century revolutions in America, France, and Haiti and with the longer history of Europe's imperial and colonial expansion over much of the world starting at the end of the fifteenth century. Working dialectically between these stories of emancipation and expropriation, he generates a regard for the revolutionary promise of universal liberty. The doctrines of the Enlightenment have licensed and inspired the disenfranchised and dispossessed to struggle against the racialized material conditions of global capitalism; at the same time, the regulative ideal of universal human rights has been used to rationalize a world order defined by relations of exploitation and deprivation.

Although the canonical reading of *Moby-Dick* associated Ahab's monomania with the authoritarian threats to democracy in America, citing the novel to critique the contemporary United States was not entirely out of step with mainstream American Studies. Contrary to James's concerns with "McCarranism," Richard Chase's influential *Herman Melville: A Critical Study* regards Ahab as an example of the kind of "doughface" or soft liberals who in their supposed pursuit of social perfection and resistance to anticommunism were unwitting accomplices to Soviet expansionism. "Ahab himself," he writes, "was a progressive American ... a terrifying picture of a man rejecting all connection with his family, his culture, his own sexuality even, expunging the colors from the rainbow, rejecting the stained imperfections of life for a vision of spotless purity and rectitude attainable only in death, drifting into the terrible future, jamming himself on, like a father turning into a raging child, toward a catastrophe which annihilates a whole world."[57] In a *Kenyon Review* article published a year after his book, Chase reiterated his concern in the practical terms of electoral politics: "if one had read and understood Melville one would not vote for Henry Wallace" because the novelist's dark vision of reality's complexity would expose as "childish and superficial" the ideas of the Progressive Party's 1948 candidate for president.[58]

Whether Ahab best anticipates Hitler, Stalin, or the American liberal who cast a lot for Progressive Party candidate Henry Wallace, the canonical thesis relies on juxtaposing this figure of destructive authority against the good example of the narrator Ishmael. James disagreed. Within the narrative that takes place on the *Pequod*, the character Ishmael poses no challenge to Ahab; he is a humble member of the crew who, like everyone else on board, is swept up in Ahab's charisma. The canonical interpretations that locate an emblem of democratic freedom in Ishmael emphasize his role as the sole survivor and storyteller. He lives to voice the tale. In *Mariners*, Ishmael does not illustrate liberty; quite the contrary, he is an "intellectual Ahab." James explains: "Ishmaels, we say, live on every city block. And they are dangerous, especially when they actually leave their environment and work among workers or live among them. For when Ahab, the totalitarian, bribed the men with money and grog and whipped them up to follow him on his monomaniac quest, Ishmael, the man of good family and education, hammered and shouted with the rest. His submission to the totalitarian madness was complete."[59] Although he compares Ishmael here to the other members of the crew in their common deference to Ahab, James follows this passage by observing that at one time or another most of the other men showed some resistance to Ahab's authority. And more pointedly, in their independent proficiency capturing whales and rendering them for use and trade, other members of the crew derive authority from their work that neither Ahab nor Ishmael is able to rival.

Before citing the passage from which he takes his title, James describes it as a "totally unexpected panegyric of the working man."[60] Appearing in the first of the novel's two "Knights and Squires" chapters, it reflects on the story of *Moby-Dick* as if it were a composition in progress:

> If, then, to meanest mariners, and renegades and castaways, I shall hereafter
> ascribe high qualities, though dark; weave round them tragic graces; if even the

most mournful, perchance the most abased, among them all, shall at times lift
himself to the exalted moments; if I shall touch that workman's arm with some
ethereal light; if I shall spread a rainbow over his disastrous set of sun; then
against all mortal critics bear me out in it, thou just Spirit of Equality, which hast
spread one royal mantle of humanity over all my kind![61]

Concerned about writing a just account of the crew, the narrator—and he
hardly seems like Ishmael at this point, but the text does not define an alternative—interrupts the progress of the story to speak a prayer that pleads with
the "Spirit of Equality" to support him against "mortal critics." The speaker's
concern is that critics of the novel may balk if, as he proceeds with the narrative, he depicts romantically the "meanest" characters to be exemplary of
"humanity."

For James, with its final pleading to "the just Spirit of Equality," this passage
discloses an unrealized potential in the text that is closer to Melville's inclinations about social relations than is the destructive resolution of the novel's
plot. In its prayerful commitment to the crew, this famous passage resonates
with the long stretches of the narrative that feature the detailed accounting of
the technical demands of whaling in combination with what James describes
as Melville's painting of "a body of men at work, the skill and the danger, the
laboriousness and the physical and mental mobilization of human resources,
the comradeship and unity, the simplicity and the naturalness."[62] His emphasis on the dignity and vitality of the men at work in Melville's novel corresponds to a signature conviction of the version of Marxism he developed over
the course of his residency in the United States. By the time of the Johnson-
Forest Tendency's split from Trotskyism in 1950, James insisted consistently
that a mobilization of the exploited or oppressed into the kind of politicized
collectivity that Marxism traditionally calls the proletariat can only take place
through the spontaneous self-organization of the masses. The idea that the
masses must be led by the vanguard of the party—that "noose around our
throat"[63]—patronizes workers by telling them perpetually that they are not
yet ready to oversee themselves. In the struggle between labor and capital that
was a generative conflict in the history of industrial capitalism, labor succeeds
most readily when the working classes organize themselves in opposition to
their exploitation and in a critical engagement with the material conditions
that enable inequality. The frustration of *Moby-Dick*, then, is that Melville's
narrative makes legible both the injustice of the crew's relationship to Ahab
and its sheer capacity for spontaneous collective action, but the story ends
with the *Pequod*'s workers' ruinous compliance to his rule. "It is clear," James
claims, "that Melville intends to make the crew the real heroes of the book,

but he is afraid of criticism."[64] The "mariners" passage shows the potential for the mutiny that would have been a justified response to Ahab's unconscionable authority. Later in the text, James elaborates that Melville does not just lack the nerve to incite complaints but in the finished novel gives priority to demonstrating "how the society of free individualism would give birth to totalitarianism and be unable to defend itself against it" (54). At odds with his typical optimism about the spontaneous capacities of workers such as the *Pequod*'s crew, here James cites Melville to claim that, in spite of the exceptionalist contention that democracy is innate to America, totalitarianism can happen in the United States. He endeavors to examine a tale of total command as Ahab proceeds to ruin the entire expedition with the single exception of Ishmael, who lives to narrate the captain's rule; yet James repeatedly calls attention to the vitality of the crew who, contrary to the resolution of the narrative, strike him as irrepressible.

James praises the "humor and the wit of the mariners, renegades and castaways," comparing their resilient joy at living to the spirit of resistance that animates "countless millions today" who are caught in loose "hangman's nooses," the "ever-present threat of destruction and a world in chaos" (25). A strictly anticommunist reading might try to understand the sense of hazard in this statement to refer to the plight of those trapped behind the Iron Curtain, but references throughout James's book to a cultural malaise in the aftermath of World War II and the atomic standoff of the Cold War encourage regarding the "millions" as people everywhere. An insider's reading from the perspective of the Johnson-Forest Tendency would infer further that James refers to global capitalism as it is dominated by the organization of the major and minor empires of the United States and the USSR, respectively.

If the "mariners, renegades and castaways" passage affirms the crew with aspirations that are legible but unrealized, the most significant representation of the crew's vitality comes in chapter 96, "The Try-Works," in which the *Pequod* becomes an industrial factory at sea for the efficient rendering of a captured whale. "The Try-Works" includes the most pointed scene of response to the historical conditions of industrial production: "In *Moby-Dick* the process of labor, though very realistically described, is presented as a panorama of labor throughout the ages. The men do not merely collect and prepare the raw material. The whaleship is also a factory. When the blubber is ready, then the try-works, huge cauldrons, are put into place, and the oil is distilled. This is really modern industry. It is the turning point of the book, for everyone is shown for what he is" (44). From this episode on, James claims, the novel discriminates between the tragic realization of the ship's ruin and the potential for resistance that the try-works makes legible.

James also asserts that this chapter establishes Ishmael's ultimate difference from the crew and his distance from radical democratic values. Ishmael's perspective on the scene of the workers and their brilliant achievement in industrial know-how marks his separation from them. He sees not how their capacity to produce represents impressive, modern knowledge; instead, he sees an uncivilized, even demonic gathering of savages:

> That at first sight is the modern world—the world we live in, the world of Ruhr, of the Black Country in England. In its symbolism of men turned into devils, of an industrial civilization on fire and plunging blindly into darkness, it is the world of massed bombers, of cities in flames of Hiroshima and Nagasaki, the world in which we live, the world of Ahab, which he hates and which he will organize or destroy.
>
> But when you look again, you see that the crew is indestructible. There they are, laughing at the terrible things that have happened to them. The three harpooners are doing their work. True to himself, Ishmael can see the ship only as an expression of Ahab's madness. The men with whom he works, even Queequeg, his splendid friend, all of them are but part of the total madness. (45)

Notice here how James distinguishes "you" from the narrator Ishmael. We readers can discern in the crew an independence that resists reification by the worst, apocalyptic machinations of industrial modernity. Informing our discerning reading is the terrible recent history of "the world in which we live," punctuated in this instance not by the Nazi death camps or the Soviet gulags but by the atomic bombings of Japanese cities by the United States. Ishmael does not share the Cold War reader's awareness. He isolates himself from the crew by reducing them to the brute force employed by Ahab's mad will. Missing from his vision is his earlier sense of fraternity and awe at both the workers' proficiency and the experienced whalemen's ability to reorganize their efforts spontaneously in response to any exigency, such as in the scene in which Queequeg dives overboard to retrieve a drowning mate from the interior of a submerged whale carcass.

From "The Try-Works" through the epilogue that follows Chapter 135, the hero of the canonical Cold War thesis is irredeemable. Ishmael only continues to view the crew as a singular instrument of Ahab's monomania. Demonizing the crew, he fails the aspirations of the earlier prayer on their behalf. James insists, however, that even the storyteller Ishmael's perspective cannot obscure from us entirely the crew's persistent difference from what the logic of totalitarianism would make of them. Recall that Arendt defines totalitarianism as an approach to governance that renders all human qualities superfluous to state rule.[65] In spite of the vividness with which he depicts Ahab's command over the men's obedience, James rejects that the crew at work together could ever be entirely reified:

> Thus, around the try-works, there comes to a head the hopeless madness, the rush to destruction of Ahab, and the revulsion from the world of Ishmael. Ahab sat in his cabin marking his charts; Ishmael, thinking of books and dreaming of how he would soar above it all like an eagle, will become in his imagination as destructive as his monomaniac leader. But . . . the meanest mariners, renegades, and castaways, remain sane and human, in their ever-present sense of community. . . .[66]

James's handling of "The Try-Works" represents his unusual contribution to the archive of Cold War writing that credits Melville with uncanny prescience about totalitarianism. Contrary to readings in which Ishmael exemplifies the exceptional democracy of the United States, *Mariners* emphasizes how the novel presents an interrupted, partial articulation of the way in which a diverse, international assembly joined together by the exploitation of its labor is able to organize itself spontaneously to create the possibility of a social order not dominated by the political economy and cultural logic of industrial capitalism. Were James to have introduced his revisionary sense of *Moby-Dick* with an unreserved account of how he viewed the democratization of work, the "mariners, renegades & castaways" would have appeared to do more than depose Ahab from a sovereign command that is the apotheosis of capital's advantage over labor. After mutiny, the crew would have constituted a council of workers to coordinate the ship's industry on the basis of their expertise and the objective of a sustainable, generalized prosperity that reproduces social conditions in which every worker thrives and all needs are met prior to the satisfaction of any private desires.

Confined and classified by a Cold War national security state that applied to every consideration a blunt hermeneutic to sort American from un-American properties, James restricted his communications about socialism after capitalism to mere implications. Removed from his direct confrontation with Cold War America, James's first book after exiting the United States, the co-authored *Facing Reality*, conveys his unabashed excitement about the popular uprising in Hungary in 1956, in which workers councils took over much of the industrial economy, at least until the USSR's invasion restored Stalinist rule. That the experiment in the democratization of the Hungarian economy was short-lived did not discourage James from proposing the efforts of the working class in that country corroborated his theory that revolutionary change aimed at overturning capitalism requires the spontaneous self-organization of multitudes of people compelled into solidarity by class exploitation, bigoted oppression, or, most likely, a combination of both.

With a chapter on *Pierre* and extended remarks on shorter works such as "Bartleby" and "Benito Cereno," *Mariners* elaborates James's claims for the social relations represented by Ahab, Ishmael, and the crew. Their associations refer to the problem of state institutions that seek to dispossess people who labor of the vitality required for radical, spontaneous democratic action and to animate them instead with exceptionalist national fantasies of otherworldly returns on the perfect catch. Most pertinent to my argument about the curriculum that is available to us in the pairing of *Mariners* and *American Civilization*, however, is how James's final chapter's personal narrative reiterates the claims he makes in his discussion of the "Try-Works" chapter of the novel. The disposition he attributes to Ahab and his unwitting, intellectual attaché Ishmael was replicated by the Department of Justice when it classified James an "alien subversive" and by the INS when it housed him as if he were a Communist. A further suggestion of a totalitarian impulse at work in McCarranism is that the subversive alien designation also stripped him of legal standing to participate in his appeal. *Mariners*, as many have observed, is illustrative of how he had lost any other recourse to be heard. Locked up on a New York island, by law he resided in a liminal space that was at once inside and outside the United States. In the indistinct, uncivil zone of Ellis Island, James found another assembly of outcasts. Over the course of the final chapter, he describes a rapport between the diverse gathering of inmates and the ordinary Americans charged with guarding them to suggest that citizenship be conceived in global terms that permit transnational mobility and ambiguate strict nativist belonging. Failing to move either the federal state or the American public to place a notion of global citizen before the priority of national sovereignty, James could not remain at home in America. The Cold War national security state of the United States was unprepared to acknowledge that the designation American "citizen" belies the ways in which the rights and privileges bestowed by that identity depend on unconscionable international disparities.

"A Natural But Necessary Conclusion"

When James turns in the final chapter to his personal experience, he identifies the non-citizens imprisoned on Ellis Island with the crew of the *Pequod*. Comparing the detention center's isolation from "the rest of society" to the whaling ship's distance from shore, he recalls how "American administrators and officials, and American security officers controlled the destinies of perhaps a thousand men, sailors, 'isolatoes,' renegades and castaways from all parts of the world." (126). Sensitive to the fact that many of the men he refers to in the chapter would still be under review by the INS or the US Department of Justice at the time of his book's publication, James is careful to preserve their anonymity. At the same time, he describes their personalities, likes, and beliefs, as well as their national, ethnic, and racial identities. He relates stories that differentiate the inmates from each other, and he conveys his personal regard for many of them. He acknowledges friendships. As if to counter the state's generic designation of each of them as one or another "detainee," he elaborates on his initial mention of their hailing from "all over the world" by cataloging their international diversity: "The whole of the world is represented on Ellis Island. Many sailors, but not only sailors; Germans, Italians, Latvians, Swedes, Filipinos, Malays, Chinese, Hindus, Pakistanis, West Indians, Englishmen, Australians, Danes, Yugoslavs, Greeks, Canadians, representatives of every Latin-American country" (151). To enrich the personal significance of this listing, he includes his private thoughts: "As I write each word, I see someone whom I knew." The administrators of Ellis Island, he charges, commit the "colossal" blunder of regarding the global assembly as "just a body of isolated individuals who are in reality seeking charity, or a home in the United States which is a better place to live than their backward or poverty-stricken countries." Presuming that the country's superior progress is the only factor pulling immigrants to America, the nationalist discourse animated by the mandates of the McCarran acts elided multiple international identities and neglected to acknowledge that the detainees may have been pushed from their homelands. For many, pressure to exit their underdeveloped countries and colonies stemmed from harsh conditions resulting from struggles against colonialism or from the persistence of colonial (or the emergence of neocolonial) social orders maintained by the affluent North over the global South. That geopolitical division of North from South was obscured in the public culture of the United States by the ubiquitous attention to the dividing line between Cold War West and East. James's anecdotes personalize the detainees, showing no single rubric can explain their presence in America. In the process, he demonstrates that the detention center's simple empiricism is stupefying in a situation that is rife with valuable knowledge that would be available if only it were engaged in dialogue (i.e., dialectically).

In James's case, the reductive misidentification was more pronounced than "detainee." While he awaited a determination of whether he would be welcome in the United States or expelled, he was assigned to a cellblock designated for

Communists. His two decades of vociferous anti-Stalinism were not meaningful because, according to the official view, one leftist belief was the same as
any other and all were comparably un-American. The identity attributed to
him on Ellis Island was a typical instance of Red Scare rhetoric that denies the
validity of any difference between anti-Communism and anticommunism.
When he was formally designated an alien subversive according to the stipulations of the McCarran-Walter Act, he also lost the right of *habeas corpus*.
In putting before the American public his best possible case for citizenship,
James confronts the emerging totalitarianism of Cold War America's McCarranism by bearing witness to the ways in which nativist anticommunism
impedes American citizens from sharing in the remarkable intelligence that
comes from the cosmopolitan insights made possible by a gathering of transnational perspectives. Self-fashioned while moving over his life throughout
the cultural and physical geography of the black Atlantic, James was himself
exemplary of the kind of transnational subjectivity that the common sense of
Cold War anticommunism would not abide. His mapping of the colonial relations of North and South in distinction from the Cold War East and West was
an alternative global imaginary that was virtually unrecognizable in the context of US public culture at the height of the postwar Red Scare. We should
note, however, that the organization of *Mariners* creates a problem for the
lessons on offer in the final chapter.

Having appropriated Ahab's fatal disposition for critical effect, James must
re-route the tragic storyline of the novel in the direction of a hopeful resolution in which his return to the United States will indicate McCarranism no
longer governs public culture. To displace the foreboding sense of devastation, his final chapter amplifies the potential for a just insurrection in Melville's narrative by elaborating the qualities of the crew in the figures of the
imprisoned detainees who, like James, await the judgment of the state. Melville's admiring but incomplete appraisal of the crew and his exhibition of
Ahab's monomaniacal drive provide the insights necessary to countermand
the ways in which the postwar Red Scare had been enlisted in nativist exclusions that bound American nationalism to white racial identity and undermined both the radical potential of spontaneous action by the masses and, as
James admits with surprise, the political resourcefulness of liberalism. Pre-
serving the pending quality of the detainees' expectations, James concludes
Mariners by opening his story to a possible redemption of American citizenship on transnational terms that are voiced in *Moby-Dick* but finally drowned
out in the novel by the impassioned totalitarianism of Ahab and the destructive consequences that entrust the narrative's dominant perspective to that of
a single individual, the storyteller called Ishmael.

As James calls on his original readers to reject McCarranism and to award him citizenship, he elaborates on the analogy between the tragic plot of the *Pequod*'s pursuit of Moby-Dick and the Cold War American national security state that defines its relationship to non-citizens in the inhospitable terms of the McCarran-Walter Act. The international assemblies of mariners in the novel and inmates in detention are both rendered instrumental by the executive authorities that preside over them. In Melville's novel, Ahab elicits the crew's passionate attachment to his cause, but in executing his pursuit of the White Whale he heedlessly treats the crew as expendable. They are a means to ends for which Ahab has only pretended to show mutual interest. McCarranism did not turn Ellis Island's detention center into a labor camp, but it did seize on foreigners residing in the United States in order to discriminate forcibly between citizens and aliens. The irony James identifies is that the predominantly nonwhite un-Americans in both locations possess superior knowledge, respectively, of the workings of the *Pequod* in the Pacific and the dynamics of the postwar United States in relationship to the rest of the world. A difference is that the crew, "federated by one keel" and "assembled by penetrating genius" of Ahab, ultimately "know nothing" of the emerging industrial society that their labors produce and symbolize (153–54). The international prisoners of Ellis Island, in contrast, "know everything" but are as yet "federated by nothing" except their common search for a "good peace" free from the Cold War and colonial dictates that deny autonomy to their "little" countries.

This analogy between the international crew of the *Pequod* and the cosmopolitan assembly of detainees prompts Pease's confidence that *Mariners* is a useful precedent for the transnational aspirations of the discipline of American Studies. He writes: "As James imagined it on Ellis Island, Transnational Americas Studies presupposed a global analytic model that would no longer move from the US center. It would entail hemispheric coverage by way of an analytic approach informed by several disciplines that would offer multicultural perspectives on the peoples and cultures of the Americas."[67] Creating his own analogy between the detainees described in the last chapter of *Mariners* and contemporary practitioners of committed, interdisciplinary scholarship according to a rubric of transnationalism, Pease alludes to James's repeated emphasis on the thoughtfulness of the men with whom he conferred during his captivity.

After the brief introduction to the chapter in which he explains that he has included an essay on his experiences in prison to teach the "inseparability of great literature and social life" as well as the pertinence of Melville's work to the "present conditions in the country which produced him," James organizes his recollections into four sections. The first concentrates initially on his trepidations about being assigned to the cellblock for Communists and then comments on how party members, especially the charismatic leader he calls M, were able to serve their political interests by adopting a humanist stance against the unfeeling and flawed bureaucracy overseeing the detention center. The following three sections then deal more directly with his personal experiences. He details in the second the ways in which the diet and medical care available at the center were insufficient to manage and then treat his chronic ulcer; in the third section, he records how his perilous deterioration required authorities to hospitalize him. He complements his tale of personal physical distress with anecdotes and portraits of how he became familiar with other inmates and guards of the detention center. He cites the support of others, including Communists and the center's employees, to underscore the contradiction between the admirable quality of his interactions with people in his immediate purview and the austere, nativist contempt for "aliens" imposed on the facility by McCarran's laws. James's final section reviews his legal case and argues that his rejection by the United States under the auspices of the McCarran-Walter Act was not only a violation of due process but an indication of how even a legitimate application of this law was tantamount to the criminalization of free expression. In sum, he puts his case forward as proof that by policing ideas McCarranism extended anticommunism toward totalitarianism. Rejecting the technical designation of immigrants housed at Ellis Island while their cases are considered, James notes that he refers to himself and other inmates as "prisoners" because using the state's term "detainee" for his legal status "would be a mockery . . . to assist them in still more deceiving the American people."[68]

Calling his original readers to attend to a damaging international consequence of the intense nativism of Cold War anticommunism, James relates how the Communist Party members in his cellblock were able to present themselves as the defenders of basic human freedoms. He writes: "On Ellis Island it was M who stood for what millions of Americans still cherish as the principles of what America has stood for since its foundation."[69] He appeals to his American captors to recognize that McCarranism's hostile treatment of non-citizens plays neatly into Communist pretense to be more charitable, humane, and democratic than American capitalism's reiteration of the racist and rapacious tenor of European colonialism. Writing while *Brown v. Board of Education* was still moving through the federal courts system, James could not have been aware of the ways in which the Cold War would influence the decision in 1954. He was on record earlier with his certain observation that the persistence of Jim Crow segregation in the United States was fodder for Soviet propaganda and a prompt for some on the left to project onto the

USSR a vision of humane social relations that lacked recognition of Russia's imperialist oversight of the other republics and the presence of racial and ethnic hierarchies that, as in the United States, were managed by state violence. Although at various points in *Mariners* James seems to invoke the normative story of the Cold War in which the USSR is the sole perpetrator of danger, his more robust commitment is to disrupt the standard coordinates of the Cold War and to expose how the Red Scare serves to insulate US public culture from an honest appraisal of the ways in which American foreign policy cites fighting Communists to cover for the country's involvement in undemocratic military and commercial exploits.

As his several references to the common Western heritage of European fascism, Soviet Communism, and postwar American capitalism make clear, James endeavors in *Mariners* to win permission to remain in the United States through the persuasive articulation of a transnational economy of belonging. That perspective could only be communicated through a critique of modernity enabled by the prior rejection of those normative stories of the Cold War that take the representation of totalitarian absolutism of the Communist East to mean that the United States epitomizes a quality of liberty integral to the democratic West. That he lapses into that same erroneous dichotomy at points has been read as a failure of integrity in *Mariners*. While not discounting that his use of Red Scare rhetoric is problematic, in this chapter I am suggesting the troubling passages of red-baiting can be read most productively as evidence of how difficult it was to formulate a non-Communist, anticapitalist perspective that could remain distinct from the discourse of anticommunism's epistemological reduction to American or un-American. Although he is careful to insist his detention by US authorities is incomparable to the inhumane conditions suffered by Germany's concentration camp victims and the prisoners of the USSR's gulags (137), James ultimately argues that, as concrete articulations of a Western heritage of instrumental reason, Nazi Germany, Stalinist "Russia," and the postwar, Red Scare United States are not different in kind but in degree. However, despite his objection to anticommunism, throughout *Mariners* his characterizations of American Communists frequently accord with those Red Scare tropes and aspersions that animate the discourse of Cold War anticommunism's elision of a meaningful distinction between Stalin's spies and people who advocate communism, whether or not they take the USSR as a positive example.

Following his statement about the ways in which M represents himself in terms of American values, he declares the man's postures to be purely cynical theatrics. Writing with a claim of unique authority reminiscent of the ex-Communist experts of *The God That Failed*, James declares M a secret despot:

"You needed a long and well-based experience of Communism and Communists to know that M in reality was a man as mad as Ahab, in all that he was doing pursuing his own purpose, with the flexibility, assurance and courage that are born of conviction. How many there knew that if it suited his purpose, in fact his purpose would demand that if he were in charge of Ellis Island, he would subject both officers and the men he championed to a tyranny worse than anything they could conceive of?"[70] James adds a footnote to this passage to indicate that he does not presume all "American Ahabs" are in the CPUSA or will join it. The Communism of the CPUSA and the USSR, he implies again, is just one variant of political reason organized to reduce human vitality to a condition of alienation. Fascism and Cold War anticommunism are others. Regardless of his disclaimer in the footnote, his depictions of dissembling, antisocial types in the last chapter of *Mariners* concentrate on Communists.

James's characterization of M's duplicity is the primary impetus for dissension in the reception history of *Mariners*. Charitable readings, which reject the accusation that James capitulates at the end of *Mariners* to the Red Scare, identify M as a proxy for the Communist Party in order to argue that James is uncompromising relative to his publication record criticizing the Stalinist Comintern and its member groups. Certainly, James is reasonable to insist that Ellis Island authorities should not have licensed M to represent him. Like planted evidence, this forced affiliation fabricates the appearance of James's guilty involvement with the Communist Party.[71] He cautions that M exemplifies the ways in which Soviet propaganda could be persuasive to people everywhere who, because their perspective is obscured by the magnitude of US failure regarding race, do not recognize that exploitation, colonialism, and imperialism are also the reality of Stalinist state-planning throughout the Eastern Bloc. Although it may be the case that James uses anecdotes of M and the other Communists to reveal how the anti-alien hyperbole of McCarranism cedes the topic of human freedom to the USSR, attributing this lesson to James's last chapter does not explain away his full employment of Red Scare rhetoric.

Even as he testifies that the Communists in detention were often kind to him, he finds in M's leadership evidence of a ruthlessness that in the manner of a Stalinist purge would see James and others of the Party's opponents "executed" for their failure to conform to Communist dictates. Identifying manifest kindness as proof of latent malice was the practice of professional ex-Communist witnesses such as Louis Budenz who instructed HUAC and other anticommunist tribunals that Communists use "Aesopian language."[72] The term meant that anything a Communist said that seemed consistent with either principles of democracy or a popular understanding of good morals had to mean the opposite. To characterize Communists as pathological liars incapable of dialogue contributes to the depoliticization of anticapitalist ideas more generally. This depiction of M along with the reductive portrayal of the CPUSA prompts Paul Buhle to call the book's ending "bizarre" and to criticize further that "[i]n this condemnation of an individual, and defence of American society against such individuals, he more nearly approached an apologia for social life under capitalism than at any other time before or since."[73] Frank Rosengarten judges similarly that "James's anti-Communism in *Mariners* could easily be used to discredit communism with a small *c*."[74] Turning again to the long letter to Padmore in 1953, we can see that James was alarmed to consider any such responses to his book. Imagining that former associates in England, including Padmore, misconstrue *Mariners* as proof that life in America lured him away from his radical political commitments, he protests:

> Now the astonishing thing about all this is the fact that the book, from the very first page, challenges in the most uncompromising terms the foundations of the official American ideology. I have lived with this for the last ten years. "Free enterprise"; "Free Institutions"; "Private Property"; "Individualism"; "The American Way"; "The Special American Capitalism which has avoided the evils of European Capitalism"; "Our Country"; "The Middle Way." I came to the United States in 1938. The country then was normal. I have seen the frenzy grow until today people have refused to endorse sentences from the Constitution and the Bill of Rights because they believed it would get them into trouble. Except for a few isolated sects, anything like radical thought is silent. The Communists alone peddle their doctrines, and under cover of the attack on Communism, whoever raises his voice against the official fetishes is a marked man.[75]

More overt than any statement in *Mariners*, this private communication characterizes Cold War culture in the United States as an atmosphere of political repression in which every idiosyncratic attitude is vulnerable to denunciation and censure. The situation he is responding to in the letter is a variation on that dynamic. Although he speaks of red-baiting in America, James is really balking at his fellow leftists taking his sharp criticisms of the Communists to mean that he has thrown in with those apologists for capitalism who equate democracy with the untrammeled exercise of commercial interest and consumer choice.

With a polemical demeanor to match James's indignation in the passage I have just cited, Pease's introduction to the restored *Mariners* purports to put an end to suspicion that James traffics in red-baiting or that his turn to memoir in the last chapter is a gratuitous addition that mars the book's otherwise interesting treatment of Melville. Pease takes umbrage at what he regards as academic police actions that prevented the book from being esteemed on par with James's other works and denied it, in particular, recognition as a legitimate production of knowledge that could be instrumental for the discipline of American Studies.[76] Building on his own account of James's extraordinary predicament as a prisoner subjected capriciously to the McCarran laws, Pease's response to the reception of *Mariners* is a complicated discussion of interpretive errors. Some he finds debatable or innocent mistakes. Others are the result of unreasonable speculation or, in one instance, poor research mixed with opportunism. The crux of Pease's defense of *Mariners* in all instances is his claim that previous interpretations have failed to recognize that James's fine reading of the "mariners, renegades & castaways" passage in *Moby-Dick* is simultaneously an incisive, original treatment of Melville's novel and a justification for the autobiographical turn at the end of his appeal. Pease's determined reading affirms the appropriately titled "Natural but Necessary Conclusion."

The final chapter, Pease argues, is necessary for the interpretation of *Moby-Dick* in the preceding chapters because it instructs us to adopt a particular stance toward James and the other detainees as a requirement for a full, retrospective appreciation of the significance James has attributed to Melville's representation of the crew of the *Pequod* in the preceding chapters. To explain this connection, Pease claims that with James's reading of the "mariners" passage the book links the first six chapters to the last through a rhetorical structure described by a counterintuitive temporality that is best defined by the verb tense "future anterior." He writes: "The temporality that James's writing might be understood to enact in the relationship he adduces between the crew's past and his own present is neither the past definite that historians deploy to keep track of completed past actions nor the present perfect, the what has been of who I am now, of the literary memoirist. It is more properly understood as the future anterior tense. The future anterior links a past event with a possible future upon which the past event depends for its significance."[77] Pease describes the link between James and the *Pequod*'s crew as if *Mariners* invites its Cold War readers to imagine that the novel's righteous promise of insurrection *will have been realized* with the felicitous acceptance of James's petition for citizenship. This reading of the temporal organization of *Mariners'* argument revisits James's situation in detention to evoke from that moment a future happening that will return to a canonical American novel a new significance. By Pease's telling, whether or not James's petition succeeds, the case he makes in *Mariners* creates a framework in which Melville's *Moby-Dick*, in the future anterior, will have meant that the transnational, multiracial, laboring mariners, renegades, and castaways are exemplary world citizens who must be welcomed and recognized without exception wherever they work and live. James's book figures a decision to release him to live in America as if it would be an act in concert with the novel's most righteous insights; a deportation order, in contrast, would mean that Cold War America has broken faith with the critical power of *Moby-Dick* and has instead reiterated the stupefying narcissism of Ahab and Ishmael's exceptionalism.

Although his interpretation does not settle the dispute over red-baiting in *Mariners* so much as overwhelm it with a reading of sufficient ingenuity to command the priority of his topic, Pease's focus on temporality is suggestive of a concern that informs much of James's work in Marxist theory and cultural criticism from the initial signs of his break with Trotskyism in the early 1940s until the end of his life. In his efforts to renovate Marxist theory to account more satisfactorily for race and the material conditions of his historical context, James endeavored to harness the urgency of Marx's representation of the historical necessity of overcoming capitalism but to do so without replicating the presumption of inevitable success that is often attributed to Marxism. James wrote in recognition of Marxism's reputation as a doctrine of inevitability, though he disagreed that Marx really claims history unfolds by laws as fixed and available to observation as the facts of nature. In "Dialectical Materialism and the Fate of Humanity" from 1947, James is strident in rejecting the suggestion that Marx's use of dialectical analysis presumes to describe unalterable facts of the natural (or supernatural) world. He writes: "The frantic shrieks that Marx's dialectic is some sort of religion or teleological construction, proving inevitably the victory of socialism, spring usually from men who are frantically defending the inevitability of bourgeois democracy against the proletarian revolution."[78] He counters that the dialectic is instead an interpretive practice that derives its legitimacy from its explanatory power regarding human social relations. It is not a means to mirror a natural order that must progress through contradictions until it arrives relentlessly at universal human liberation. To write away from the positivist subtext that presumes capitalism will necessarily be superseded by some form of socialism, James revises "necessity" to signify not the inevitable but the imperative: not what must be in a predictive sense, but what we must make of social life because both the status quo and the barbaric alternatives are unconscionable.

Contrary to Pease's complaints about those who claim *Mariners* is not a fitting representative of James's work in general, I concur that the book is atypical. For our examination of Cold War black radicalism, it has a distinction more important than the contradiction between its objection to anticommunism and its use of Red Scare rhetoric. In the contentious reception history of *Mariners*, the focus on how to read the implications of James's use of Red Scare rhetoric has diverted attention from his unusual admission of a new-found respect for liberalism. For all of its creativity, Pease's reading extends the neglect of this unexpected confession. In the final section of the last chapter, James acknowledges that his captivity has stirred him to reconsider the tenets of classic liberalism:

> Above the correspondence in the *Herald-Tribune* is printed Voltaire's famous statement: "I wholly disapprove of what you say and I shall defend to the death your right to say it." In years past I have smiled indulgently at the grandiloquent statements and illusions of these old liberals. But recently in light of modern events I have been re-reading some of them and the conditions against which they struggled to establish the principles by which only a few years ago we thought we lived. Today it is not their limitation I am conscious of, but rather the enormous service they did to civilization, as decade after decade they struggled for the right of *habeas corpus*, freedom of assembly, freedom of speech, went to jail for them, died for them.[79]

Before his imprisonment, James admits, he was bemused and disdainful of the discourse of rights at the heart of classic liberalism. Put bluntly, the standard Marxist critique holds that in the absence of equitable resources, the discourse of equal rights or civil liberties involves an insufficient description of freedom.[80] Moreover, the dedication of politics to rights is a ruse that diverts notice from the real action happening outside the political sphere in the exercise of economic advantage. And the individual subject of rights is an abstraction denuded of particularities of class, race, sex, age, gender, sexual orientation, and any other identifying details of personal disposition and historical context that are "sacrificed at the altar of abstract humanity," as Costas Douzinas writes in a provocative essay on the prospect of a positive relationship between communism and rights.[81]

Rather than reprise the conventional line of Marxist complaint and disparage rights claims as a distraction that facilitates the interests of capital over labor, in the fourth section of his conclusion James embraces a critique of the Cold War national security state based in liberalism's account of inalienable rights. As evidence of the Red Scare disrepair of constitutional democracy, he points to the disjunction between the principles of liberalism inscribed in the foundational documents of the United States and the judgment made against him on the basis of his writings. Noting that worry over the subject matter of his books outweighed consideration of his actions in the United States (including supporting his family), James concludes that the Department of

Justice has strict designs on what he should think and which historical facts should be acknowledged. Pointing to the hypocrisy with which American nationalism claims unique dominion over human freedom while the federal state, which derives legitimacy from the consent of the US citizenry, prosecutes independent thought, James alludes to *The Black Jacobins* to ask if his history of the Haitian Revolution should have lamented the end of slavery or the success of the French Revolution: "Should I have deplored the freeing of the slaves in San Domingo, or marshaled arguments to show how the Bourbons and the landed aristocrats should have triumphed over the great revolution in France? Would I have been more welcome as a citizen? Unfortunately, that would compel me also to denounce George Washington, Thomas Jefferson, and Benjamin Franklin.... This is my chief offense, that I have written books of the kind that I have written."[82] Agents of the Cold War national security state were not bound by law to extend rights protected by the Constitution to a non-citizen such as James, but that is precisely his grievance. Denying James free expression and then adding the injunction against *habeas corpus*, the national security state reveals the exceptions to democratic principle it accords itself in the emergency called the Cold War. Against such injunctions, James argues that he should be recognized to voice his case not on the basis of a national identity he has yet to be assigned but as an irreducible preroga-tive of his status as a human being who presents himself before the state as a petitioner. His claim, à la Arendt, is that the inalienable "right to have rights" must be independent from and prior to identification by a nation-state. Fig-uring the national state in a position of obligation to receive entreaties from mariners, renegades and castaways like him who propose only their being human and present to justify their license to demand recognition from the state, James endeavors to counter the ways in which McCarranism depoliti-cizes the interaction between Cold War America and those citizens and non-citizens deemed un-American, a term that when applied with juridical force reduced the person so labeled to the status of international criminal conspira-tor. When a person's writing is all that is required to prove she warrants such infamy, then the public culture informed by that regulation may be protected against any suggestion that the political order should be altogether different. Such constraint is a prohibition against democracy according to James's radi-cal conception in which all ideas are permissible and every institution must be ruled by popular consent.

If we were to extract James's admiring reference to liberalism from the context of his autobiographical final chapter, it might seem a desperate con-cession to status quo pieties of democratic capitalism. However, in the orga-nization of his concluding appeal, he precedes his attention to liberalism with the prior section's visceral demonstration of how the separation of the abstract subject of rights from the physical facts of a person lends itself to punishing circumstances that show equal rights are only of equivalent value with parity of material conditions. James invites us to reconsider liberalism's discourse of rights only after he has guided us through a reflection on the explanatory power of his particular experience of physical distress on Ellis Island. When James refers in *Mariners* to the work of writing the book in detention, he speaks more about his body than his thoughts. He refers specifically to his stomach and how the food served to the inmates aggravates his chronic ulcer. His condition had been diagnosed in England a few weeks before he arrived for the first time in the United States; four years later, he collapsed outside a movie theater in New York City with a perforated ulcer. Emergency surgery saved his life. In the ten years between this near-death experience and his incarceration, managing his health with a careful diet was a daily preoccupation. On Ellis Island, he struggled to sustain the routine that was necessary for him to live and work:

> My chief trouble was the food. I do not wish to go into any detailed description of it. I believe that a country like the United States should spend more on the materials and thus relieve the cooks from having such poor meat to work on and such small quantities of it, that, they have to resort to chop sueys, heavily spiced meat loaf, meat-sauces of the same kind, sardines with soy bean oil, etc. It was very difficult for me, particularly because of the way I have been eating since my operation. But Ellis Island is not a pleasure resort. I did not intend to live there permanently, and I knew from long experience that if I wanted to be well, and do my work, I had to avoid two things: worrying about my situation and getting a food complex. I ate with a will. One of my Communist roommates told me that I should be more careful with that food. But I was determined to eat it.[83]

Echoing the alimentary anxiety that McCarran used to denigrate "indigestible" alien subversives, James reverses the accusation, arguing that INS policies forbidding "special" treatment of any foreign detainee are prejudicial in their refusal to consider that the humane care of inmates must acknowledge what is necessary to sustain each of them. James's hunger and pain impeded his progress on *Mariners*. "If I could get some ordinarily decent food," he writes, "I hope to be able to stave off attack and pull myself together in a few days ... But it cannot be done on milk. You can live on milk for a while but that diet demands that you stay in bed, keep still and have everything done for you."[84] Sharing the deleterious effects of the Ellis Island meal plan on his ability to think, write, and live, James teaches Marxist conceits in accessible terms and examples: social being determines social consciousness, material conditions inform a person's capacity for creativity, individuality is a capacity for action contingent on others' activities, and any conception of liberty that does not account for starting conditions is illusory (and likely an alibi for persistent inequality).

The manner in which his lawyer's initial appeals for medical assistance were rejected enables James to include an insight into the persistent relevance of colonialism in depriving him relief and, ultimately, recognition. In reaction to a formal request from his attorney, he reports, "Mr. Shaughnessy said that I could leave any time I wanted and go and 'drink my papaya juice.' I was not being detained, I could leave any time I pleased. The legal theory behind this is that my status in the Courts in a case of this kind is one of grace and not of right."[85] Papaya juice, like James, is presumably alien to America. Director Shaughnessy's unsubtle insinuation is that the delicate constitution of James's ailing black body would be better kept in the West Indies. James's reference to rights rather than privileges (i.e., "grace") in relation to both his physical treatment and his legal standing is suggestive of how the last two sections of "A Natural but Necessary Conclusion" attempt to reconcile his Marxist political philosophy with core convictions of liberalism. His story of physical distress leading into his remarks on liberalism's mandate of rights communicates that the presumption of equality motivating a demand for political recognition insists on a conceptual space—a public—of universality. James affiliates his portrayal of individual autonomy with the anticapitalist redistribution of resources rather than with notions of possessive individualism that have historically made liberalism, in effect, an asset to capitalism.

James narrates how his detention imposed on his autonomy. For a month, he can eat almost nothing. He takes to his bed, too weak to write, and worsens. Sympathetic prison personnel who express their willingness to help fail to surmount what he calls "bureaucratic stupidity," such as the stipulations that disallow alternative diets. Only when he becomes so ill that an intervention might have been too late do the authorities admit the urgency of his condition and deliver him to a hospital where he has to recuperate for twice as long as he had been starving. In attending to this key image in *Mariners* of the wasting James, I credit the text with presenting his precarious experience as a lesson: an accident of his body voiced a spontaneous protest that became ungovernable by the standard procedures through which he had been rendered to prison in the guise of a confirmed enemy of the state. His emergency unsettles the state's representation of him as a mere alien subversive whose every need can be rejected as so much clamoring for unwarranted entitlements or, worse, as an inscrutable effort toward sabotage and terror. If the final section's invocation of liberalism's provisions for political recognition insist that James be treated as a subject bearing inalienable rights, the preceding depiction of his inadvertent hunger strike suggests that the value and exercise of rights is contingent on our being well enough to fortify our bodies. At a time that Cold War liberalism won preeminence by supplementing civic identity with an ethos of anticommunism, James's *Mariners* charts a procedure from physical concerns to civil rights to suggest instead that liberalism could be a valuable supplement to Marxism.

I have presented James's autobiographical turn at the conclusion of *Mariners* as an impressive pedagogy that conveys radical insights through the common topics of *Moby-Dick*, totalitarianism, and liberalism that he incorporates most powerfully in the presentation of his physical emergency. Although the anecdote of his ulcer and hospitalization describes solidarity sparked by common concern for the exigencies of his imperiled body, the story of inmates and personnel rallying to his well-being is pretty thin, even unthreatening as a portrait of collective political action. James's tale of Ellis Island reiterates the unrealized insurrection on board the *Pequod* with a description of potential tested provisionally in an emergency that may serve as an allegory of spontaneous collective action against the proscriptions of McCarranism. However, the minor revolt of James's person and affiliates still sees the detainees waiting on either the immediate judgment of the state or a public uprising against Cold War America that cannot be imagined easily in reference to the exceptional populace of Ellis Island inmates through which *Mariners* attempts to bring the weight of the world to bear against the nativist and still colonial racism of Ahab's America. *American Civilization* offers comparable lessons but in a more impressive scale and with a demeanor that would have been obviously imprudent for James's appeal for citizenship.

Moby-Dick is also essential to the argument of *American Civilization*'s chapter on nineteenth-century intellectuals, but the novel is not in itself exemplary of collaborative, spontaneous, popular human striving for liberty against totalitarianism that James depicts in *Mariners* as the work necessary for a new socialism to supersede capitalism. Instead, Melville's novel satisfies an intermediate step in James's dialectical presentation about nineteenth-century intellectuals in the United States that culminates with the abolitionists.

Melville in the Dialectic of *American Civilization*

In contrast to the relatively isolated conditions in which James composed *Mariners*, his two "notebooks"—*Notes on Dialectics* and "Notes on American

Civilization"—were written in collaboration with other members of the John-son-Forest Tendency. Grace Lee and James Boggs recall James's forceful, personal influence on the group's eclectic research itinerary and its simultaneous involvement in the practical considerations of factory workers:

> Projecting the American revolution and the American working class as the heir to all the achievements of Western civilization, he inspired a few of us, known as "the Johnson-Forest Tendency" first inside the Workers' Party and then inside the Socialist Workers' Party, to fantastic studies. We struggled to understand Marx in the light of European history and civilization, reading *Capital* side by side with Hegel's *Logic* in order to get a sense of dialectical and historical materialism. We explored the world of Shakespeare, of Beethoven, of Melville, Hawthorne and the Abolitionists, of Marcus Garvey and Pan-Africanism.
>
> At the same time most of us worked in the plant, struggling to squeeze every ounce of revolutionary significance out of what American workers were saying and doing.[86]

The manuscript on dialectics was completed for circulation within the group in 1948, but was not published as a book until 1980. In retrospect, it may be read as a contribution to the extensive literature by European and diasporic African intellectuals on the left who participated in the mid-twentieth-century revival of interest in Hegel. Following Kojeve's famous lectures from the 1930s on the "master/slave dialectic" in *The Phenomenology of Spirit*, figures such as Sartre, Marcuse, and Fanon sought to rejuvenate historical materialism after World War II through a reconsideration of Hegel's importance for Marx. Although generally in concert with this effort to revive radical thought by revisiting Hegel, James led the Johnson-Forest Tendency to a different text. He answered Lenin's admonition that Marx's chapter on the commodity form from the first volume of *Capital* could not be understood without a thorough knowledge of the *Science of Logic*.[87] An extensive treatment of James's difficult *Notes on Dialectics* would divert from the primary concerns of this chapter, but I call attention to the manuscript because it is indicative of the expert command of Hegel, Marx, and Lenin expected of those whom he asked two years later to review "Notes on American Civilization." His private audience for that prospectus had been prepared by working through the previous manuscript he referred to as a "kind of basic training" in dialectical thought.[88]

American Civilization includes instances of Hegelian-Marxist vocabulary and unexplained references to conventional wisdom in that tradition, but its more significant influence appears in the book's organization. James employs the dialectical thought process of Hegel's *Science of Logic* as a rhetorical procedure to trace the ways in which revolutionary episodes punctuate American history, which he reads through constellations of productive technologies, political events, state policies, public unrest, popular culture, key personalities, and happenstance. The chapter I discuss here, "The American Intellectuals of the Nineteenth Century," for example, examines Whitman, Melville, and the abolitionists, in turn. For each topic in the sequence, James puts his finger on a failed attempt to contend successfully in writing or action with vexing material conditions. He locates textual evidence of social contradictions that require he take up new texts that address the problems more satisfactorily. The last lines of the chapter restate emphatically that its presentation has advanced dialectically:

> It is possible now with extreme brevity to sum up a lengthy chapter:
>   1. Whitman: a singer of loneliness and Democracy with a capital D
>   2. Melville: prophet of destruction
>   3. Abolitionism: advocates of mass revolution
> The further economic and social development of America into the present must now occupy us.[89]

James uses a blunt Hegelian formulation for rhetorical purpose with his coterie of readers. Whitman's poetics of individualism were an intelligent response to the historical conditions of his moment, but its limitations are displayed by Melville's true critique of Ahab as the ruinous apotheosis of that individualism. In a third move, the abolitionist movement, tapping into popular unrest against slavery, is a corrective to the excess of Melville's negation of Whitman.[90] Yet even in its impressive reconciliation of direct action and social theory, the abolitionist movement remains incomplete. Gesturing toward the book's further chapters, the last sentence reinforces his finding that for all of the unprecedented gains experienced by African Americans after the Union victory over the Confederacy, the basis of Reconstruction's termination in 1877 was already prepared by the failure at the end of the war to follow through on the full anticapitalist promise of abolitionism. Instead of presenting at length on Melville's uncanny exemplarity for the crisis of the Cold War, James situates Melville between Whitman and the abolitionists in a demonstration of how the partial victory over slavery in the nineteenth century should instruct a just political response to modernity's degradation still taking place under industrial capitalism a century later. As in *Mariners*, James's discussion of Melville in *American Civilization* concentrates mainly on *Moby-Dick*, and in both books his claims for the novel are much the same. *American Civilization* does not invite us to adopt a future anterior optimism

about James's text realizing the implicit promise of the novel, but its account of the narrative does rely on a reading of the tragic vitality of the crew in combination with a claim for the prescience with which Melville figures Ahab's monomania.

James opens the chapter by rehearsing a thesis premised on a description of US history as a continuous, rare state of freedom importantly distinct from the feudal past of Western Europe:

> *Because of the peculiarly free conditions in the United States, the American intellectuals as a social group were the first to face as a practical question the beginnings of a problem which has been fully recognized during the last twenty years—the relation of individualism to democracy as a whole; while in Europe the question was narrowed and at the same time concretized by all kinds of conditions.... But now as society faces its fundamental problems, the work of these writers and the Abolitionist politicians assumes a new significance ... World War II already seems to have lifted the American literature of the middle of the nineteenth century to a new level.*[91]

With the expression "peculiarly free conditions," James alludes to an idea of American exceptionalism that was dear to his contemporaries in postwar American Studies and their academic fellow-travellers the "consensus historians," most notably Louis Hartz.[92] James admires the literature of the American Renaissance for its pertinence to social conditions after World War II, and he invokes the long-standing conceit that, notwithstanding the enslavement of Africans and the dispossession of American Indians, the unique quality of personal freedom in the United States was such that revolutionary anticapitalist movements would only fail to find purchase in the body politic.

As the chapter proceeds, this idea about the exceptional freedom of individuals in America is revised twice. The sequence maps onto Hegel's discrimination of modes of thought in his critical remarks on Kant in the preface to the first edition of the *Science of Logic*. In the book on dialectics, James glosses Hegel's presentation of a dialectical movement through understanding, reason, and speculative reason:

> Take the passage clause by clause: "Understanding makes determinations and maintains them." That we know. "Reason is negative and dialectical because it dissolves into nothing the determination of Understanding." That we know too. "Reason is positive because it is the course of the Universal in which the Particular is comprehended."

There you get the distinction in Reason which on the one hand negates the determinations of Understanding and at the same time *creates* a higher truth by speculation. So that Reason is both negative and positive.[93]

Again, as we have it, *American Civilization* is a draft of a prospectus for a primer intended to be accessible to a popular audience unschooled in Marxism. In the meantime, James's confidence in his actual readers' common preparation in dialectics is on display when he translates Hegel's specialized vocabulary into the proper names of literary artists and a social movement in nineteenth-century America. Whitman's poetics of individual freedom and equality attempt to maintain a transhistorical category of "Democracy, with a Capital D." The problem with Whitman's verse, for James, is that he develops poetic methods to preserve his "fantastic thesis" that understands equality among individuals, in the United States and the world, in order to "overcome the potent fact that men were not equal" in standing.[94] Whitman's poetic understanding of individual freedom, James suggests, anticipates Cold War propaganda that touts American freedom to be the only viable alternative to the fetters of the USSR.

Melville, James contends, "is the exact opposite of Whitman." His narratives portray individuals in intricate webs of social relations, and he reasons that unchecked individualism is an existential threat to any society. "The prototype of this," James writes, "was Ahab. The modern dictator whose prototype he is, is best exemplified by Adolph Hitler" (76). Whitman's understanding of a capacious individualism is seen, from the perspective of Melville's reason, in truth, as Ahab. Contrary to the sheer possibility of insurrection he will attribute in *Mariners* to the crew under Ahab's command, in *American Civilization* he concedes that Melville's vision provides no solution to the problem of authoritarianism. The middle section of James's chapter on nineteenth-century intellectuals runs aground with Melville's suggestion that "society was doomed."

Revolutionary aspirations are articulated through James's examination of the political program of the abolitionists, especially Wendell Phillips. Consider this long passage in which James explains his plan to revise "Notes" into the primer:

A finished book will have to relate Emerson, Thoreau and the Transcendentalists to Whitman, Melville, and the Abolitionists. It cannot be done here. Sufficient to say that even Parrington says that the soil which produced Emerson also produced Garrison—they were complementary parts of the same movement. What we have to show is that if Whitman anticipated the loneliness of the American character, its passion for the old free association which it was losing, the powerful but false ideals which it tries to substitute and did substitute for many years; if Melville brushed aside the slaves and painted a picture of impending catastrophe for America and the whole world, whose significance we are only today able to see; then the Abolitionist intellectuals in their political action showed a solution or rather a method of solution that corresponded in range and intensity to the inspired vision of Melville. If Melville saw the totalitarian dictator as the ultimate end, the Abolitionist intellectual embodied an American anticipation of the most radical political action that the nineteenth and twentieth centuries have known. (87)

Notice here that Melville's significance involves truth and error. He writes discerningly about the perils of totalitarianism, but in doing so he "brushed aside the slaves," neglecting the most visceral contradiction animating the tension in the US republic between Enlightenment postulates of inalienable human value and the dispossession of enslaved black Americans. The first element of the abolitionists' "method" that excites James corresponds to his conviction about the need for popular spontaneity in any movement for revolutionary change. Unlike Whitman and Melville, the abolitionists arrived at their ideas and objectives through their interactions with—and as—escaped slaves who pursued freedom to the north. James explains that the abolitionists were the means "by which a direct social movement expressed itself," and therefore any analysis of the abolitionist intellectuals must begin with the slaves (85).

James starts his discussion of how slaves were involved in the abolition of legal slavery in the United States by offering a brief genealogy of slave revolts, the Underground Railroad, and the publication of *Freedom's Journal*, "the first Negro newspaper in the United States," all of which marked the "Age of Jackson" with division, violence, and struggle (85–86). Consensus historians characterized the same early-nineteenth-century period as a time of expanding democracy that saw the common people use electoral politics to wrest authority from rich elites, but they paid little heed to the rash of slave revolts or the displacement of American Indians that gave Jackson's populism a white supremacist demeanor.[95] James disrupts praise of democracy's progress by emphasizing that the irrepressible force of the abolitionist movement is a more vital truth than Jackson's advocacy for democratic governance in defiance of traditional, moneyed interests.

James surveys the efforts of renowned movement leaders such as William Lloyd Garrison and Frederick Douglass, but he concludes the chapter on nineteenth-century intellectuals with extended remarks on and long extracts from Phillips. The oratory, writings, and public actions of Phillips represent, for James, a unique vision for extending the abolitionist movement after the resolution of the US Civil War. Garrison, in contrast, argued that the passage of the 13th Amendment to the Constitution fulfilled the purpose of the American Anti-Slavery Society. Phillips's famed quip about the Emancipation Proclamation—it "frees the slave but ignores the negro"—captures neatly his perspective on the joined priorities of political recognition and social equality. By the time of the Civil War, he saw the abolition of slavery as not only a moral imperative but also as a necessary precondition for a political reorganization of the social order that would redistribute property to freed slaves and impoverished whites. James complains that Phillips's political program "to this day remains ignored and almost forgotten. Yet seen in its context, it is perhaps the highest peak reached by the United States intellectuals in the foreshadowing of the future of the world today."[96] In an influential book from 1949 that is not cited in *American Civilization*, Richard Hofstadter shares James's opinion, including Phillips among the twelve "men who made" the "American political tradition." He opens his admiring chapter on the "Patrician as Agitator" by acknowledging that Phillips's "reputation stands very low ... the standard writers have been handling him roughly for forty years."[97] Hoftstadter and James's comparable efforts to restore Phillips's reputation were not on trend with American history in the late 1940s. Outside the American Anti-Slavery Society in the years after the Civil War, his demands for the comprehensive reorganization of social life in America were regarded as rash and unreasonable. And the fortunes of his ideas were not much different during the reconversion of the US economy after World War II, a time characterized by the passage of the anti-union Taft-Hartley Act, the failure of federal full employment policies, and a backlash of violence in defense of white supremacy against efforts to transfer the moral authority of America's victory over fascism in Europe to the struggle against Jim Crow. Rehearsing Phillips's development from his early opposition to slavery on moral grounds to his later objection to capitalism writ large for its irreducibly exploitative character, Hofstadter compares his stance at the end of the Civil War to that of a contemporary: "Karl Marx, looking upon slavery as a socialist, had said that white labor could never be free while black labor was in bondage. Phillips, approaching socialism as an abolitionist, was arriving at the conclusion that black labor could never be truly free until all labor was released from wage slavery."[98]

American Civilization records Phillips's vision for Reconstruction as a history of the possible that should instruct the US citizenry after 1945 to acknowledge that democracy is a value with radical demands that are not satisfied by electoral franchise and which may be pursued most effectively in moments of tumult:

But one thing is clear. The great national crises in social upheavals are caused by challenges to revolutionary governments, not to established ones. It was the challenge of Lilburne and the Levellers to Cromwell; of the Paris Commune to the Committee of Public Safety and Robespierre which marked the most desperate crises of the revolutionary regime. It never came to this in the Civil War. But the Abolitionists and Phillips in particular show that in the United States, such an embryo, such an anticipation of extreme revolutionism had developed. Phillips in his context and in his political programs showed the same breadth of view, the revolutionary conception of democracy, and political ruthlessness which are associated with what is loosely called Bolshevism. His ideas for America, and he was prepared to go through blood and fire for them, should be indicated.[99]

James goes on to single out Phillips's conviction that the resolution of the Civil War must be followed by the appropriation of lands in the South for newly liberated African Americans. His "revolutionism," as James describes it, refused any compromise with the South to end the Civil War because "that would mean an agreement on the South's terms and those terms would inevitably mean the nationalization of slavery, and the subjugation of free speech and democracy in the North to aristocratic tyranny."[100] Phillips's neglected, alternative version of Reconstruction was based in reparations that would have enabled newly liberated African Americans "to be the very basis of the effort to regenerate the South."[101] Even after passage of the 13th Amendment, Phillips remained adamant that former slaves should be granted suffrage in every state and that, at a minimum, property, education, unpaid wages, and dignified work were all owed to the freed African Americans whose forced labor had been instrumental in generating the prosperity of the United States. With the slogan "Forty Acres and a Mule," General Sherman's Special Field Order 15 was better preserved in public memory, but James recalls in *American Civilization* that, in the years just after the Civil War, African Americans used the term "a Wendell Phillips" to refer to the allocation of land and a furnished cottage for a freed family.[102]

Mariners invites its reader to imagine rectifying the capricious sovereignty of Cold War America under the influence of McCarranism by rescuing James from the unjust fate of the mariners, renegades, and castaways who drowned for Ahab's capricious leadership in *Moby-Dick*. By Pease's reading, the stance James charts for us involves inhabiting a future that realizes a significant and righteous revision to the past. That the example of the past is taken from fiction is not insignificant, especially when we read *Mariners* alongside *American Civilization*. That earlier text, in its treatment of American intellectuals in the nineteenth century, obliges us to consider actual historical events that, akin to the mutiny that might have deposed Ahab, remain possibilities lost, in this case to the long, twinned history of reactionary capitalism and anti-black racism. As an essential point of mediation in the development of an argument that ultimately reclaims Phillips's abolitionist philosophy as a usable past to orient the critical evaluation of the reconversion of the US economy after 1945, *Moby-Dick* helps James to revitalize the claim that the unfinished program of Reconstruction after the Civil War must entail reparations for the unremunerated labor of African American slaves. From his confined position as a subversive alien hoping for the US national security state to relax its judgment against him, it would have been foolhardy for *Mariners* to tout Phillips's version of abolitionism and the reparations it entailed. Needless to say, the agents of Cold War America that took issue with his earlier writings on revolutions outside the United States would never have entertained James's admiration for the homegrown Bolshevik Phillips's ideas for the annihilation of the "Spirit of the South." And yet, James was not ultimately protected from exile by devoting *Mariners* to a canonical American writer while understating his own anticapitalist convictions through an allegory of his body's rejection of being a detainee. James's restraint in *Mariners* relative to *American Civilization* signifies the ways in which anticommunist discourse was an impediment to acknowledging in public that, to satisfy democratic principles, political recognition would have to be accompanied by the redress of punishing social inequalities. The Red Scare rhetoric confronting James equated recognition to liberation and tainted complaints about social inequality as if they were un-American abuses of civic standing. His unrestrained admiration for Phillips informs *American Civilization*'s more robust pedagogy of social protest that, paired with *Mariners*, should appeal to an American Studies discipline that remains interested in reckoning with damages wrought by state and commercial institutions of imperialism made prosperous by, among other means, the dispossession of black people in and out of the United States.

CHAPTER FOUR

Black Is Red All Over Again: President Obama's Father Figure Frank Marshall Davis

From now on I knew I would be described as a Communist, but I had reached the stage where I didn't give a damn. Too many people I respected as Freedom Fighters were listed as Red for me to fear name calling . . . . The genuine Communists I knew as well as others so labeled had one principle in common: to use any and every means to abolish racism. From now on, I would join hands with anybody going my way.
—**Frank Marshall Davis**[1]

Prominent in Chicago's African American arts renaissance of the 1930s and 1940s, journalist and poet Frank Marshall Davis has been lost to cultural history and found again more than once. As I detailed uncomfortably in the opening pages of this book, his most recent recuperation followed perversely on his appearance as a character of President Obama's acquaintance in the memoir *Dreams from My Father*. Davis's personal association with Obama's family provided fodder for the return of Red Scare invective and Cold War iconography in reaction to the first African American president of the United States. Publications that contest the legitimacy of Obama's citizenship and describe his election as a deadly serious hoax invoke the image of Davis as a role model of black masculine anger, depraved sexual license, unremitting resentment at America, and ultimate loyalty to the USSR during the Cold War. The impetus for this chapter is this fantastic, anticommunist refashioning of Davis into a father figure whose alleged dreams of a Stalinist world order supposedly reverberated in Obama's innermost thoughts as he insinuated himself into the White House in 2008.

The resurgence of Red Scare racism aimed at Obama represented a return on the work of anticommunist discourse during the long 1950s. Exemplified by the use of Davis, the complaints about Obama's alleged communism served once again to disconnect political recognition from socioeconomic redistribution, predictably coding the former as an American value and the latter as a treacherous, alien idea that has no place in the public culture of the

United States. Without acknowledging the irony, those reviving this argument in its Cold War form to attack Obama typically supplemented their claims by insisting this most American distinction was a central tenet of the civil rights movement. The ubiquitous depictions of King as a Communist were forgotten. A descendant of Davis and others of his ilk, Obama had no claim on King's legacy, which the New Right has endeavored for years to reduce to an impassioned campaign to render "colorblindness" to race an inviolate precept of law and custom in America. Also missing, then, was the late revelation of King's radicalism.

A sketch of Davis's political affiliations and his reception history will be instructive for our efforts in this chapter to relate the harm of anticommunism during the long 1950s to its damaging resonance several years after the end of the Cold War. Of particular interest is the way the appropriation of Davis's life story proffers a direct and personal connection between Obama and un-American activities during the Cold War. Embodying communism as if it were a mere expression of black anger, the image of Davis advising a teenage Obama diverts attention from the anachronistic tenor of representing the president after 2008 as if he were deliberately carrying on with the plans of a state that ceased to exist in 1991. Reactionary polemicists use Davis to demonize leftist political convictions that they attribute incautiously to Obama. Never minding how different is Davis's characterization in Obama's book or the ways the Obama administration's positions share in the neoliberalism that has characterized the attitude of the White House without interruption since Reagan's first inauguration, the self-appointed investigators of Davis's influence clamor that the president's mentor was literally a figure of black Communist menace from another age.

After reviewing the disjunction between Davis's identity in literary and cultural studies from what his work and person mean in publications about Obama, I take a more extensive look at the most successful and prosperous single production in the veritable culture industry devoted to disparaging Obama's presidency and the leftist ideas he was erroneously said to have advocated. A unique contribution to the archive of New Right histories of the struggle for civil rights, Dinesh D'Souza's film *2016: Obama's America* seizes on the international travels and affiliations of Obama's autobiography in order to craft an alternative life story purporting to expose that the president secretly keeps faith with an anti-Western, un-American ideology inspired by his father's involvement in anti-colonial struggles in Kenya. Undistracted by the farcical quality of D'Souza's psychological profile of Obama, I concentrate on the historiographical subtext of the film in which the supposed exposé of Obama serves to endorse a narrative that conveys an unembarrassed apology for European colonialism and the North Atlantic bequest of global hegemony to the United States. *2016: Obama's America* insists that the civil rights movement in the United States was the natural extension of the precepts of the American Revolution and is therefore incomparable to the ultimately anti-American efforts of decolonization that took place across Africa and Asia in the years following World War II. Davis appears in the documentary as one of Obama's five "Founding Fathers" who prompted him to cultivate animus toward the doctrine of American exceptionalism. More specifically, D'Souza claims, Davis represents precedent for the ultimate hazard threatened by Obama's serving a second term: the fulfillment of a plot to surrender the United States to anticapitalist "collectivism" and to engender a new Cold War in which America cannot prevail.

After I examine the returns on Cold War anticommunism enjoyed by efforts to degrade Obama's presidency with reference to Davis and to take his election as an opportunity to trumpet anti-statist market fundamentalism (i.e., neoliberalism) as if it were the logical extension of the values behind the civil rights movement, I turn to Davis's writings. Good-faith appraisals of his committed journalism and radical literature demonstrate that his twinned critique of racism and capitalism teaches that black liberation can only follow from the dispossession of those socioeconomic advantages that in their routine, historic bestowal made whiteness into a valuable property. Although the postwar Red Scare made such a critical enterprise exceedingly more difficult, "Frank-ly Speaking," Davis's newspaper column from 1946 to 1957, takes the exigency of anticommunism as a chance to lay bare the collusions of capitalism, racism, and nationalism and, in Hawaii, to champion the efforts of the International Longshoreman's and Warehousemen's Union (ILWU) to free the territory from the "Big Five" corporate monopolies that effectively ruled the islands in colonial fashion from the end of the Spanish-American War until 1954. For a Hawaiian readership, "Frank-ly Speaking" contends with Cold War anticommunism in order to link the struggle for civil rights with labor activism and against the role of postwar US imperialism in hampering decolonization. Exile from the continental United States enabled Davis to sharpen his criticisms of the Red Scare in a context of labor union activism and interracial opposition to white supremacy that did not simply acquiesce to the criminalization of Communists.[2] Anticapitalist ideas remained legitimate political considerations during the eight years Davis volunteered his radical opinions to the *Honolulu Record*, a weekly newspaper dedicated in its inaugural issue of August 5, 1948, to speak "for the common man." If the postwar Red Scare impeded the socioeconomic imperatives of the civil rights movement in the United States by expelling black radicalism from public culture, in the

US territory of Hawaii anticommunism was instead confronted by a forceful collaboration of labor union and anti-racist activism. In Hawaii's volatile public culture from the end of World War II until statehood in 1959, claims for the affinity between anticapitalist convictions and democratic principles could be taken seriously. The anticommunist partnership between Jim Crow's proponents and the major corporation's interests could be exposed for crying "un-American" to cover efforts to perpetuate colonialism in Hawaii whether or not the territory became the 50th state.

Receptions of Frank Marshall Davis

Davis disappeared from literary esteem for two decades largely as a consequence of the postwar Red Scare. He published his third and last full volume of poetry in 1948, the critically acclaimed *47th Street: Poems*. When federal investigations of un-American activities intensified in Chicago that same year, Davis and his wife Helen moved to the territory of Hawaii. Paul Robeson encouraged their decision, advising Davis that the racial diversity and multicultural styles of life on the islands would see the couple's interracial marriage treated with less hostility than they faced in the continental United States. Davis's wife was Helen Canfield, a member of a prominent Chicago family that disowned her over the marriage. Their partnership across the racial divide of black and white, in combination with her seemingly dramatic contempt for her family's wealth, was just the most visible indication that anticommunist authorities would label them un-American.

Davis served on the board of directors and taught a course on the history of jazz at the Abraham Lincoln School. Anyone associated with the school was certain to be investigated. Targeted for disloyalty by US Attorney General Tom Clark in 1947, the school would later be placed on the official list of subversive organizations. Davis was also suspicious for his affiliations in the late 1930s with Popular Front literary groups, such as the League of American Writers, which was founded by Communists after the termination of the party-affiliated John Reed Clubs. He published poetry in journals reputed to be in line with the party's philosophies, and he contributed to the league's *Writers Take Sides*, an anthology in support of the fight against fascism in the Spanish Civil War that also featured statements by Countee Cullen, Langston Hughes, James Weldon Johnson, Alain Locke, and Wright.

As a journalist and editor, he was outspoken on incidents of white supremacist bias and Jim Crow violence that also prompted the Communist Party to assist those targeted for being black, including the trials of the Scottsboro

Boys and Angelo Herndon.[3] Before World War II ended, Davis became a board member of the Civil Rights Congress and would remain active in the Hawaii chapter until the pressure of repeated federal prosecutions finally broke the national organization. Worse for his standing with the FBI or investigative tribunals such as the Senate Internal Security Subcommittee, after the war, as the NAACP began to purge Communists and their sympathizers, Davis moved further to the left with a new publication. He became founding editor of the *Chicago Star*, a weekly labor newspaper committed to reporting in support of workers' struggles for fair pay and a real say in the management of their workplaces. The paper closed after two years, when Davis moved to Hawaii. There, he discovered the new *Honolulu Record* had much the same mission. He volunteered "Frank-ly Speaking" to the weekly's editorial page for free from May 12, 1949, to May 16, 1957.

Davis was indeed a Communist.[4] Contrary to the essentialist logic of the latter-day anticommunists who cite him in their screeds against Obama, becoming a Communist did not subsume every aspect of his identity. The quality of his involvement in the party is another indication the CPUSA was not a monolithic institution. After years of fellow-traveling in appreciation of the party's activism for civil rights, he joined officially not long after the so-called Detroit Riots of 1943. He was dedicated enough to the party to find Wright's original publication of "I Tried to Be a Communist" to be an unforgivable breech of solidarity. Wright and he had agreed that black liberation required fighting capitalism, so the public airing of grievances with the party in Chicago struck Davis as too obviously an asset to those opposed to the African American freedom struggle. In his memoir, however, he relishes observing that the public break with the party did not alter Wright's basically Marxist perspective.[5] And, like Wright, Davis was always an embattled party member, criticizing policies when he disagreed and refusing to compromise his independence as a poet and a journalist.

Davis was, in summary, an exemplary figure of the black cultural front of the Great Depression era,[6] and his deepening interest in communism after 1943 contradicts the narrative that says African American artists on the left came uniformly to realize that the Communist Party was never a sincere ally in the struggle for civil rights. At the same time, his exile to Hawaii and the resulting disappearance of his presence and his poetry from literary institutions in the United States during the 1950s and early 1960s is a further reminder that the image of African American support for anticommunism and confidence in racial progress was cultivated by significant elisions.

Davis's literary obscurity in the 1950s was not, however, entirely the result of Red Scare politics. A shift of aesthetic values in the late 1940s favored high modernist difficulty over proletarian literature of all kinds, including the naturalist mode of the Wright school of narrative fiction and Davis's style of social realist poetry. His unadorned depictions of the indignities African Americans suffered as a consequence of anti-black racism were more like the accessible low modernism of Carl Sandburg, whom Davis admired, than the rarefied formal difficulty of Eliot and others so perfectly suited to the ostensibly disinterested, apolitical interpretive practices of the New Criticism. The proletarian sensibilities, didactic racial politics, and vernacular sound that were deemed insufficiently literary by official verse culture in the 1950s were instrumental to his first rediscovery in the late 1960s.

Propelled by Black Arts and the wave of radical social movements that coalesced through opposition to the American war in Vietnam, the academic discipline of Black Studies encouraged the recuperation of forgotten artworks that were viable precedents for scholarship and creative arts intent on demonstrating the autonomous value of black art and experience, independent from the Western canons of white esteem. As Davis recounts in *Livin' the Blues*, he was surprised and pleased when in 1967 he began receiving requests to reprint poems in new anthologies intended for classroom use.[7] In Dudley Randall's influential *The Black Poets*, for example, Davis's poems appear in the "Post-Renaissance" section between selections from Melvin Tolson and Robert Hayden.[8] This renewal of interest and the offices of the influential Margaret Burroughs, art director at the DuSable Museum of Afro-American Art in Chicago, brought Davis back to the mainland United States for the first time; in 1973 he toured several cities and campuses to give poetry readings. Davis's cultural front credentials meant he was prized in the ethos of the emerging discipline of Black Studies, which sought alternatives to what was regarded as the accommodating decorum of celebrated African American texts of the 1950s such as Ellison's *Invisible Man*. Davis's hiatus from mainland literary scenes during the early Cold War was a feature of this first, Black Arts recuperation. An interview with Davis in 1974 was entitled "Mystery Poet,"[9] alluding to his relative obscurity as a writer rather than any quality of his blunt, didactic, and darkly comic poetics.

Davis's second recuperation was more academic in tone. After select poems were collected in significant anthologies in the late 1960s and early 1970s, particular interest in Davis's work quieted. His books remained out of print, and his editorial writing was available only in libraries or other archives holding back issues of the black press. Mainly as a result of the archival research and editorial work of literary scholar John Edgar Tidwell, Davis's poetry, memoir, and a representative selection of his newspaper columns are now available as books. Starting with the posthumous publication of *Livin' the Blues* in 1992,

Tidwell's ongoing commitment to recovering Davis as a subject of literary significance has been instrumental for scholarship in cultural politics that over the past two decades has rectified the historical record concerning the relationship between the organized left and the black freedom struggle. For research into the cultural front in Chicago during the 1930s and 1940s, Davis's writings have been especially useful to rebut the Red Scare story that dictates all black Communists were simply duped.[10]

Unrecognized in literary scholarship at the time, in 1995 Obama's *Dreams from My Father* introduced a characterization of Davis that would become the source for his reception history's third episode of rediscovery. After Obama's emergence in 2007 as a candidate for the Democratic Party's presidential nomination, the radical historian Gerald Horne was the first scholar to identify in print that "Frank" from his first memoir was Davis.[11] Further research into this "revelation" of the president's teenage rapport with a black Communist poet and journalist was undertaken primarily by self-described political conservatives who usually contributed to print, radio, and television venues addressed to a right-wing audience. I place "revelation" in quotations because Davis's identity in Obama's *Dreams from My Father* is not a secret, though without exception anticommunist publications about the connection between the men claim references to "Frank" without his last name are an attempt to hide his identity and a sign that Obama was cognizant at the time he was writing that any association with Davis would be embarrassing. Paul Kengor's *The Communist: The Untold Story of Barack Obama's Mentor* is typical. Referring to Davis's CPUSA membership, Kengor declares: "I have no doubt that this is why Obama was careful to never once give Frank Marshall Davis's full name in *Dreams from My Father*."[12] Age 34 and working as an attorney when he published this first memoir, Obama omitted the last names of several characters who lacked sufficient personal or historical importance to warrant fuller identification. Much has been written since 1995 to restore Davis to relevance for the study of African American literature, but at that time it was unreasonable to expect a non-specialist would recognize or be interested in his work. Among the books Davis authored, only the posthumous *Livin' the Blues* was in print. Moreover, for readers with expertise or research know-how on twentieth-century African American literature, Obama's book provides all the information necessary to identify "Frank" as Davis. No one else named Frank remotely fits the profile of place, publications, and personal associations with canonical figures such Hughes and Wright, both of whom are mentioned in the first appearance of Frank in *Dreams from My Father*.[13] The suggestion that Obama's use of only Davis's first name is purposeful dissembling can only be either obtuse or a willful error made with the assumption that the audience for publications charging the president with being a secret Communist would not give Obama's original memoir fair consideration.

The other obvious error of the documentary films, books, articles, book reviews, television and radio appearances, and countless blog posts (followed by interminable threads of commentary), is that, without exception, they ignore or misunderstand the unsubtle rhetorical function of Obama's characterization of Frank in *Dreams from My Father*. Unlike failing to acknowledge that Obama made no effort to hide Davis's true identity, this point is open to interpretation, a little. No reasonable account of the description of Frank can deny that Obama is dismissive of his politics.[14] While Obama does acknowledge the poet was an important contact in his teen years, one of the very few African American adults with whom he was acquainted at the time, he does not depict him as a mentor deserving of emulation. Nor is his text pregnant with suggestions of a deeper rapport. He is forthcoming about Frank's place in his life; he was a well-meaning, affable, older African American man who explained his attitudes on the difficulty of being black in the United States to the teenage Obama. However, when Obama recalls thinking of Frank at critical junctures later in his life, each time he is instructive as a bad example. In *Dreams from My Father*, Frank is an obvious foil for how Obama's thinking on racial politics is incomparable to familiar tropes of protest and discord that carry connotations of late-1960s counterculture.

Perhaps the conservative pundits who attacked Obama with the image of Davis were so committed to replicating Hoover's depictions of all Communists as a single malignant and evil influence on the body politic that they did not discern that Obama also resuscitated the anticommunist strategy of depoliticizing leftist convictions. *Dreams from My Father* does not follow the Red Scare invective of McCarthy, McCarran, Hoover, or even the registered Democrat Kennan. Instead, Obama writes in the manner of Schlesinger's version of Cold War liberalism, which discredits Communists and communism with ridicule and condescension rather than virulence. In the case of Davis, Obama's decisive judgment against the older man's attitudes is tempered with personal affection. Recounting his last conversation with Frank before he left Hawaii to begin college at Occidental, Obama quotes Davis telling him that he could expect nothing of higher education but lessons in conformity and obligatory capitulation to norms and traditions of white culture. For an African American man of Davis's age and anti-Western biases, attending college in the United States was racist training that even for successful black professionals would lead ultimately to a crude reminder that "you may be a well-trained, well-paid nigger, but you're a nigger just the same."[15]

As Obama narrates their exchange from this key moment in his young adulthood, Frank's diatribe goes nowhere. In spite of all of his pronouncements, he concedes with "shoulders slumped" that Obama should nevertheless go to college but "[s]tay awake."[16] Davis's resignation that his sweeping denunciations of the white supremacist designs of college instruction should mean no more for the young Obama than the vague admonition to "keep your eyes open" tells the reader of *Dreams from My Father* that all of the Black Studies fire and brimstone sounding in Davis's monologue is an echo from an era of social protests that are exhausted. Obama amplifies his generational difference by casting Frank in a recognizable caricature of authentic identity politics: "It made me smile, thinking back on Frank, and his old Black Power dashiki self. In some ways he was as incurable as my mother, as certain in his faith, living in the same sixties time warp that Hawaii had created."[17] Obama and Frank were familiar and may even have been friends, but writing a few years after the poet's death he trusted his portrait to imperfect memory and popular caricature. Nothing in the book suggests he did his homework on Davis's actual political attitudes. If he had, the referential pact of autobiographical writing would have required he acknowledge that Davis's own memoir protests his unequivocal difference from Black Nationalism.[18] With more intensity after he took up exile in Hawaii, Davis's race politics were pluralist, though his radical critique of racist capitalism and white supremacy— virtual synonyms in his thinking—always pointed to anti-black racism as the organizing precedent for America's other racisms.

Of course, precision regarding Davis's political imagination is not Obama's purpose. Frank's recurrence in *Dreams from My Father* marks a pattern in which the narrating Obama discloses that he came to maturity, in part, through an ever-increasing appreciation for how inappropriate and even silly the race politics of the late 1960s had become. He neglects that Davis was a cultural front warrior from the 1930s who paired Old Left Marxist optimisms to his indignation at white supremacy in order to fight for an idea of anticapitalist radical democracy that the postwar Red Scare rendered virtually illegible in US public culture after *Brown v. Board of Education*. Obama's political trajectory to the presidency could not have been expected at the time he published this first memoir, but the narrative testifies to an adult political imagination in accordance with the disposition of the Clinton administration: the era of big government was over, and it was high time to end welfare as it had been known. In other words, for all the vitriol aimed at Obama on account of Frank, his *Dreams from My Father* is more than the catalyst for others' disfiguring portrayals of Davis. His memoir affirms the prejudice that says leftist convictions result from dysfunctional feelings and not from political reasoning.

The consistent misrepresentation of how Obama's *Dreams from My Father* names and characterizes Frank is sufficient reason to discount the more elaborate fabrications of Obama's un-American identity that followed in all of the publications and productions concerning the Davis connection, but arguing the merits of these attempts to assassinate the president's character with the smoking-gun evidence of Davis's CPUSA affiliation was rather beside the point of the anti-Obama culture industry. These arguments found their warrants in the visceral appeal of tropes, narratives, analogies, and optics for an audience persuaded already, for whatever reasons, of Obama's treachery. Most visibly in D'Souza's film and most respectably in Ronald Radosh's admiring book review of Paul Kengor's *The Communist* in the *National Review*,[19] speculations about Davis's influence on Obama did creep into mainstream public notice during the presidential contest of 2012. Radosh's piece was published October 29, in the week preceding Election Day. Moreover, calling Obama a Communist, socialist, Muslim socialist, and the like was routine for his opposition throughout his presidency. In his presidential campaign, Governor Mitt Romney characterized Obama's un-American sensibilities as typical of European socialism.[20] The less temperate accusation that Davis was and remains Obama's direct connection to the dream of the United States being supervised by the Kremlin was, however, generally reserved for a reactionary counterpublic identifiable by its common contempt for the idea that Obama's election was legitimate and a related certainty that his intentions for the presidency were malevolent toward America. Internal to this counterpublic, division arose only over how best to characterize the malignancy of his presidency.

Again, my concern in this discussion is not to disprove arguments that are at root conspiracy narratives and therefore constructed to adjudge contrary evidence, incredulity, and disrespect with an infinite regress of incrimination according to which my insistence on the differences between criminal spies in Stalin's employ, American Communists, the anticapitalist left outside the CPUSA, and Obama's neoliberalism can only be read as a sign of either my involvement in an un-American plot or my unwitting accommodation of America's enemies. Formulated into narratives of existential threat, the discourse of Cold War anticommunism makes every US citizen an unabashed capitalist, dupe, or traitor. My interest is instead in the ways in which the Red Scare invective aimed at Obama carried on in the countersubversive tradition of demonizing leftist political ideas. Moreover, reuniting anticommunism with anti-black racism encouraged a synergy of panic between the threat of un-American terrorists hiding in the body politic and the presence of African Americans residing in the White House with authority to imply that black slaves and their descendants have been the most vital of American citizens all along. To employ this discursive strategy, Obama's far-right opponents availed themselves of monolithic historical premises about the CPUSA that were invented in the propaganda initiatives of Hoover's FBI, HUAC, and many other state, civil, and commercial institutions that transformed a real concern over Stalin's espionage apparatus in the United States into a potent social fiction about the emergency of a criminal conspiracy of limitless reach, permanent endurance, and pathological compulsion.

Although his account of Obama's supposed radicalism shares in the most common Red Scare complaints about the president, Kengor's *The Communist* is novel for its re-investigation of Davis's un-American activities. Most striking about the book is Kengor's fidelity to the postwar Red Scare, which he treats neither as a discourse nor even as an object of study examined and debated by historians. Cold War anticommunism was, for Kengor, an axiomatic and heroic posture of national defense that received its final vindication with the dissolution of the USSR. Showing no regard for the extensive scholarship on the complicated history and character of the CPUSA, especially in relationship to civil rights, Kengor resurrects without revision the FBI's characterization of the CPUSA from the time that Hoover appeared before HUAC to school the committee on how to spot a Communist. The book's insinuations about Davis's influence on Obama are routine examples of guilt by association, but the book takes on a higher degree of complexity in the way it uses Davis's life story to reinstitute Hoover's vision of the CPUSA: a vast criminal conspiracy in which every member was tantamount to a spy aiming to destroy the United States and every fellow-traveller was an unwitting, but responsible accomplice to that ruinous plan. In the service of that historiographical objective, Kengor endeavors to reorganize the substance of the memoir *Livin' the Blues* so that the decision to join the Communist Party defines Davis's identity. A precocious intelligence born into racist circumstances, Davis, by Kengor's retelling, might have followed a different path were his misfortunes not compounded by poor judgments at crucial moments resulting in an ultimate instance of abject failure when he joined the party. Traumatic and trivial incidents of his childhood, viewed through the lens of Cold War anticommunism à la Hoover, become telling prelude to his ultimate decision to go with the Reds. Deciding to join the CPUSA, he became forever after a different kind of person, and as a Communist, he could not have resisted the lure of Obama's youthful malleability and potential to serve a cause that Davis was incapable of seeing for its inhuman malice.

Kengor is right that Davis's decision to become a member of the CPUSA calls for explanation. For a US citizen to join in 1943 meant coming to terms with or overlooking starkly negative reports about the USSR, including

well-circulated testimony about the 1936 show trials and the arresting fact
of the short-lived 1939 non-aggression pact between Hitler and Stalin. As we
discussed in relation to Wright's "I Tried to Be a Communist," the CPUSA's
wartime suspension of opposition to racism in America for the sake of military unity was an immediate betrayal of African Americans' needs, and it
undermined confidence in Communists' historic involvement in civil rights
prior to World War II. How, in the face of that record, could Davis determine
that in 1943 it was time for him to become a card-carrying member of the
party and, as the passage I cite in the epigraph recalls, to undertake the risks
of membership?

Kengor's answer imagines that Davis's resentment at years of racism and
the absence of a Christian faith to direct his insecurities more constructively
finally culminated in his conversion to the unholy dogma of the Communists. As he does throughout his book, he draws on *Livin' the Blues* to single
out a moment that in retrospect throws light on Davis's later ability to implicate himself with an organization that Kengor holds responsible for perpetrating crimes against humanity all over the world. In 1922, after learning of
the lethal mob violence against African Americans in Tulsa, Davis prayed
that the perpetrators would be brought to justice.[21] Repeating this response to
other incidents of racial violence to no avail, the young Davis determined that
"the Christian religion was a device to keep black subservient to white. Very
well. Then I was through with it."[22] He qualifies, however, that he still kept
close contacts with the church for social reasons, and that he never hesitated
to partner in a cause with people motivated by religion. For Kengor, Davis's
early turn to agnosticism denied him the Christian foundation that braced so
many African Americans in the fight for civil rights. He concludes, "among
the rancid fruits of this separation from Christianity may have been communism."[23] This phrasing is clever. The separation from Christianity undoubtedly
produced rancid fruits, but whether it caused his Communism specifically
is a mere speculation. In a book called *The Communist* that rewrites Davis's
autobiography to orient its every episode to the defining event of his becoming a member of the party, a decision he continued to enact with world historical consequences when Obama fell under his tutelage, Kengor can afford
to hedge from strict, tenable claims of causality. He can trust that his audience
will assuredly make the connection he wants with confidence: the godless
incline to communism, and Communists must be godless. Agnosticism may
not have made Davis a Communist, but it was a condition of possibility that,
added to racism, became probable cause. If *The Communist* had taken into
account influential scholarship that professional academic historians of the
interaction of the CPUSA and civil rights in the twentieth century are bound

by professional expectations to consult, Kengor would have had to qualify his uncomplicated association of unbelievers with un-Americans. Kelley's *Hammer and Hoe*, to cite a single landmark of research into the black left, reports that a "radical, prophetic tradition of Christianity was a major factor in drawing blacks into the Communist Party and its mass organizations."[24] For a time, black Communists in Montgomery, Alabama, even opened their party meetings with a Christian prayer.[25]

Having identified Davis's preparation for conversion to Communism with reference to experiences of racism in combination with the absence of a Christian faith, Kengor proceeds to characterize Davis's belated decision to enroll in the party as a symptom of his resentful tendencies finally becoming too intense to resist. His erratic passions and animus at white society needed an outlet; the CPUSA provided one, and in hindsight his interest can be traced back to his days at Kansas State. Reviewing the section of *Livin' the Blues* in which Davis reflects on his involvement with the Communist Party starting in the middle of World War II, Kengor correctly observes that Davis (writing around 1982) shows surprising naïveté about the USSR. Davis mistakenly believes it is opposed to imperialism and free of domestic racism; in fact, the USSR and the Eastern Bloc were an imperial confederation held together by forceful command that had the ancillary effect of disguising ethnic and regional conflicts that have often exploded into racialized violence in the years since the breakup of the USSR.

Kengor is, however, entirely dismissive of Davis's suggestion that his antiracist political activities in cooperation with the Communist Party brought him to the attention of the FBI and HUAC. Kengor insists: "It was Frank's scathing words on Churchill and Truman and the Marshall Plan and much more—not Scottsboro or lynchings—that got him noticed. Frank's attempt to paint his accusers as motivated by racism is irresponsible. It was deeply divisive. And yet, Frank flung these race charges in self-defense for forty years, especially in his commentaries, always insisting that it was the alleged racism of congressmen, not his pro-Soviet communism, that raised flags in Washington."[26] Kengor's aspersions at Davis are explicit here; he was guilty of a treasonous affiliation, investigated for Communism and not for his antiracist politics, and was himself a divisive race-baiter. In the 1950s and again in the 1980s, Davis supposedly played on racism to impugn the motivations of the federal authorities who investigated him. For Kengor, Davis is the racist: not Senator Eastland, who denounced the Supreme Court's *Brown v. Board of Education* decision as a Communist plot, called for Chief Justice Earl Warren's impeachment, and in 1956 brought the "SISS" to Hawaii to investigate subversives in the territory. Ordered to testify, Davis exercised his Fifth Amendment rights, which Kengor, like Hoover before him, takes as an admission of guilt.[27] A year later, the US Supreme Court would finally declare the criminalization of Marxist ideas to be unconstitutional. Davis and thousands of other card-carrying Communists who committed only Orwellian "thought crimes" prior to 1957 maintained all along that Smith Act prosecutions were an unconscionable violation of the First Amendment of the US Constitution, which is to say genuinely un-American. Purporting to teach the nature of Davis's influence on Obama, Kengor instructs his credulous readers (and presumably his Grove City College students) to look back on FBI policing, Congressional tribunals, and the practice of democracy in Cold War America as if they were a lock-step combination in pursuit of the ideals of equal rights for all citizens and governance by popular consent. Considering all that has been made public about the FBI's decades of institutionalized suspicion of anyone African American and the prevalence of Dixiecrat legislators using HUAC and "SISS" to defend Jim Crow, Kengor's self-righteous assertion that national security agencies and Congressional investigators discriminated cleanly between Davis's Communism and his racial activism (and his racial identity) is incorrect and irresponsible about the particulars of Davis's case and the procedures of anticommunist institutions in general. He paints a willfully naïve picture of anticommunist initiatives in the long 1950s as if they were carefully circumscribed police actions that targeted criminal activity. He does not entertain the possibility that the Red Scare was employed to suppress and punish political dissent. As we will see when we turn to Davis's "Frank-ly Speaking" columns, Kengor's account of the non-racist propriety of the anticommunist activities of the US federal government is most obviously impossible to sustain when considering events taking place in Hawaii between World War II and statehood in 1959.

Kengor's presentation of Davis's decision addresses the records that confirm he became a party member, speculates about the psychological formation that could enable his choice, and judges the conversion a moral failing. But he avoids Davis's explanation in *Livin' the Blues* of the events that compelled him to formalize his relationship with the CPUSA after so many years of active sympathy and occasional cooperation. In *Livin' the Blues*, Davis reflects at length on his decision to join the Communist Party.[28] In the first couple years of US involvement in World War II, he remembers his only interest outside of work was photography. He wrote little poetry and disengaged from politics. Then, he explains, two incidents of racial violence jolted him back to action. A lynching in Missouri not far from where he grew up and the Detroit Riots of 1943 prompted him to reflect on the hypocrisy of the United States fighting for democracy against fascism in Europe and Asia while permitting in America "the same kind of atrocities found in Hitler's Germany" (276). While Davis had been supportive of the Double V campaign, these events persuaded him that African Americans' contributions to an eventual victory for the United States and its allies would not result in the surrender of white supremacy in America. To rejoin the struggle against anti-black racism in anticipation of the persistence of Jim Crow rule during and after the war, Davis determined that he could not go it alone. "I resolved," he recalls, "to join hands with others seriously interested in curing the disease of American racism." He knew that he would be labeled a Communist, but he no longer cared. Herndon, Ben Davis Jr., Wright, and Patterson had all been Communists who sought in that capacity "to use any and every means to abolish racism."

To counter readers' suspicions that his decision to join the Communists meant he began taking "orders from Moscow," Davis offers a detailed explanation of his attitude toward "Russia." Like any other American raised after 1919 on a diet of Hearst press publications, Davis grew up convinced that the Bolshevik Revolution was an offense against human liberty and the USSR a hateful state. Later, evidence that the USSR's official policies were anti-racist and that the state had no colonies in Africa or Asia shook his faith in mainstream reporting about the Communists. He writes: "Like the vast majority of Afro-Americans who thought about the issue, I considered Red Russia our friend" (277). However, Davis's affiliation with the Communist Party was not seamless or one-sided. He characterizes his participation as just one of his political associations among others, all of which he engaged as parts of a constellation of resources to use in contending against white supremacy.

Davis reports that even without public acknowledgment of his CPUSA membership, he was nearly certain at the time that he "had attracted the special attention" of HUAC. Had that been confirmed, he boasts, he would have accepted "any resultant citation as an honor" (279). For Kengor and others investigating the supposed mentor to President Obama, Davis's inclusion on a list of subversives slated by J. Edgar Hoover for internment camps if the Cold War were to turn hot is indisputable proof of his treason. In contrast, two years into President Reagan's first term, Davis recalls with pride that he had been on the wrong side of HUAC even before the outbreak of the Cold War. To warrant HUAC's attention and ire was a positive sign that he "was beginning to upset the white power structure" (279). In the literature on Davis's alleged un-American mentoring of the teenage Barack Obama, nowhere is there any acknowledgment, let alone embarrassment, that neither HUAC nor "SISS" ever investigated the un-American activity of organized, massive, terrorist resistance to the civil rights movement.

In Davis's view, being investigated by HUAC was less remarkable and more expected than the response of other Communists to his writing. Refusing to subscribe to Earl Browder's call for the party to "soft-pedal harsh criticism of American racism for the sake of 'national unity'" during the war, Davis was accosted by Communists for his anti-racist poem "War Quiz for America." Appearing in the April 1944 issue of the NAACP's journal *Crisis*, the long poem was composed as a dialogue in several voices, including a chorus. For party leaders and members more compliant with official policy than Davis was, his verse dialogue communicated too harsh a critique of race relations in the United States. He includes in his memoir an excerpt of the just over two pages from the poem that "made them [Communists] tear their hair out." Consider the following stanza from the middle of his selection:

1st Voice: Uncle Sam, Uncle Sam
            Why send me against Axis foes
            In the death kissed foxholes
            Of New Guinea and Europe
            Without shielding my back
            From the sniping Dixie lynchers
            In the jungles of Texas and Florida? (280)

A single rhetorical question in seven lines, this stanza confronts us with the speaker's inarguable knowledge. The doctrines of racial superiority that animate the fascist states of Germany and Japan are indistinguishable from the racial apartheid in the United States. African Americans, without exception, are more or less susceptible every day to the mortal danger of Jim Crow rules that license their discrimination, abuse, molestation, and murder. If, as anticommunists then and now claim, becoming a Communist is a conversion of subjectivity to a compulsive state of perfect compliance and un-American disdain for human liberty, then Davis's indoctrination failed. His defiance of the wartime policy against anti-racist agitation is on display in this poem delivered to the membership of the NAACP, a group founded by the black radical Du Bois and which Kengor invokes as supposed proof that the Communist Party was not necessary in the struggle for civil rights. Whether it was necessary or not, the party made ample, positive contributions to the black freedom struggle, and Davis's involvement sharpened his attention to a necessity Kengor and others of his mindset cannot abide: black liberation entails two forms of redress, anti-racist political recognition and anticapitalist socioeconomic redistribution.

Davis's reflections on becoming a Communist in *Livin' the Blues* imply that he anticipated an Allied victory in World War II would be followed in the United States by a redoubled commitment to racial segregation to counteract public recognition of the Double V campaign and the impressive record of African American contributions to the war effort. The column he began to write for ANP around the time he joined the party, "Passing Parade," provides detailed explanations of his apprehensions for the postwar period, for which he foresaw not only a resurgence of anti-black racism in America but also US foreign policies of antagonism toward the USSR and of support for Europe's colonial powers. Rather than the hoped-for termination of Jim Crow rule in the United States and decolonization without European resistance across Asia and Africa, Davis effectively predicted the Cold War and was wary of the advantages it would afford the doctrine and colonial system of white supremacy. In "Passing Parade," which he wrote for several months in 1943 and 1944, he identified the links between the politics of race in the United States and an international order that he feared would resume white supremacist colonialism the moment the Allies won World War II.[29] The so-called Detroit Riots of 1943 and other incidents of racial violence in the United States at the time presaged for Davis the domestic racial politics that with the instrument of anticommunism would delay and disappoint the promises of the Double V campaign. Looking outside the United States, in a three-part series of "Passing Parade" columns, he identified alternative visions of postwar geopolitics with reference to, on one side, the colonial imperialism endorsed by Winston Churchill and, on the other, the international plan for peace advanced by Henry Wallace.[30]

Davis's too-optimistic expectation was that the CPUSA could be enlisted in the fight against Jim Crow racism, European colonialism, and the interests of capitalism in such a way that would not map onto a polarized geopolitics of capitalist West against communist East. As it turned out, his exile to Hawaii to avoid the crush of anticommunism in Chicago afforded him the opportunity to be active in a public culture that, unlike that on the mainland United States, accepted that communist ideas were viable for political consideration and that the divide between industrialized nation-states and the underdeveloped colonies and former colonies was as crucial an axis as the Cold War divide of East from West. In Hawaii, a vibrant, interracial, working-class majority population discerned that anticommunism was a campaign of political repression intended to break the ILWU and sustain the apartheid-like political economy of Hawaii that was ruled by the "Big Five" corporate monopolies. Those companies had grabbed local authority in the wake of the US military colonizing the islands by force in the Spanish-American War. Their influence, plus a track record of white Republican men controlling Hawaii's electoral politics, inspired US representatives and senators wedded to either corporate interests or Jim Crow to initiate support for Hawaiian statehood in the late 1930s. Preferences would shift in 1954 after the popular backlash against the Red Scare disrupted decades of stasis in party politics and swept the Democratic Party into all major offices.

With the Red Scare subjected to popular protest and small-c communism more politicized than criminalized, Hawaii was like no place in the mainland United States during the early years of the Cold War. According to the overt and implicit claims about US history that inform the anti-Obama chapter in Davis's reception history, we are expected to believe that nothing like the political events and culture of Hawaii in the 1950s ever took place in the United States or any of its other territories. Davis's communist dreams of a political coalition moving against both capitalism and racism in the pursuit of radical democracy were at home in Hawaii, and his exile there afforded him critical purchase on how, especially in the years just before *Brown v. Board of Education*, the federal officials fighting for the survival of Jim Crow in the American South and the capitalist interests of monopoly control on the islands were in unsubtle accord in their opposition to the democratization of Hawaii's racial hierarchy, electoral politics, and local economy. With "Frank-ly Speaking," he was able to bear witness to how anticapitalist, anti-racist principles supported by the formidable energies of the ILWU were moving Hawaii away from colonialism and toward democracy. In denial of the fact that the colonialism of Europe and the United States in the nineteenth and twentieth centuries was systematically an anti-democratic, racist, and exploitative means to prosper at the expense of others whose descendants and homelands still bear consequences of that history of deprivation, D'Souza never permits his film *2016: Obama's America* to acknowledge that Davis was a participant in Hawaii's liberation struggles in the 1950s or to admit that the Red Scare was met there by massive and righteous resistance.

D'Souza's *2016: Obama's America*: Un-American Anti-Colonialism after Racism

Released to theaters in the summer of 2012 in time to alert voters of the disaster that would follow if Obama were elected to a second term, *2016: Obama's America* proposes to expose the president's unhealthy fixation on the decolonization of Africa and his unacknowledged plans to redress the historical crimes of the West by purposefully undermining America's global authority. Omitting the term decolonization from his discussion of anti-colonialism,

D'Souza purports to teach the difference between the attitude motivating the American Revolution and another kind of anti-colonialism that fomented national liberation struggles in Africa and Asia following World War II. Proven virtuous over time, the first type of anti-colonialism stemmed from Enlightenment principles of individual reason and republican self-determination. With the leadership of America's founding fathers, this eighteenth-century anti-colonialism overthrew Great Britain's unconscionable rule, opening the transatlantic community and, eventually, the world to a commercial infrastructure better able to reward merit and encourage enterprise than was possible under monarchy. The second anti-colonialism, a dead enterprise according to D'Souza, is an anti-American, anticapitalist variety that he suggests incited a conflagration of violence, unrest, and enduring social ruin across Africa and parts of Asia in the middle of the twentieth century. Obama, he claims, is party to this latter mindset and legacy; his personal feelings of abandonment compelled his secret dedication to Barack Obama Sr's dreams of his home country free from British influence and overseen by an elite state bureaucracy in which he would hold a prominent position. Kenya did finally rid itself of British occupation, but the national and personal attainments the senior Obama envisioned did not come to fruition. As a consequence of his deceased father's grip on his psychology, the film argues, the president could not be more removed from the revolutionary heritage of America's original opposition to colonialism. Even worse than being un-American, the first black American elected president derived his ideas from an obsolescent philosophy of political violence that sought to undermine the authority of his own country. The seditious Obama has long been in pursuit of a geopolitical vision that would roll back the world historical progress D'Souza regards as President Reagan's triumph over Communism and the related ideas of collectivism.

Among the many anti-Obama productions in various media, 2016 was distinguished by its impressive distribution, revenue, and notice in news media across the political spectrum. While it opened at a limited number of theaters on July 20, 2012, word of mouth and social media publicity, in combination with well-placed reviews, generated enough interest to win it a wider distribution. At the time of the Republican national convention in Tampa, Florida, in the last week of August, the film was appearing on more than 1,800 screens at movie theaters across the United States. Two weeks later, its distribution peaked at 2,107 screens, making it the seventh most profitable film in the United States over the weekend of September 9. With ticket sales in excess of $33 million total at the time it closed in October 2012, it was the second most prosperous political documentary ever, behind Michael Moore's *Fahrenheit 911*.[31] Virtually every major print publication in the United States carried either news of the film's financial success and message or an extended review. Outside of avowedly conservative publications that characterized the film as insightful or, at least, suggestive and brave, appraisals of the film were in the main hostile, dismissive, and sarcastic. Audiences were undeterred. The film surpassed all revenue expectations for documentaries.

The film's prosperity may reflect on the appeal of its argument for audiences inclined to dispute the legitimacy of Obama's presidency while, at the same time, trying to maintain a belief in being reasonable when in disagreement with others. Purporting to identify the foreign, un-American roots of Obama's politics, D'Souza asked viewers to consider a psychobiographical interpretation of Obama's personality, but he did not traffic in "birther" or other conspiracy theories that are indisputable only through the paranoid rejection of incontrovertible evidence (e.g., the release to the public of Obama's long-form birth certificate from the state of Hawaii). Some paranoia about Obama's intentions is requisite for approving of D'Souza's film, but it is not necessary to accept that Obama's achieving the presidency was the culmination of a plot that dates back to his birth. The film's argument also banks on D'Souza's particular status as a conservative public intellectual who worked in the Reagan administration and who is a person of color. Proponents of the film's thesis can cite D'Souza's identity and life story to imagine that race is not a factor in their conviction that President Obama seeks to bring about the end of America's international authority because of his deep-seated, pathological attachment to the anti-colonial aspirations of the socialist father who abandoned him.

My interest in the film concentrates instead on its troubling and ambitious historiography. Obama's presidency provided D'Souza with an opportunity to fashion a novel, dynamic, and seemingly urgent version of an apology for European colonialism that has been a recurring feature of his writing since the early 1990s.[32] D'Souza's *2016: Obama's America* may have failed in its seeming objective of interfering with Obama's re-election in 2012, but its more durable and harmful accomplishment is the dissemination of two stories it tells as if they were the incontrovertible histories of both the civil rights movement and the resolution of the Cold War. Whether or not its audience agrees with its argument about Obama's anti-colonial political philosophy, the film communicates that the civil rights movement in the United States was unrelated to decolonization elsewhere and that the end of the Cold War vindicated the Reagan administration's domestic and foreign policy attacks on welfare programs everywhere.

In the two best-selling books that cover the same position as the film, D'Souza poses as if his investigation were an academic exercise.[33] He presents the hypothesis that Obama has adopted his Kenyan father's anti-colonial philosophy and then tests it against the evidence, such as it is. While committed to the same claim, the film is organized like a personal essay. It begins with D'Souza's voiceover reflection on how as a child growing up in India he understood America to be an imperial power unlike any that preceded it; not an expansionist, acquisitive, and martial occupying presence inside and outside of its borders, America is, he explains, "an empire of ideas." After describing how coming to the United States to attend Dartmouth College advanced him from limited prospects in India to the diverse opportunities of the American Dream, D'Souza arrives at the proper subject of his film with a series of observations about the coincidences between Obama's and his life stories. They were born in 1961. Each spent years of his childhood in a "Third World" country that was formerly a European colony. Both attended Ivy League schools. They married US citizens in the same year. Neither of the men is white. In a shot that hints at D'Souza's willful neglect of facts about racial discrimination in America, the camera shows us the brown arms of two different men while his voiceover tells us that Obama and he have nearly identical complexions. The film says nothing about the significant historical differences between being of African and Indian descent in the United States. The litany of similarities is prelude to how over the course of the film D'Souza uses his own biography as a foil to bring into relief how different is his romantic faith in the American Dream from what, prior to his ground-breaking research, had been Obama's well-concealed antipathy toward the idea that the United States is an exceptional nation-state that merits its advantages over most of the world. At the outset of the film, their differences are merely entrée for D'Souza to mull over his confusion about Obama's behavior after taking office in 2009. "Baffled," he explains, by several of the president's initial decisions, he sets out to travel the key sites identified in Obama's memoir *Dreams from My Father* in order to uncover "How Obama Thinks," which was the title of the 2010 *Forbes* magazine cover story in which he debuted his tendentious and lucrative argument.

Retracing Obama's life story on location in Hawaii, Indonesia, Chicago, and Kenya, the film also tells a story of its own production in the guise of a detective narrative. The befuddling quality of his initial decisions as president persuade D'Souza that the common understanding of Obama's life story must be mistaken, so he travels in pursuit of the man's real identity. D'Souza's voiceover represents how the investigation proceeded, while throughout the film he also appears in each location to gather information. He surveys the key sites identified in Obama's book and conducts interviews with people who possess firsthand knowledge of the president, his family, and his upbringing.

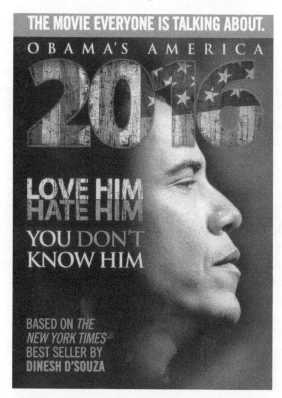

3. DVD cover image for *2016: Obama's America* (Lionsgate 2012)

He also consults a succession of professedly conservative scholars whom he acknowledges only as leading authorities on topics that pertain to his effort to uncover the truth behind Obama's mysterious identity: the psychology of people abandoned by their fathers, the history of the Cold War, the sociology of race in US electoral politics, international relations in the Middle East, and the US economy.

Despite reporting that he became aware of then Illinois State Senator Obama when his acclaimed speech at the 2004 Democratic National Convention launched him into national prominence, D'Souza maintains that on the cusp of the 2012 election Obama remains an enigmatic character who was able to become president because voters had so little awareness of him. Citing Obama's public prominence and referring to his best-selling autobiography while, at the same time, denying that anyone could have known much about him, is typical of the unacknowledged contradictions that recur in *2016*. Below, I will discuss how, according to the film, Obama's 2008 election victory was both a consequence of racial anxiety *and* testament to the public culture of the United States finally becoming truly post-racial. The claim that Obama is an unknown figure gives the documentary a narrative trajectory for the detective plot that runs parallel to the film's rendition of Obama's biography, complete with long excerpts from the audio edition of *Dreams from My Father* read by Obama that in the framework of the film imply the president has incriminated himself.

D'Souza shepherds us from ignorance to awareness so that he can rectify the problem stated in the slogan on the film's promotional poster and DVD cover: "Love Him. Hate Him. You don't know him." Beneath the symbolism of the tarnished flag that fills the date by which he will have satisfied his ruinous intentions, Obama appears out of character in half profile. He does not face us as we study his image; he does not meet our eyes. His image is reminiscent of that genre of expressionless photography in which people are routinely expected to turn ninety degrees to the side: the mug shot taken when a suspected criminal is "booked" by the police. At a glance, this famous man we supposedly do not know appears to be more dubious than inscrutable. Like the JBS billboard campaign against King more than four decades earlier, promotional materials for D'Souza's *2016* were distributed widely to insinuate that the authorities behind the film had captured evidence of Obama's illicit, un-American activities.

Near the conclusion of the film, D'Souza invites us finally to judge for ourselves whether to love or hate the president. Considering his ultimate claims for Obama's psychopathological motivations and the havoc his re-election will bring to the world, the concluding gesture of equanimity toward both sides of a stark divide of feeling can only be disingenuous. D'Souza's Obama is an enemy of American prosperity. At the same time, the gesture inviting us to make our own judgment is representative of how D'Souza plays with conventions of reasonable deliberation between well-informed interlocutors who can regard each other with respect in spite of irreconcilable differences of opinion. In the end, the film assures us that D'Souza knows Obama to be a closeted anti-colonialist who denies the value of the intellectual legacy of the West, but he acts as if he asks us to consider rather than accept this thesis. As was the case with anticommunist discourse in its early Cold War moment, convincing the audience of the veracity of the claim that a particular person is integral to a treasonous conspiracy is less important than winning serious attention for a narrative that represents the United States as subject to an existential threat residing inside the country. For the dangers identified in *2016*, D'Souza maintains that Obama must be held responsible whether we agree that he plotted against America or argue instead that he was merely an unwitting accomplice to others' anti-American designs. Moreover, to regard the film as thought-provoking but ultimately wrong about Obama's particular motivations still gives unwarranted credibility to a historical narrative that denies decolonization in Africa and Asia after World War II was primarily a movement for national self-determination against the rule of Europe's colonial powers. The film's narrative redeems colonialism and rejects that racism was a substantial impetus for the cruel tenacity the European powers exhibited in their attempts to retain their rule over indigenous, nonwhite populations living on the periphery of their dwindling empires.

In spite of D'Souza's claims that his theory is distinct from conjecture about Obama's secret Marxism, the film is a variant of Cold War anticommunism's return, albeit with a twist. According to D'Souza, Obama seeks reparations for colonialism through the redistribution of private wealth in America to the state coffers of the postcolonies in the Global South, and this means that he is also in pursuit of centralized state power. These objectives show Obama to be an anachronism, a throwback to the great problem of the twentieth century: collectivism. When D'Souza's voiceover talks admiringly of President Reagan, we learn that the New Deal welfare state in the United States and centralized state planning in the former USSR were collectivisms different in degree but not in kind. Such a sliding-scale association is a typical maneuver of anticommunist discourse's reprise after the Cold War. In the 1950s, Cold War liberals such as Schlesinger insisted on the contrary that FDR's New Deal was incomparable to the socialism of the Soviet Bloc. So, D'Souza is more resonant with the depoliticizing tactics employed across the anticommunist consensus during the early Cold War when he attributes Obama's motivations to an irrational compulsion to win the love and regard of his deceased, abandoning father. The well-hidden frailties of Obama's psychology are akin to those deficiencies in outlook and nationalist "community spirit" that Kennan cautioned would enable parasitical Communism to flourish and spread. Call that un-American sensibility "anti-colonial collectivism" and you are still trafficking in tropes, narratives, and arguments that have been and remain constitutive of the discourse of anticommunism. Allusion to the former Soviet Union is an option in that discourse but not a requirement. More pressing are the epistemological strictures by which the anticommunist discourse reductively sorts people and places into friends and foes of an American way of life. It may be formulated vaguely as the exercise of freedom but, ever since Reagan popularized the idea that "government is the problem,"[34] in practice the "American way" has been reliably advantageous to those whose economic self-interest is served by neoliberalism's insistence on the deregulation of commercial enterprises, especially those involving financial speculation. And when the deregulation of government oversight facilitates the privatization of public enterprise, infrastructure, and resources, it follows that the unification of workers' interests into a common voice will be treated not as the exercise of the right to assemble a union but instead as an offensive display of collectivism.

For our consideration of how anticommunism contributes once again to the disavowal of systemic racism, the most pertinent feature of the film is D'Souza's argument that what he calls anti-colonialism was absolutely distinct from the civil rights movement in America. For this distinction to bear on his thesis about Obama's anti-colonialism, he has to disrupt the popular idea that Obama's election realized the dream of civil rights for which King and so many others made sacrifices. In his voiceover, D'Souza laments that Obama was "chosen as the fulfillment of the civil rights movement"; this "insecure kid ... whose life is shaped by his father's ghost, whose ideology could not be more remote from what Americans believe or care about is now the president of the United States." To understand how Obama could successfully appropriate the legacy of the civil rights struggle, D'Souza turns in the film to Shelby Steele, a sociologist of race in the United States renowned for his political conservatism. According to Steele, Obama was able to seize the mantle of King's legacy for two main reasons. First, from a very young age Obama learned to adopt a civil, bargaining attitude in his relations with whites. Unlike figures such as the Reverend Jesse Jackson who, according to D'Souza and Steele, assumes the racism of white Americans and then makes charges against public culture and state policy on that basis, Obama shrewdly ingratiates himself to white Americans who are surprised and pleased to encounter African American political interest expressed without aggression. Steele's second reason is that the appeal of Obama's bargaining demeanor paved the way for white Americans to take advantage of an unprecedented opportunity to exorcise bad conscience. In a dynamic like an inversion of the Bradley Effect that sees exit polls outpace actual results for African American candidates, guilty white liberals gave Obama a substantial bump in the polls. Many white Americans grabbed the chance to show just how not racist they are. Or so Steele claims. Statistical analyses of the results in both 2008 and 2012 indicate that race was a factor in the elections and that being African American cost Obama votes that would have likely gone to a white Democratic Party candidate.[35] Without any mention in the film of empirical evidence to the contrary, Steele's expert speculations help D'Souza to trivialize Obama's 2008 victory with the suggestion that a significant number of votes only came to him through a compulsive desire on the part of whites to think well of themselves. Presented as a phone call from D'Souza on location outside the United States to Steele in the intellectual climate of Stanford University, this exchange undermines D'Souza's insistence elsewhere in the film and his other writings that race has become irrelevant to public life in America.

D'Souza follows his conversation with Steele by resuming his voiceover narration while the imagery on screen shows the Washington Mall in D.C. morphing from a black-and-white shot of the masses assembled to hear King's "I Have a Dream" speech to a full-color scene from Obama's first inauguration. Cutting back and forth between brief scenes from the inauguration and a shot of D'Souza on a couch continuing the voiceover in conversation with someone off camera, the film presents a disjunction between the optics of an African American being sworn in as president and D'Souza's explanation that an inauguration much of the world witnessed with jubilation was the culmination of a magnificent bait and switch. He explains:

> For white America, a majority white country, to turn over the ultimate power and to entrust that to an African American only 35 years after the civil rights movement ... Now that is a stunning accomplishment. That's not Obama's accomplishment. That is America's accomplishment.
>
> Still, for Obama to make himself acceptable to America, he had to hide major elements of his past. He had to hide the group I call Obama's Founding Fathers. And who were his founding fathers? Well, let's just say they were not Jefferson, Washington, and Franklin.

While the imagery suggests the ease with which popular imagination projected Obama into King's position, D'Souza's commentary insinuates that Obama has stolen a legacy to which he has no title, which has not informed his experiences, and which his presidential agenda betrays. Inconsistent with Steele's cynical vision that he had invoked moments before to minimize Obama's importance in the 2008 victory, D'Souza gives the electorate full credit for entrusting the highest office to an African American. The admirable post-racial citizenry he imagines is not, it seems, also responsible for being duped into bestowing their faith on an African American who only appears to be a legacy of the righteous struggle for civil rights. Speaking in defense of that struggle, the history of which he embraces as an integral feature of American national identity, D'Souza points a finger at the interloper Obama. In the book *The Roots of Obama's Rage*, he performs a comparable sleight of hand in contrasting Obama to King: "Obama is not fundamentally guided by Martin Luther King's dream. The best evidence of this is that he rarely talks about that dream, and he does not seem to be moved or motivated by it. When is the last time you heard Obama speak with conviction about the importance of a color-blind society?"[36] Whatever debate D'Souza might invite about the distance of Obama's personal aspirations from the inspiration of the civil rights movement, he presumes that King marched for "colorblindness" in regard to race. Repetition has made this canard a truism within a conservative public that is inured against King's actual words to the contrary. Not even the signature line about "content of my character" as opposed to "the color of my skin" that conservative appropriations of King typically cite entails becoming oblivious to social facts. But the difference between what King said and what he can be said to mean to the right audience is not a consideration for D'Souza. In the more seductive presentation of the film we are shown that, beneath the veneer of respectability, the deep meaning of Obama's presidency veers away from the trajectory of just social reforms and colorblind ethics that were touted by King and, by D'Souza's reading, then installed by every successful effort to reduce those provisions of the New Deal welfare state that supposedly taught dependency to the recipients of federal assistance.

D'Souza purports to uncover Obama's real direction by exposing the five figures he credits with fathering the president's ideology: Davis; former Weather Underground terrorist turned radical professor of education William Ayers; Brazilian socialist and Harvard professor Roberto Unger; "leading anti-Zionist" Edward Said; and the Reverend Jeremiah Wright, who damned America with sermons that claimed violence visited on the United States at home was reciprocation for its malfeasance abroad. Although Obama assuredly had personal or professional connections with each of these individuals, he may be the only substantive point of connection between them and there is precious little resemblance between the Obama administration's positions and the kinds of recommendations that we might infer from the writings and statements of these alleged mentors. An open letter by Ayers is representative of the pronounced difference between the various leftist orientations of these intellectuals and Obama's positions as president. Published right after the 2012 election, the letter is a detailed plea that Obama reverse course on virtually every significant policy detail and personnel appointment related to the federal "Race to the Top" education program initiated by his administration in its first term.[37] Ayers's catalog of grievances characterizes Obama's approach to education policy as a discouraging capitulation to the corporate drive to transform public schooling into a commercial business.

Roberto Unger did not wait until after Obama's re-election to communicate his public disapproval of the President's first term. Quite the contrary, in May 2012 he posted online a video entitled "Beyond Obama,"[38] which denounces the platforms of the Republican and Democratic parties but then appeals to the US electorate not to vote for Obama in 2012. Speaking directly into the camera for more than eight minutes, Unger explained that the very idea of leftist political alternatives to the status quo of global capitalism were ridiculed to the point of meaninglessness by the disjunction between Obama's reputation for democratic populism and the reality of his administration's imperialist military operations and pro-corporate neoliberal economic policies. He declared that unless Obama "is defeated there cannot be a contest for the reorientation of the Democratic Party as the vehicle of a progressive alternative in the country." The cost of allowing Romney to win, he acknowledged, would be considerable but worth it.

Obama's public break with the Reverend Jeremiah Wright was a major news story in April 2008, when the Democratic primaries were still a tight contest between him and Senator Hillary Clinton. Those who invoked Wright to paint Obama an angry radical saw Obama's public statement against the minister and the decision to leave his church as political expediency. However, Wright's public appearances and sermons in the first months of Obama's second term became especially critical of the president. On multiple occasions, he alluded to the Obama administration's program of high tech, "unmanned" US military attacks around the world with this pithy discrimination: "King had a dream. Obama has a drone."[39]

Davis and Said died in 1987 and 2003, respectively, but their writings suggest that they each would have enthused at Obama's breaking the color barrier to the Oval Office but then been dismayed by his administration's inability or unwillingness to make more of a difference in the comportment of the presidency. Of course, substantive disagreements with Obama from the left are incidental to D'Souza's argument, which is intent on fashioning a portrait of un-American identity predicated on Obama's association with individuals that the film pretends are a cabal.

Again, the epistemology of Cold War anticommunism suspends the logical interdiction against arguing guilt persuasively on the basis of associations. As the tropes of disease and contagion that routinely characterized communism in the 1950s and 1960s imply, the condition was imagined to be catching. Ignoring that Obama might be fairly judged for his affiliation with people he actually appointed to positions of authority, D'Souza paints him un-American with reference to five radicals from his past. Through these associations, Obama is known to be an un-American, anti-capitalist, collectivist opponent to Western civilization. Although it administered a punishing colonialism to much of the nonwhite world outside of Europe, this West, which Obama supposedly opposes, D'Souza insists is to be lauded for how it generated the civilizational achievements to which all the world now aspires and for which the United States may remain emblematic, provided Obama does not have his way in a second term. In *The Roots of Obama's Rage*, D'Souza gives "two cheers" for colonialism and explains: "I say 'two' and not 'three' in deference to my ancestors, who had a hard time under colonialism. But while colonialism was bad for them, it has been good for me."[40] In D'Souza's sense of history, European colonization was a trial that saw the suffering of the colonized redeemed by the delivery of their descendants into a world finally made for and by America. And the heritage of inalienable rights and providential nationalism bequeathed to the United States by the proper founding fathers has arrived in its inevitable trajectory to the place where racism has been diminished to a fact of history and untimely personal prejudices that we should all regard as trivial. In D'Souza's post-racial America, to take notice of racism is to be both un-American and the real racist.

Obama's failure to be post-racial is insidious, according to the film, because his anti-colonial commitment to the non-Western world involves a reversal of neoliberal reasoning about the proper role of governance. Neoliberal piety dictates that "the state" should oversee security (through mercenaries whenever possible), facilitate the creation of ever more commercial markets, disempower labor, and socialize the losses that come from the risky business of a too-big-to-fail financial sector, which it bails out with public funds.[41] At the time I am writing, Obama's presidency has not substantially disrupted any of these tendencies of the executive branch. Regardless, D'Souza's penultimate gesture to delegitimate the president and with him any notion of a state not regulated by market fundamentalism points to a future map of the Middle East and North Africa. It ostensibly symbolizes one of Obama's top priorities in his second term: to bring into being the United States of Islam.

An obvious attempt to incite panic in credulous audiences, this map of the Islamic world is alleged to illustrate the inspiration from his father that Obama favors over the dream of America's civil rights movement. The details of the image are plainly Orientalist. Green shading surrounded by a border barbed with thorns and decorated with crossed scimitars threatens the American movie audience with a militant pan-Islamic super-state garrisoned against the outside world. Viewed in a theater, only the keenest eyes could notice that Israel still exists as a sliver of grey pinned in isolation between the black border and the Mediterranean Sea. The more likely impression of the map is Israel's eradication.

The map of the future United States of Islam suggests that the Red Scare resurgence in reaction to the first African American president did more than recycle imagery, tropes, arguments, and narratives that were more at home in the long 1950s. D'Souza insinuates that the anti-colonialism Obama adopted from his father and honed with the influence of his five mentors will give rise to

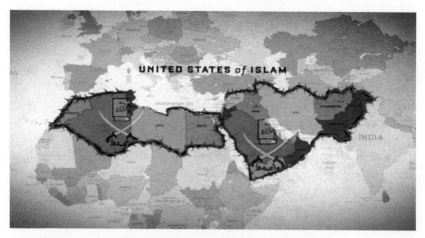

4. Image from *2016: Obama's America* (Lionsgate 2012)

a supranational political enemy of the United States and thereby initiate a second Cold War. Confronted with this apocalyptic vision to rival *The Manchurian Candidate*, it might be tempting to take a cue from Marx and describe D'Souza's attacks on Obama as the farcical return of the tragic history of the Red Scare persecution of the civil rights movement in the 1950s and 1960s. However, with his further assertion that the chief executive of the United States is purposefully burying American prospects in debt in order to feed a monstrous political agency rising across North Africa and the Middle East, D'Souza's speculations take on the quality of a narrative form that is neither tragedy nor farce. In the moral absolutism of the conflict between a virtuous United States of America, weakened by Obama's betrayal, and a vicious United States of Islam preying on its advantage, D'Souza replays Cold War anticommunism, with Islamophobic and neoliberal twists, in a generic form that is actually the best designation for Cold War Manicheanism from its first appearance in the late 1940s: melodrama. That genre of hyperbolic feeling and contrived crisis affords D'Souza a shrill advantage on the topic of race. An anticommunist epistemology retrofitted for Reaganism's objection to government is ready to meet any insistence on the enduring pertinence of racism with the charge that identifying America as post-racial is a requirement for being on the right side of the new Cold War between America and the upstart United States of Islam. The opposition between patriots of free enterprise and the dependents of thieving states is fundamental to that emerging geopolitical conflict.

Davis's "Frank-ly Speaking" columns from his position of exile constitute an archive of commentary that reveals D'Souza's global imaginary of

twentieth-century anti-colonialism cannot make sense of Hawaii. The territory's political culture, in which Davis's editorial writing thrived, cannot be
mapped plausibly onto D'Souza's sense of geopolitical history at midcentury.
The obvious reason is that the lessons on anti-colonialism D'Souza threads
through *2016* as if they were incontrovertible are weak, idiosyncratic fictions
he invented. He peddles errors to an audience that must be unfamiliar with
the history of decolonization, but his narratives resonate with the premises
of stories of American exceptionalism that record the early years of the Cold
War without cognizance of the project of the "Third World" or the spirit of
Bandung. In the years following World War II, Hawaii transitioned from a
colonial territory dominated by five corporate monopolies and a Republican
white minority stranglehold on electoral politics to become perhaps the most
progressive place in the United States and its territories. The CPUSA did dis-
solve there under Red Scare pressure from the mainland, but the ideas of
communism and individual leftists, including known Communists, met with
approval and resistance in public. Largely as a result of the ILWU's refusal to
be cowed by the Red Scare, anticommunism on the islands was associated by
many with white supremacy and monopoly capitalism. In Hawaii, Davis was
able to address his particular anti-racist radicalism in response to the circumstances of the Cold War for a supportive audience that understood labor
union activism and the struggle for civil rights to be the same fight. An irony,
then, of D'Souza attaching his romantic historiography of the achievement of
neoliberal post-racial America to a cautionary tale about racial insurrection
that includes Davis as a bad example, is that a closer look at the poet and journalist's political activities confirms the importance of radical anticapitalism
for the black freedom struggle in and out of the United States.

"Frank-ly Speaking": Frank Marshall Davis Contends with the Cold War

In *Livin' the Blues*, Davis acknowledges that his friends in Chicago regarded
his move to Hawaii as a retreat from the Red Scare, accusing him of "desert-
ing the battle."[42] While he anticipated living in the multicultural environment of Hawaii would mean his interracial marriage received less resistance
from others and he hoped that he would be able to give more time to writing poetry, he also prepared to carry on politically. He understood Hawaii to
have troubles of its own, though he could hardly have imagined how inviting
the volatile public culture would be for his particular disposition of political conviction and plainspoken complaint. Before leaving Chicago, he contacted the head of ILWU, Harry Bridges, to inquire about opportunities for

employment and activism. Based in San Francisco and a formidable union on the West Coast, the ILWU was the largest and most powerful union in Hawaii. Communist Party members were instrumental in its founding in 1937 and remained integral to its operations even after the party went underground in the United States and ceased operations in Hawaii. Bridges referred Davis to Koji Ariyoshi, the founding editor of the *Honolulu Record*. Ariyoshi was also a Communist, but as editor of the *Record* he provided an independent voice on the left. His bias toward the concerns, opinions, and activities of the ILWU's rank and file members was actually a source of tension between him and key union leaders, especially Jack Hall.[43] However, their differences were unimportant to the anticommunist authorities who prosecuted the two men together with five others in the Smith Act case known locally as the trial of the "Hawaii Seven."

The Red Scare trifecta of the Taft-Hartley Act in 1947, HUAC investigations in Hawaii in 1950, and the Smith Act convictions of the "seven" in 1953 disappeared the CPUSA from political relevance as an institution in the islands. Despite the party's absence, anticommunist activities did not abate. The trade association IMUA lobbied government and the public on the dangers of unions' Communist sympathies, and in 1956 the US Senate convened Internal Security hearings in Hawaii. However, as Horne documents throughout *Fighting in Paradise*, anticommunist aggression at leftist ideas, institutions, and individuals was met with equally fierce defiance. In 1950 HUAC's extensive report on the *Honolulu Record* held that it was unequivocally Communist propaganda aimed at the violent overthrow of the United States.[44] Neither that denunciation nor Ariyoshi's Smith Act conviction could deter the newspaper. Begun in 1948, it ran ten years before folding as a result of financial difficulties that Ariyoshi attributed to the ILWU's leadership deciding to initiate a newspaper owned and controlled by the union. That paper failed quickly but not before Ariyoshi retired the *Record*, which generally had 7,000 subscribers, mostly ILWU members. The regular readership of the paper is harder to estimate, but its reporting and editorials were a routine feature of life in the ILWU and ally labor unions. In 1946 the ILWU alone boasted 35,000 members in Hawaii.[45]

The newspaper's importance for the labor union ethos of the working-class, mostly nonwhite majority of the islands indicates that the dissolution of the CPUSA as a formal organization did not mean that Communists and anticapitalist ideas were shunned, stigmatized, or even quieted in Hawaii's labor disputes, electoral politics, or public culture more generally. Labor strikes, for example, were a negotiating tactic of last resort in contract disputes, but the unions also walked off the job in response to political abuses meted out to alleged subversives by anticommunist government officials either in cooperation with or at the encouragement of the Big Five corporate monopolies. When the Smith Act sentences of Hall, Ariyoshi, and the others were announced, 20,000 ILWU members struck in protest.[46] "It was difficult," Horne summarizes, "to convince the Hawai'i working class that the Smith Act trial was about subversion of the colony, as opposed to subverting a radical movement that had uplifted the dispossessed."[47] On the mainland United States, the arrest, prosecution, and conviction of suspected Communists met with virtually no public outcry. The execution of the Rosenbergs in June 1953 sparked public demonstrations in some major cities in the United States, but appeals and placards for clemency were matched by shouts of good riddance and posters cheering their electrocution.

The reason for the different response to the Red Scare in Hawaii was no doubt overdetermined, but race was a major factor. Hawaii was and remains majority nonwhite, and at the outset of the Cold War the "haole" (white) population was composed primarily of military personnel on temporary assignments, vacationers, or a minority of elites who were prosperous through colonial legacies and/or their employment by one of the Big Five corporations. To put it bluntly, Hawaii in the first half of the twentieth century was a US colony organized in a system of racial apartheid and exploitation that served the interests of the five monopoly corporations that dominated the territory's political economy and relationship to the United States. If the circumstances of racialized inequality and corporate malfeasance were abhorrent to Davis, they also represented what from the mainland may have seemed an exaggerated corroboration of his longstanding complaints in poems and newspaper columns about the mutual support racism and capitalism afforded each other to the detriment of everyone lacking wealth and whiteness. Exiled to Hawaii, his pugnacious and confident criticisms of big business, white supremacists, and Red Scare demagogues were at home. "Frank-ly Speaking" bore witness to the ongoing contest between the massive, interracial, multiethnic, and unabashedly leftist ILWU and the predominantly white Big Five that, with their colonial history, monopolized the islands' agriculture, docks, and shipping. Davis used that oversized relationship of opposition between the ILWU and the Big Five as a basis for communicating further instructions about how the postwar organization of Cold War America was harmful both for decolonization and the related struggle against Jim Crow.

His column debuted in the *Honolulu Record* on May 12, 1949, with a head-shot photograph and a biographical note touting his poetry books, his posts as editor for the *Chicago Star* and executive editor for the American Negro Press, and his position on the National Executive Board of the Civil Rights

Congress. This last item would have suggested to anyone on either side of the Red Scare that he might be a card-carrying Communist. While not every installment of "Frank-ly Speaking" concerns political affairs, his initial column for the *Record* established the precedent that his frequent attention to politics would challenge US public culture's normative Cold War story of containment.[48] And while the anti-Obama literature citing Davis would have us understand that his editorial writing parrots Soviet propaganda, his first "Frank-ly Speaking" concentrates not on the Cold War standoff but instead on how the United States comports itself relative to "oppressed peoples," by which he means Europe's colonies in Africa and Asia. Davis confirms the appropriateness of his column's title from the candor of his opening lines. He declares: "For a nation that calls itself the champion of democracy, our stupendous stupidity is equaled only by our mountainous ego. Our actions at home and abroad are making American democracy synonymous with oppression instead of freedom."[49] He goes on to explain that, in the four years following World War II, the United States squandered an opportunity to maintain the international reputation for defending liberty that it won by vanquishing Nazi Germany and imperial Japan. That opportunity was lost, Davis argues, with the Marshall Plan.

It was consistent with the USSR's publicity campaigns against the United States to characterize the Marshall Plan as a threatening show of solidarity on the part of the aggressive United States and Western Europe, and the USSR's propaganda operations made powerful impressions across Africa and Asia with evidence of Jim Crow apartheid in the American South. However coincident with Soviet propaganda, Davis's views on the Marshall Plan were rooted firmly in a politics of race that understood the fight to preserve Jim Crow in the American South to be in synch with English, French, Belgian, and Dutch postwar efforts to sustain or reclaim supervision of their colonies in Africa and Asia. Injuring America's pronouncements about defending democracy from totalitarianism were the Marshall Plan subsidies that made it possible for the colonial powers of Western Europe to rebuild infrastructure and rejuvenate their economies, with both undertakings entailing the further accumulation of resources through the dispossession of the colonies and the colonized. Writing in 1949, Davis explains to his Hawaiian readership that the American state is subsidizing the renewal of European colonialism.

Popular history and standard school curricula in the US view the Marshall Plan retrospectively as if it were an extension of the "Greatest Generation" saving Europe and the world from the ultimate evil of Hitler's Nazi regime. It is credited correctly with providing for the long-term reconstitution of Europe as well as immediate assistance to a populace in dire need of resources—from water, food, and shelter to employment, education, and investment. Kengor takes full advantage of the seeming preposterousness of complaints about the Marshall Plan to declare Davis a stooge of Stalin's regime. And he takes repeated note of Davis's animosity toward President Truman who, Kengor reminds us, was a Democrat. He does not bother to inform his readers that many Americans on the non-Communist left, along with American Communists such as Davis, objected to Truman replacing Henry Wallace as Roosevelt's vice president in 1944 and then supported Wallace's Progressive Party candidacy for president in 1948. Kengor regards Wallace as a Communist dupe too, of course. But my point is again that Davis is deemed outside the parameters of reasoned political deliberation through a combination of significant omissions from the historical record and a belief in the general validity of Hoover's capricious and racist classifications of un-Americans.

The benefits of the Marshall Plan for America's allies in Europe may be inarguable in hindsight, but Davis's grievance was not about the simple fact of foreign aid. His column complains that no comparable assistance was forthcoming from the United States for the restoration of African and Asian countries and regions that had been dispossessed of wealth and denied self-determination by their European colonizers for a century or longer. Moreover, with reference to the Cold War, the European states' redoubled efforts to command colonies after 1945 had been undertaken in the name of democracy. Davis's first objective with "Frank-ly Speaking" in Hawaii was to identify the Marshall Plan as a racial project. It was consistent with the long history of white supremacy justifying the organization of the rest of the world into Europe's keeping. Even as the United States would eventually become nominally supportive of some decolonization efforts in the late 1950s and 1960s, American foreign aid or the assistance of the international agencies established at the Bretton Woods conference in 1944 imposed patronizing conditions on the recipient nation-states. While Europe enjoyed American stimulus at the cost of friendship, trade relations, and non-binding, yet persuasive influence on its domestic affairs, in Africa and Asia, the colonies and former colonies of Europe were subject to loan arrangements that denied them autonomy and, in the long run, saddled them with impossible debt.[50]

In numerous columns, Davis continued to disparage the Marshall Plan as well as Truman's containment doctrine. Two months after introducing "Frank-ly Speaking," he began a seven-part series of columns on the topic "Depression and War." At several points in this series, he is romantic about the USSR. He applauds the country for surpassing race problems, and he implies that the United States is the more responsible party in stoking Cold War animosities. He recommends that opening trade with the USSR and other countries in the Eastern Bloc would be beneficial for the US economy and conducive for peaceful international relations. Some of his laudatory remarks on the USSR at the time are off-putting from this side of the revelations about Stalin, but the critical response to the Cold War worked out in his series is not an endorsement of the communist East over the capitalist West. Aided, I think, by his purview from exile in an American territory with a palpable colonial history that still informed everyday conflicts of political economy and race relations, Davis's seven-part series warns against a global imaginary dividing Soviet East from American West without sufficient regard for anywhere else except as proxy to that primary bifurcation. Disaster looms with this impression of two foes that, in consideration of the other, seek to secure advantages of growth and prosperity by comparable, excessive investment into their militaries of public funds, national infrastructure, international relations, human capital, higher education, and so on. In sum, Davis's series on "Depression and War" suspects that commercial interests see arms production as the surest route to surplus profits, while the US government seizes on Red Scare anxieties to cover for the most explosive means of stimulating the economy: military spending for a permanent state of emergency. In a slow presentation over several weeks, Davis lays out a curriculum with the objectives of remapping the geography of global politics described by Cold War containment narratives and teaching a core idea President Eisenhower would famously capture in his farewell address just over a decade later. From the former general become president who, among other military exercises, expanded the covert operations of the CIA to overthrow democratically elected governments in Iran and Guatemala, the belated warning about the growing power of the "military-industrial complex" remains disorienting. From Davis, the critique is just another example of the way he combined investigative journalism with a most practical version of historical materialism to track the way capitalist and racist institutions reproduce the social conditions under which they and their proponents flourish and the world's nonwhite, underdeveloped majority populations struggle and suffer. While provocative in Hawaii, on the mainland United States his perspective in the "Depression and War" series would have been cause for more significant consequences than the regular monitoring conducted by the FBI's Honolulu office.

In the third part of "Depression and War" on July 28, 1949, Davis describes how Red Scare rhetoric is "poison for democracy." Corporate interests use anticommunist aspersions to disguise their profit motives as if they were matters of national security: "The propaganda organs of Big Business have made Communism synonymous with all that is vile and evil. With this premise established, those who disagree with the master plans of the billion

dollar corporations are called 'Communists' and made to appear as outlaws to the general public. As outlaws, they have no rights which society is bound to respect."[51] He makes no overt connection in this passage to the regularity with which the red-baiting he describes is joined to xenophobic appeals to base racism, but his last line invites that connection with its allusion to the Supreme Court's *Dred Scott* decision, which notoriously ruled that African Americans "had no rights which the white man was bound to respect." The opinion's author, Justice Taney, then adds, "the negro may be justly and lawfully reduced to slavery for his benefit."[52] Although Davis did not generally imply the analogy of labor struggles with abolitionism (i.e., make references to "wage slavery"), his writings on the Big Five in Hawaii take note of the implicit paternalism of arguments denying workers title to living wages and a voice in adjudicating the value of their labor. The presumption of white superiority that animated the Big Five's postures of condescension toward their manual laborers resonated with echoes of the supremacist *Dred Scott* decision.

As "Frank-ly Speaking" proceeds from week to week, Davis's ease with residing in Hawaii becomes more pronounced. His debut column for the paper seems written for mainland readers who were unaware of how colonized peoples view the United States and Western Europe, unlike his actual readers in Hawaii, many of whom had direct experience of European or American colonialism in the Pacific. Over time, Davis comes to use local conflicts as good examples with which to teach his readers the extent of the Red Scare's damaging accomplishments on the mainland United States. Part six of the "Depression and War" series, for example, holds up the ILWU as an increasingly rare example of a labor union that refuses to be intimidated by demands that Communists be expelled from the membership rolls and that anticapitalist ideas be shamed out of common usage.[53] Davis targets his ire at the CIO. Accommodating itself to the Truman administration's various demands, including support of its foreign policy, the CIO, he argues, secured the president's regard and the good graces of the National Labor Relations Board (NLRB). By the CIO's "swooning at the proper times to the slick siren songs of the Truman gang," he scolds, "labor is now saddled with Taft-Hartley."[54] Davis's language play may cover a bit for a strain in his claim; Taft-Hartley only became law over Truman's veto. But Davis's more general point is that Truman's centrist appreciation for "Big Business" and his reserve relative to Roosevelt's more progressive efforts with the New Deal—as well as Truman's extreme difference from Henry Wallace—contribute to a Red Scare environment in which union leaders stave off suspicions of disloyalty by yielding labor's authority to the interests of capital. The ILWU and a handful of other unions are different: "bright spots on the dark labor horizon."[55]

Davis's insistence on the significance of the ILWU's difference from the CIO would be confirmed the following year, when the CIO expelled the ILWU for its Communist influences. Unlike unions purged from the CIO in the forty-eight states, the ILWU's loss of association did not weaken it in Hawaii.

In the aftermath of *Brown v. Board of Education*, the final three years of his column attend frequently to the emergence of the civil rights movement in "Dixie." As Langston Hughes did in his "Simple" stories for the *Chicago Defender*, Davis brought acerbic wit to bear on the incongruity and hypocrisy of ongoing Congressional investigations of un-American activities that targeted alleged Communists but showed no interest in the massive, violent vigilante and state-sponsored resistance to the Supreme Court's desegregation ruling. By this time, the FBI had enriched its surveillance of Davis with a routine, quasi-scholastic practice of "close reading." He was listed as a subversive on the Bureau's Security Index for years prior to relocating to Hawaii. Agents in the FBI's Honolulu offices were tasked with keeping him under regular investigation from 1948 until 1963, when his name was removed from the Security Index. His complete FBI file runs hundreds of pages.

In 1953 the Bureau introduced a procedure for documenting the Communist nature of the writings of subjects under investigation. Bureau personnel assembled an encyclopedic document entitled "The Communist Party Line," which included representative excerpts from publications overseen by the CPUSA or related groups. Updated every few months, citations were compiled from the *Daily Worker*, the *Worker*, *Political Affairs*, *Masses & Mainstream* (*Mainstream* after 1956), and *Party Voice* (of the New York State CP).[56] The volume covering January to April 1955 includes sixty-four pages of citations pertaining to twelve topics: foreign policy; domestic issues; labor and industry; agriculture; colonialism; legislative and judicial affairs; armed forces; minority (national and racial) groups; education; culture, science, and religion; women; and youth. The quotation records were then used in what must have been a tedious procedure of identifying similarities between passages authored by a security risk such as Davis and citations in the party line. Matches were not determined by verbatim repetition of the language; instead, an FBI agent's interpretations of the suspect's writings and of the party line quotations were necessary to determine if ideas were analogous. During the period that Davis's "Frank-ly Speaking" was under review for its ample correspondence to the party line, reports were prepared by Special Agent Leo S. Brenneisen, though nothing in his records on Davis seems a unique viewpoint. Brenneisen read for the Bureau; his documentation includes no explanation of his judgments on particular passages from either Davis or the party line database. Simple juxtaposition of quotes from both sources deems

Negro Question and Integration

"Why has not the Federal government seen fit to use the Smith Act in Tennessee and Texas where certain elements of the local citizenry are determined to prevent the integration of white and Negro students in public schools? . .

"The leaders of the White Citizens Councils have not only conspired but have led others into using force and violence against the government. What more can you do to violate the provisions of the Smith Act? .

"Of course there were no Communists leading the conspiracy, so there is little chance that the Smith Act will be invoked. This gives rise to an interesting question. Are we to assume that a person labelled as a Communist--and who reads books available in most well stocked libraries-- is a danger to America and should therefore be jailed even though he is not guilty of one overt act against the government, while a person who forms a mob to violently defy a high court ruling is not a danger to America?. . "

(Issue of September 6, 1956, p. 8)

"Most of the segregated schools which were declared illegal on May 17, 1954, and again on May 31, 1955, are still segregated. White supremacists, using legal technicalities and terror, including murder, have challenged the authority of the high court and federal law and order. Congress has refused to legislate in support of Supreme Court decisions, and the Department of Justice has kept its hands folded while the Constitution and the Supreme Court have been defied.

". . . the situation demands a vigorous enforcement policy to carry it into effect."

(Editorial, "Daily Worker", November 9, 1955, p. 5)
  - - -

"THE SILENCE of President Eisenhower in the face of the orgy of racist violence in Tennessee is inexcusable. . . .

"This is not an ordinary mob which has threatened law and order, life and limb in Clinton, Tennessee-- it is a racist mobilization to prevent the enforcement of a federal court order." . . .

- 12 -

5. Excerpt from FBI file for Frank Marshall Davis

passages to be essentially identical. Any differences, the reports imply, are merely incidental. The party line reading procedure justified suspicions of un-American activities on the basis of agreement. Guilt by association would have been a higher standard.

While Davis had a sizable audience for "Frank-ly Speaking," Brenneisen and other agents working his case must have been his most dedicated following. Reading Davis with the rubric of "The Communist Party Line" entailed organizing columns of correlation. Statements from "Frank-ly Speaking" were transcribed on the left side of the page; matching quotes from the party line database were typed on the right. In the example reproduced in Figure 5, the FBI reader, Brenneisen, takes excerpts from a "Frank-ly Speaking" column critical of the federal government's neglect of massive resistance to *Brown v.*

Board of Education and juxtaposes them to citations from two earlier *Daily Worker* editorials that make the same complaint.

The agent made a fair judgment. Davis's criticisms of the federal government abiding violent massive resistance to school desegregation is comparable to the *Daily Worker*'s objection to President Eisenhower's silence and inaction "in the face of the orgy of racist violence in Tennessee." The *Daily Worker* editorial and Davis's column share critiques of the federal government's inaction toward realizing the desegregation of schools and protecting the vulnerable African Americans and their allies who pursue school integration in good faith observance of the Supreme Court ruling. Adding to the grievance a critique of the Smith Act persecution of suspected Communists, Davis implies unmistakably that the differential treatment of the CPUSA and the White Citizens Councils results from two prejudices at once: anticommunism and anti-black racism. Both columns allude to the events in Clinton, Tennessee, in August and September 1956. The court-ordered integration of the city's high school was met with protests, intimidation, and violence led initially by a White Citizens Council member, John Kaspar. The state's governor ordered the Tennessee National Guard into the city to end the violence, and 600 guardsmen would remain in Clinton to keep peace for the rest of the month. Davis was writing before the National Guard entered the city, but his column still seeks a broader legal response than peacekeeping. His more biting point in reference to the Smith Act is that if there were ever a time to prosecute individuals for being un-American subversives intent on the violent overthrow of America, it would seem to be in the aftermath of mob violence organized for the express purpose of both denying the legitimacy of the federal government and arresting actions taken by the judiciary in accordance with the Constitution. Instead, he observes, the Department of Justice directed Americans to be wary of those who read subversive literature. The inclusion of Davis's criticisms in the FBI report alongside quotes from "the CP Line" means that Brenneisen determined that his complaints invited suspicion of criminality. By the FBI's account, there can be no validity to a grievance from Davis whether or not he correctly points to glaring evidence that the Smith Act is exploited by the federal government selectively and with prejudice.

Three months after Davis published his column calling out Smith Act prosecutors and other investigators of un-American activities for their hypocritical neglect of the illicit defense of Jim Crow, Senator Eastland of Mississippi brought the Senate Internal Security Subcommittee to Hawaii. Davis was called to testify before the committee and in a private hearing exercised his Fifth Amendment right not to incriminate himself. His FBI file records an informant saying that Davis believed he was interviewed in private because of the subcommittee's apprehension that in public session he would have insulted Eastland directly, thereby turning news media to the race matters that the subcommittee was attempting to pretend were not at issue in its investigations. The senator's fears were not misplaced. "Frank-ly Speaking" did testify on the topic of the Senate's forthcoming investigation of subversive activities in the islands. In a November 22 column subtitled "Our Coming Fraud," he ridicules the subcommittee, declaring that it should be renamed the "Eastland Committee to Promote Reaction and White Supremacy."[57]

In the same issue of the paper, an article on the subcommittee's plans cited recent reporting by the *New York Times* and other sources to confirm that by all accounts the CPUSA had no presence in Hawaii and that the senator's real motivation was to sow distrust of the territory that would impede its progress toward statehood.[58] Again, federal legislators supportive of Jim Crow segregation were keen in the 1930s about the prospect of statehood for Hawaii. At the time, conventional wisdom in Washington said the islands would assuredly elect white Republican men to Congress, and Dixiecrat representatives could count on those officials to support *de jure* segregation. From the outset of the Cold War, confidence in Hawaii's utility for Jim Crow wavered. And Eastland's commitment to segregation was in the deepest tradition of white supremacy. Alongside Davis's "Our Coming Fraud," the *Honolulu Record* reprinted a statement Eastland made in 1954 in reaction to the *Brown v. Board of Education* decision: "We are witnessing the beginning of a great controversy—one which will last for years. The issue is: Shall the white and Negro retain their racial identities? The future greatness of America depends upon racial purity and the maintenance of Anglo-Saxon institutions, which still flourish in full flower in the South. Who says the South will not win?"[59] The Mississippi senator's comment for the press extols white supremacy and its exceptional bastion in the American South. Sympathetic readers of the *Record* were keen to voice an answer to his last question. Horne describes hundreds of ILWU members marching in protest to greet the arrival of the subcommittee. "One of their number," he reports, "was clothed in a white robe with a pointed hood—a replica of the outfit of the terrorist Ku Klux Klan—and carried a sign bearing a skull and crossbones insignia on a black field, along with the words 'Eastland is Our Leader—White Supremacy.'"[60] Such displays must have gratified Davis in his choice of exile in Hawaii. On the mainland, satirists and cartoonists did meet Red Scare demagoguery with mockery on occasion, and Joseph Welch roasted McCarthy with a curt line of indignation. But in Hawaii, dark comic responses came with an unusual show of numbers.

Davis's FBI file includes many pages of the double-column accounting of his alleged obeisance to a "Communist Party Line" that in the United States by

Suez Crisis

Excerpts from
"Frank-ly Speaking"

CP Line

"To me, an atrocity is an atrocity no matter who commits it. I cannot consider wanton killings in Budapest any more horrible than wanton killings in Port Said. And I feel reasonably certain that a corpse in Egypt is just as cold and dead as a corpse in Hungary.

"The Suez Canal runs through Egyptian soil. It was built by Egyptian hands, and Egyptian blood—the blood of those who died building it—was merged with its waters. In nationalizing the Suez Canal, the Egyptian government is only correcting an historical injustice which permitted Western governments and investors to plunder colonial Egypt of almost a century ago.

6. Excerpt from FBI file for Frank Marshall Davis

1955 was probably nowhere more coherent than in the FBI's indexing. There is no disputing that CPUSA members who worked in the USSR's employ as spies often demonstrated an ascetic devotion to their cause and the dictates of the party. The espionage network including numerous CPUSA members and those Central Committee officers who received directives from the USSR were typically religious about party doctrine and discipline. But Davis is representative of a different and altogether common, non-doctrinaire approach to being an American Communist, which in Hawaii proved fundamental to the decolonization of its apartheid political economy and to its eventual entry into the United States as a state with a progressive influence on federal efforts to curb racial segregation. Measured, cut, and transcribed with the single-mindedness of the FBI reading him alongside "The Communist Party Line," Davis's writings would seem unlikely to admit the kinds of independent convictions and idiosyncratic ideas that a holistic appreciation of his work reveals. But even the mechanical reading protocols of the FBI provide occasional evidence that Davis, while a Communist, was not possessed of the aberrant subjectivity identified by the discourse of Cold War anticommunism.

Disregarding the possibility that the agreement between the left and right columns in Davis's file could state a truth or involve significant differences, the FBI's interpretive protocol was assiduous but obtuse. Although employed by an institution that must be said unequivocally to have wielded repressive authority in its efforts to deter the black freedom struggle, this practice of reading for "The Communist Party Line" also illustrates the regulative dynamic of the power/knowledge discourse of Cold War anticommunism that disciplines public culture with rhetorical power. Consider, in Figure 6, the comparison of Davis and the *Daily Worker*'s attitudes on the "Suez Crisis" in 1956.

The *Daily Worker's* editorial of July 30, 1956, defends Egypt's sovereign right to determine the use of its territory, including the Suez Canal. Siding with Egypt in objecting to England and France's military actions to retake the canal from Nasser, who pledged to nationalize its revenue, the CPUSA's newspaper is indeed in line with the USSR's reaction to the conflict. Also critical of England and France's joint military intervention to recover property taken from Egypt in the first place, Davis's column can be aligned with the Communist Party. Fully invested with a knowledge of Communists that insists the passages from the "CP Line" have been published solely for their instrumental value to the USSR's interest in world domination, the FBI reader quotes a passage from "Frank-ly Speaking" to show resemblance. Having noted a claim by Davis that reiterates a certified Communist complaint, the report's juxtaposition indicates that the common assertion is Davis's real meaning and that, whatever Davis's intentions, his editorial serves the same ulterior motives as the "CP Line." Unnoticed by the FBI is Davis's critical difference. The Bureau's surfeit of anticommunist know-how is generative of a failure to recognize a stance that is idiosyncratic to the Cold War opposition of East and West.

Davis's column is precipitated not by events in Egypt so much as mainstream reporting in the United States on the USSR's military suppression of the Hungarian revolt. Calling the European attacks on Egypt "wanton killings" gets him written up by the FBI scribe, but Davis's interest does not end with Egypt. He also indicts the USSR's invasion of Hungary. He does not play at moral equivalencies in order to excuse the USSR with reference to the wrongs of America's allies. Neither attack can be justified. In both cases, national sovereignty was transgressed, and many civilians were injured or killed. Lamenting these comparable atrocities, Davis sees a disparity in news coverage by American media: the Soviet invasion is shown correctly to be unjust and an international tragedy, but the British and French invasion of Egypt to reclaim lost property is treated as a non-event. Within a few weeks of his column, the United States would demand that the English and French relent and defer to Egyptian sovereignty, an action that complicates the circumstances beyond his interpretation at this earlier point. But in the full column as it appears in the *Honolulu Record*, he is astute to note that the United States reneging on aid for a construction project to facilitate the Nasser government's development plans was a motivating factor in Egypt's seizing the Suez Canal.[61] Those complexities and the United States' generally tepid, self-serving support for decolonization went mostly unremarked in mainstream news reporting.

In his column, Davis attributes the neglect of news media coverage of events in Egypt to two reasons. First, reporting on England and France in a negative light would be inconsistent with the anticommunist alliance among the North Atlantic states. And, a related point, to allow other atrocities to distract focus from the USSR's aggression in Hungary would interfere with the news media's opportunity to show support for the West in the Cold War. Second, Davis observes that the news coverage bias toward Hungary to the neglect of Egypt is another instance of Western media communicating more concern for the plight of majority-white populations than of imperiled nonwhite peoples. "Hungarians," Davis writes in Hawaiian parlance, "are fellow-haoles . . . and white America has not learned to weep for the colored people of the world unless there is a political motivation."[62] To corroborate this point, he adds to his disappointment about the news media's neglect of Egypt a complaint about the virtual absence of any reporting in the United States on current events in Kenya. The FBI file includes five complete paragraphs from Davis's column, but it does not excerpt additional passages that compare the news media's neglect of Egypt to the even more comprehensive failure to report on the efforts of the British government in Kenya to suppress that country's anti-colonial revolution. Too knowing about how the topic of the "Suez Canal" serves as a litmus test to define the un-Americans, the FBI reader does not take note of Davis's claim that events in Egypt and Kenya bear a remarkable similarity. Their common neglect in news reporting in the United States, Davis suggests, means that US public culture conducts itself aware of the Cold War but oblivious to decolonization struggles. The national liberation movements in Africa and Asia were inseparable in practical terms from the Cold War, and Davis's column gives his readers an opportunity to recognize that familiar stories of containment are, in effect, an epistemology. For all it knows, the expertise of anticommunist discourse cannot apprehend those freedom struggles devoted to carving out conceptual space and material conditions for real people striving, with too little success, to describe and enjoy lives after colonialism and outside the parameters and imperatives of the Cold War. Davis informs his reader that "in Kenya, the British are holding some 40,000 native Africans in concentration camps after slaughtering thousands of others for trying to get back a reasonable share of their ancestral land taken from them at gunpoint by Europeans. Yet you see nothing of this in the daily press."[63] The American news media's preferential treatment of Hungary over Egypt and Kenya rewards institutional and audience biases. It also creates deficits of knowledge that exacerbate ignorance with further misrecognition of the meaning of this West that after 1945 is led by the United States. Through its antagonism with the USSR, the West appears in US public culture to be a purveyor of freedom and never a progenitor of a racial world order in which white supremacy is disclaimed but the lion's share of its advantages are organized to ensure whiteness remains an unearned asset and a bulwark to capitalist institutions. In Hawaii, at least, these institutions were unable to use blithely the Red Scare to obscure the contradiction between pronouncements in support of liberty and the practice of exploiting the vulnerabilities of labor and race.

In "Frank-ly Speaking," Davis's recurring attention to the ways in which a romantic image of Cold War America's international identity interferes in public culture with cognizance of decolonization, partners with his similar concern for the ways in which the Red Scare is a resource for blunting the potential of the civil rights movement. Anticommunism obscured and deterred initiatives to win a full exercise of franchise for nonwhite Americans and to disrupt the increasing power of the kinds of massive corporations that held sway in Hawaii. Mobilizing support incited by the Big Five's investment in white privilege, the ILWU managed to push back against systemic racism and economic exploitation. Davis writes with concern that readers uninformed about decolonization taking place outside the United States need to recognize that the civil rights movement corresponded to that larger context of global rebuke to white supremacy. Citing Davis for his ideas as they were arranged by the FBI, D'Souza would have his audience understand instead that the civil rights movement was somehow antithetical to the transnational struggle of decolonization that his film depicts so contemptuously as the un-American kind of anti-colonialism.

CONCLUSION

Back to the Billboard: The Long Civil Rights Movement Still

Circulated within days of the events at the Highlander Folk School that it depicts, the photograph of King on the JBS billboard was taken by a covert operation orchestrated by the Georgia Commission on Education. Chartered in 1953 by an act of the state legislature and administered by the governor, the GCE was a public agency charged with finding a way for the state to preserve its segregated schools. Faced with the setback of *Brown v. Board of Education* a year after its founding, it persisted in its mission by adopting an aggressive strategy of surveillance and propaganda against the civil rights movement.[1] The GCE employed photographer Edwin Friend to infiltrate Highlander's twenty-fifth anniversary celebration in 1957 with the pretense of making a freelance documentary about the school's efforts for social justice. Myles Horton, Highlander's director, welcomed him to record whatever he liked of the proceedings. Friend was perhaps the only one in attendance to learn during that weekend that the other reporter present, Abner Berry, was a writer for the *Daily Worker* and an active member of the CPUSA. For a journalist also on site to observe and report, Berry appears in a conspicuously high number of Friend's photographs.[2] The picture on the billboard is a good example. Friend was asked to take a photograph of Horton, King, Rosa Parks, and the legendary activist Aubrey Williams seated together. Horton hoped for an image to commemorate the gathering and to use in Highlander's promotional materials. But Friend positioned the shot to feature Abner Berry in the foreground. The billboard names only King, but versions of the picture appearing on other segregationist propaganda invariably identify CPUSA member Berry as if he were a close associate of the others and a key organizer of Highlander events.

The first publication to include the photograph was a four-page newsletter published by the GCE that declared the Monteagle, Tennessee, school to be a Communist institution.[3] The billboard's photograph is just one of fifteen supposedly incriminating images spread across the newsletter's interior pages.

191

7. "Labor Day Weekend at Communist Training School," Broadside created from photographs taken at the Highlander Folk School, 1957 (courtesy S. Ernest Vandiver Papers, Richard B. Russell Library for Political Research and Studies, University of Georgia)

munist Training School

C. H. PARRISH (on left) who was panel moderator on the question "What is the impact of Integration on the People?" is shown with Rosa Parks (3rd from left) and Maurice McCracken (4th from left).
Rosa Parks was one of the original leaders of the Montgomery Bus Boycott. This agitation has resulted in strife and violence in the Alabama capital and continues to maintain tension and distrust. Maurice McCracken is affiliated with Neighborhood House, 901 Findlay Street, Cincinnati, Ohio.

THIS PICTURE of a station wagon lettered FINDLAY STREET, NEIGHBORHOOD HOUSE, CINCINNATI, OHIO, is included for the purpose of illuminating how many units of the Communist apparatus are cloaked by organizations purportedly charitable or religious in nature.
Reverend Maurice McCracken of Neighborhood House, Cincinnati, who is pictured elsewhere attended the Communist Training School. Apparently he used this station wagon as transportation. Neighborhood House is located at 901 Findlay Street, Cincinnati, Ohio, and is supported by the Community Chest. This same address is also the address of Friends of Koinonia Farms.

ROSA PARKS, who precipitated the Montgomery Alabama Bus Boycott, and Ralph Tefferteller of New York's Henry Street Settlement listen to group training under the watchful eye of Abner Berry of the Central Committee of the Communist Party.
Berry reported the meeting of this Communist Training School in his column in the Daily Worker of September 10, 1957.

PICTURED HERE are leaders of first recent scenes of racial disturbance and violence.
Septima Clark, presently director of Highlander integration workshop was associated with the South Carolina NAACP School Teachers incident.
Conrad Browne is a leader of inter-racial Koinonia Farms, Americus, Georgia, the scene of boycotts, disturbances and violence.
David H. Brooks was a leader of the Tallahassee Bus Boycott. This incident was commenced only after a psychological survey of the area had been made to determine the outcome.
Rosa Parks was the central figure in the agitation which resulted in the Montgomery Bus Boycott.
Charles Gomillion, Dean of Students at Tuskegee Institute, was the leader of the Tuskegee Boycott.

MARTIN LUTHER KING addresses the assemblage. President of the Southern Christian Leadership Conference for his activities in the Montgomery Boycott, Prayer Pilgrimage Association and the March on Washington associated with Bayard Rustin. The Daily Worker lists those who attended the 1957 convention of the NAACP. Bayard Rustin is identified in the Daily Worker as adviser to Reverend Martin Luther King.

That Reverend Martin Luther King represents the embodiment. It is doubtful that Reverend King can push such a program without outside leadership. Bayard Rustin is perhaps the leading expert on this country.

The Christian Leadership Conference is a new organization. Reverend King for region-wide agitation of strife.

CHARLES GOMILLION, Dean of Students at Tuskegee Institute, was the leader of the Tuskegee, Alabama, Boycott, his agitation in large part responsible for this disturbance.
Gomillion has been most vehement in his defense of Communists and the Communist Party. His principal areas of agitation and infiltration have been among educators, Negroes, and youth groups.

PICTURED HERE (foreground) is Abner W. Berry on the Central Committee of the Communist Party. On the first row are Reverend Martin Luther King (3rd from right) of the Montgomery Boycott, Aubrey Williams (2nd from right) president of the Southern Conference Education Fund Inc, and Myles Horton (on from Right) the director of Highlander Folk School.
These "four horsemen" of racial agitation have brought tension, disturbance, strife and violence in their advancement of the Communist doctrine of "racial nationalism".

With a mailing list of two million "opinion leaders," the GCE circulated news of the "Communist training school" eight years earlier than the JBS billboard campaign. Copies were "sent to every daily and weekly newspaper in the United States, to other federal and state investigating committees, and to veterans' posts, patriotic groups, citizens' councils, and businessmen."[4] A late October article in *Human Events* on Georgia's supposed discoveries about Highlander spurred thousands of additional requests, and by the start of 1958 the GCE had to order an additional printing of 300,000.[5] In the same year, the CPUSA's membership nationally had shrunk to three thousand, down from seventy thousand at the end of World War II, and its political influence in the United States was assuredly nil.[6] Five years later, when the party's status in the United States was basically unchanged, Governors Ross Barnett of Mississippi and George Wallace of Alabama gave the photograph more public exposure when they used posters of it before the US Senate in their testimonies against legislation that would become the Civil Rights Act of 1964.

I sketch these details from the history of the photograph's early appearances to recollect the extraordinary lengths taken by states to resist the movement for civil rights in defiance of the federal government and, in the case of the GCE, outside its jurisdiction. Of course, Tennessee issued no complaint about Georgia's unauthorized, secret reconnaissance operation over its borders. On the contrary, its state legislature seized on the GCE's publications to initiate an investigation into Highlander. Friend served as a witness, and his photographs and film footage were introduced as formal evidence of the school's subversive activities.[7]

The GCE newsletter's design foregrounds the sovereign authority of Georgia and insinuates the state is within its rights to undertake national security initiatives. It includes a commentary signed by Governor Marvin Griffin that suggests the state of Georgia has satisfied a patriotic obligation by informing the American public of the "Communist infiltration and the direction of Communist movements." While the billboard suggests that the meeting it depicts was held in secret at an undisclosed location and discovered late, the newsletter impresses on recipients that the Communists train brazenly in the open but that Georgia is on the job, keeping watch and meticulously documenting every detail of the un-American activities. Dense columns of information about the weekend's participants and long lists of the subversive organizations to which they belong appear on the first and last pages to corroborate beyond doubt that the school only supports civil rights in service to the CPUSA. According to the arrangement of images in the interior photo spread (see Fig. 7), the open secret of the party's priority for social life in America is to foment "miscegenation." At the center of the page appears an image of interracial dancing. It is the only picture in the layout without an accusatory caption; its meaning is a self-evident threat.

The photograph that would appear later on the JBS billboard is in the bottom right corner. Its caption refers to Berry, Horton, King, and Williams as the "'four horsemen' of racial agitation [who] have brought tension, disturbance, strife, and violence in their advancement of the Communist doctrine of 'racial nationalism.'" That Berry was virtually unknown to the other three was, obviously, unimportant to the GCE, as was King's unequivocal disagreement with the CPUSA's "black belt" thesis. Unlike the version appearing on the JBS billboard, the image is cropped to show the high ceiling and a row of well-lit windows. Shameless audacity, public immorality, and planned insurrection are the message, rather than the billboard's suggestion of espionage that may be coming quietly to a newly integrated community or organization near you. The ease with which these Communists meet to plot their dissidence is a further offense for the segregationist audience for the newsletter whom Governor Griffin's "Editorial Comment" praises as those Americans who "oppose the alien menace to Constitutional government." Like better-known shows of state sovereignty such as Governor Orval Faubus's last stand in front of Little Rock's Central High, the GCE newsletter presumes that Georgia's executive branch knows best about American security interests. While the newsletter relies on lists compiled by federal agencies, it seeks nonetheless to persuade its massive readership to regard officials in Atlanta as the legitimate national authorities.

By the time of the JBS billboard, such efforts had already become less common, and passage of the Voting Rights Act in August 1965 would drive home to officials in the South that the federal government would no longer share sovereignty on the topic of *de jure* segregation. As Louis Menand recalls in his elegiac response to the US Supreme Court's 2013 decision in *Shelby County v. Holder*, the Voting Rights Act of 1965 was a more substantial, if less symbolic, landmark in the slow death of overt Jim Crow laws than even *Brown v. Board of Education*. The VRA destroyed the "central pillar of Jim Crow": the white supremacists' complete control over the political systems across the states of the former Confederacy.[8] To express how consequential the denial of franchise was to African Americans, Menand recalls that jury pools were typically selected from voter rolls. The "near-ubiquity of all white juries" meant, he explains, that the "Southern judicial system … was turned into a rubber stamp of approval for police and vigilante actions against African-Americans."[9] The addition of 740,000 new African American voters in the Deep South between 1965 and 1968 may not have been sufficient to swing statewide elections or to disrupt the realignment of the Southern states to the Republican Party in national elections, but it was a visible transformation of sovereignty in the South. After 1965, segregationists no longer enjoyed an uncontested monopoly on the legitimate use of violence in the region.

Unhappy clamoring about the secret un-American roots of civil rights may have persisted in chatter fixed on the notion that the South was once again forced to change at the behest of outside interests. But, as King surmised with a too-optimistic sense of timing in 1957, popular opinion and key officials in the South did concede finally that the Cold War, among other factors, required that the United States make a show of racial democracy before the world by undoing *de jure* segregation. To do otherwise would have been too costly by all accounts. With this historical transition from *de jure* to *de facto* segregation in mind, we may regard the JBS billboard as one of the last unsightly examples of an unembarrassed collaboration between state and civil institutions to mobilize Red Scare rhetoric in order to keep racial segregation lawful.

Another way of looking at the billboard is to see in it the emergence of new ways to color anti-racist initiatives un-American Red. They are with us still. After the fight against Jim Crow was no longer defined so obviously by the civil rights movement's confrontation with massive resistance and the corresponding opposition between the federal government's gradual support for desegregation and those states confederated again to defend anti-black apartheid in America, anticommunism remained resourceful for preventing the remarkable legal achievements of the movement for civil rights from becoming the kinds of material differences that could dispossess whiteness of its value as an unearned asset. Cold War anticommunism worked to ensure white privilege remained a capital advantage. And it should be needless to say that the fact of white privilege does not mean every American identified as white enjoys comparable or even satisfying proceeds. While the minimum of information presented on the billboard does associate the civil rights movement with the criminal reputation of the Cold War CPUSA, it also represents the billboard's source as anonymous. In contrast to the GCE's direct-mail efforts, the billboard does not name its authority to lead government, commercial, civil, and individual partners in the fight against the un-Americans. Instead, it announces King's exposure as if it were new information transmitted to become common knowledge. The billboard's alert is to be received by people on the move in their daily lives across the American South who, depending on their attitude about the civil rights movement, may find it fantastical, threatening, provocative, or familiar. Whatever the response, the short-circuit association of King with the charge of Communist was kept in circulation, readying observers of any sensibility to expect that in every cultural conversation around his ideas, as in his every television interview, it would be compulsory to appraise what he had to say against the stupefying litmus test of Communist or not. Only because of the retrospective, public neglect of the actual content and character of his most reaching claims is King's iconic status mostly free of such associations today. At the time that his Riverside Address modeled for US public culture how to conceive of political concerns free from the imaginary, nationalist geography that coded every place in the world as either American or un-American, the domestic landscape was still dotted with these signs advising citizens to keep to the blunt coordinates of anticommunism.

I have suggested that King's opposition to the American war in Vietnam and his belated revelations about the Cold War stories used to excuse the "conflict" resound more meaningfully if we attend to radical antecedents represented here by the writings of Wright, James, and Davis. In the years prior to *Brown v. Board of Education*, their correct expectations that the Red Scare would obscure and exacerbate the collusion of anti-black racism and class exploitation were espoused more readily from exile. In America, their most discerning ideas travelled mainly among counterpublics. Returning these examples of Cold War black radicalism to the purview of the civil rights movement before, during, and after the King years, in this book I have offered a cultural rhetoric studies account of evidence that demands the black freedom struggle in the United States and elsewhere be characterized as long, unfinished, and presently in need of repair.[10] After 2008 this conviction must stand against the wrong attitude that Obama's presidency, whether in good faith or bad, is the legacy of a civil rights struggle that was essentially completed in the 1960s. Among its errors, any such story about the post-racial character of the United States after civil rights must entail forgetting the exigency of Cold War anticommunism, which facilitated a split decision between winning political recognition and losing the anticapitalist purchase necessary to lay claim to socioeconomic redistribution.

Notes

Preface

1. Obama, *Dreams from My Father*, 76.
2. *Dreams from My Father: A Story of Reds and Deception*, directed by Joel Gilbert (Los Angeles: Highway 61 Entertainment, 2012), DVD.
3. Valerie Richardson, "Anti-Obama best sellers speak volumes," *Washington Times*, September 10, 2012. www.washingtontimes.com; Michelle Goldberg, "The Obama-Bashing Book Bonanza," *The Nation*, October 22, 2012: 24–26.
4. Rogin, *Ronald Reagan, the Movie*, 68–80.
5. Hofstadter, *The Paranoid Style in American Politics and Other Essays*, 3–40.
6. Warner, *Publics and Counterpublics*, 65.
7. Ibid., 66.
8. Ibid., 119.
9. Ibid., 121–23.
10. Harris, "Whiteness as Property," 1713.

Introduction

1. Like other scholars who write critically about US Cold War culture, I distinguish anti-Communism from anticommunism. The former refers to government programs to police espionage activities undertaken by members of the Communist Party. Small-c anticommunism has two meanings in this book. It refers to government, commercial, and civil volunteer initiatives to demean all manner of liberal and leftist critiques of capitalism without regard for whether the institutions or people targeted had a formal relationship to the USSR that involved criminal acts of espionage, sabotage, or terrorism. Anticommunism also signifies a discourse that has enjoyed normative force in the public culture of the United States. In both senses, anticommunism entails denying that there can be a meaningful distinction between anti-Communism and anticommunism.
2. Marable, *Race, Reform and Rebellion*, 19–25.
3. Von Eschen, *Race against Empire*, 2–3.

4. Lipsitz and Tomlinson, "American Studies as Accompaniment," 1–30.

5. Roediger, *How Race Survived U.S. History*, 194. Explaining how the postwar Red Scare contributed to the perpetuation of systemic racism, Roediger also points to the removal from the United States of key black left intellectuals, including James, Paul Robeson, Alphaeus Hunton, Claudia Jones, and W. E. B. Du Bois.

6. Storrs, *Second Red Scare*, 1–15.

7. Foucault, *The History of Sexuality*, 94–96.

8. Ibid., 100.

9. Mailloux, *Reception Histories*, ix.

10. Mailloux, *Rhetorical Power*, 58–61.

11. Warner, *Publics and Counterpublics*, 160.

12. James Thompson, "Should I Sacrifice to Live 'Half-American'?" *Pittsburgh Courier*, January 31, 1942 (3), Black Studies Center.

13. Winant, *The World Is a Ghetto*, 31.

14. Ibid., 2, 31–33.

15. Ibid., 35.

16. Dudziak, "Desegregation," 61–120.

17. Frederickson, *Racism*, 113.

18. Fraser and Honneth, *Redistribution or Recognition*, 9.

19. Lipsitz, *The Possessive Investment in Whiteness*, 1–23.

20. Davis, *Writings*, 86.

21. Harrington, *Bootsie and Others*, n.p.

22. May, *Homeward Bound*, 1–9.

23. Harrington, "Why I Left America," 96–109.

24. Dickson-Carr, *The Columbia Guide*, 38–39.

25. Burke, *Rhetoric of Motives*, 105–7.

26. In recent years, there has been a remarkable development of scholarship on women writers and activists who have been important to black radicalism. The following books concentrate at length on the early years of the Cold War and the work of Claudia Jones: Weigand, *Red Feminism*; Davies, *Left of Karl Marx*; McDuffie, *Sojourning for Freedom*; Gore, *Radicalism at the Crossroads*; Higashida, *Black Internationalist Feminism*.

Chapter One

1. Branch, *At Canaan's Edge*, 130–31. The ruling stipulated that the group reduce its number to 300 when it traversed the two-lane section of Highway 80.

2. Garrow, *Protest at Selma*, 31–132; Branch, "Selma: The Last Revolution," *At Canaan's Edge*, 3–202.

3. Woods, *Black Struggle, Red Scare*, 12.

4. Heale, *McCarthy's Americans*, 246–53, 256–65. A study of Red Scares in the state politics of Michigan, Massachusetts, and Georgia, Heale's book includes a detailed account of

the Georgia Commission on Education, which was the original source for the billboard's photograph.

5. Kelley, *Hammer and Hoe*, 227.

6. Branch, *Pillar*, 305; *At Canaan's Edge*, 183–84.

7. Garrow, "The FBI and Martin Luther King." This article is a succinct account of the FBI's persistent efforts to incriminate King for involvement with Communists. For more detailed accounts of FBI overreach in reaction to the civil rights movement, see O'Reilly, *Racial Matters*.

8. Glen, *No Ordinary School*, 170–71.

9. Melamed, *Represent and Destroy*, x–xi.

10. Phelan, *Living to Tell about It*, 214. Phelan defines a cultural narrative as a "story that circulates frequently and widely among the members of a culture; its author, rather than being a clearly identified individual, is a larger collective entity, at least some significant subgroup of society. Cultural narratives typically become formulas that underlie specific narratives whose authors we can identify, and these narratives can vary across a spectrum from totally conforming to the formula to totally inverting it."

11. HUAC, *100 Things You Should Know About Communism*; Leo Cherne, "How to Spot a Communist?"

12. Glen, *No Ordinary School*, 220.

13. Pease, *New American Exceptionalism*, 25.

14. Rogin, *Ronald Reagan, the Movie*, 44–80.

15. *Atomic Age Classics*.

16. Ctd. in Schrecker, *Age*, 133.

17. Ross, *No Respect*, 45.

18. Kennan, "Moscow," 63.

19. Dolan, *Allegories of America*, 71–75; Kim, *Ends of Empire*, 40–56; May, *Homeward Bound*, 16; Whitfield, *The Culture of the Cold War*, 33.

20. Morgan, *Literary Outlaw*, 289.

21. Schlesinger, Preface, *The Vital Center*.

22. Schlesinger, "The US Communist Party," 85.

23. Ibid., 84.

24. Corber, *Homosexuality*, 20.

25. Ibid., 127.

26. Johnson, *The Lavender Scare*.

27. Schrecker, *Many*, 24–25.

28. Dies, *The Trojan Horse in America*.

29. Nadel, *Containment Culture*, 4.

30. Dyson, *I May Not Get There with You*, 230.

31. Whitfield, *Cold War Culture*, 21. Whitfield cites Albert Cantwell, the chair of the Washington State Legislative Fact-Finding Committee on Un-American Activities: "If someone insists that there is discrimination against Negroes in this country, or that there is inequality of wealth, there is every reason to believe that person is a Communist" (21).

32. King, "Look," 271.

33. Ibid., 276.

34. Ibid., 272.

35. Selby, *Martin Luther King and the Rhetoric of Freedom*; Miller, *Voice*, 13–28. Selby and Miller discuss King's use of the Exodus narrative in sermons, speeches, and writings other than "The Look to the Future."

36. King, "Look," 272.

37. Ibid., 273.

38. Ibid., 274.

39. Ibid.

40. Dudziak, *Cold War Civil Rights*, 79.

41. Ibid., 104–6.

42. Ibid., 107.

43. Goldfield, *The Color of Politics*, 269.

44. Dudziak, *Cold War Civil Rights*, 102.

45. Melamed, *Represent and Destroy*, 56.

46. Cf. Mills, "Racial Liberalism," 1380–97. Mills uses "racial liberalism" as a critical term to name the underestimated racist underpinnings of classic liberalism and the neglect of race by its successors in contemporary political philosophy (e.g., John Rawls).

47. Myrdal, *An American Dilemma*, 1015–16.

48. Ibid., 24.

49. Singh, *Black Is a Country*, 39.

50. Pease, *New American Exceptionalism*, 7–23.

51. Melamed, *Represent and Destroy*, 53.

52. Bhabha, "DissemiNation," 291–322.

53. Sommer, "Irresistible Romance," 73–74.

54. Bhabha, "DissemiNation," 297.

55. Ibid., 200.

56. Ibid., 199–209.

57. Melamed, *Represent and Destroy*, 238 n. 7.

58. King, "Look," 275.

59. Ibid., 276.

60. Branch, *At Canaan's Edge*, 581–604. Branch describes how in the days and hours prior to his appearance at Riverside, King and several close advisors made revisions to his speech, which was drafted initially by Vincent Harding.

61. King, "Time," 231.

62. "Dr. King's Error," *New York Times*, A36 (April 7, 1967); "A Tragedy," *Washington Post*, A20 (April 6, 1967); "NAACP Decries Stand of Dr. King on Vietnam," *New York Times*, 1, 17 (April 11, 1967); "Dr. King's Disservice to His Cause," *Life*, 4 (April 21, 1967).

63. Dyson, *I May Not Get There with You*, 230; Thomas Jackson, *From Civil Rights*. Dyson asserts that "King was sorely compromised in his progressive thinking by the realpolitick of the civil rights movement." Contrary to the conventional distinction between King's early reform period and his late radicalism, Jackson argues that King's attention to class discrimination was apparent throughout his career in public.

64. Ctd. in Dyson, *I May Not Get There with You*, 87.

65. Thomas Jackson, *From Civil Rights*, 26.

66. King, "If the Negro Wins, Labor Wins," 206. Delivered before the Fourth Constitutional Convention of the AFL-CIO in 1961, this speech is a good example of King's early attention to the intersection of race and class (but not gender) as grounds for coalition politics.

67. King, "Time," 243.

68. Ibid., 241–42.

69. Ibid., 232–34.

70. Ibid., 233.

71. "Dr. King's Disservice to His Cause," *Life*, 4 (April 21, 1967).

72. King, "Time," 233.

73. Ibid.

74. Ctd. in Marqusee, *Redemption Song*, 214.

75. King, "Time," 235.

76. King, "'Face to Face,'" 409.

77. King, "Time," 241.

Chapter Two

1. Said, *The World, The Text, and the Critic*, 26.

2. Adorno, *Notes to Literature*, 3–23.

3. Said, "Reflections on Exile"; *Culture and Imperialism*, 51, 66–67.

4. Crossman, "Introduction," 2.

5. Mullen, *Popular Fronts*, 21.

6. Said, *Representations*, 113.

7. Ibid., 111.

8. Ibid.

9. Scott-Smith, *The Politics of Apolitical Culture*, 167–68. An appendix includes the text of the CCF manifesto.

10. Engerman, "Foreword," vii.

11. Norman Thomas, "Review of *The God That Failed*," *The Call*, Box 6, Folder 110, Richard Wright Papers; Rebecca West, "Roads to Communist and Back: Six Personal Histories," *New York Times Book Review*, January 8, 1950, 3, 29. Thomas's excited notice that the anthology promotes socialism was a rare exception to the standard reception, but *The Call* was a socialist newspaper in New York with a small leftist readership. West's article is a more typical example of how reviews in mainstream publications took the anthology as an occasion to promote anticommunism.

12. Arthur Schlesinger Jr., "Dim Views of the Red Star," *Saturday Review of Literature*, January 7, 1950, 11.

13. Said, *Representations*, 86.

14. Bruce Robbins, "Socialism," 25–38.

15. Said, *Representations*, 110.

16. Ibid., 113–14. Said is careful to acknowledge that an even worse incidence of political religiosity overtook the Soviet Union at this time. He writes: "The battle for the intellect has been transformed into a battle for the soul, with implications for intellectual life that have been very baleful. That was certainly the case in the Soviet Union and its satellites, where show trials, mass purges, and a gigantic penitentiary system exemplified the horrors of the ordeal on the other side of the Iron Curtain" (ibid., 111).

17. Crossman, ed., *The God That Failed*, 114.

18. Ibid., 195.

19. Ibid., 272.

20. Ibid., 273.

21. Rowley, *Richard Wright*, 519.

22. Saunders, *The Cultural Cold War*, 382.

23. Ibid., 5.

24. Coleman, *Liberal Conspiracy*, 10.

25. Lasch, "Cultural Cold War," 198–212.

26. Saunders, *The Cultural Cold War*, 3.

27. Coleman, *Liberal Conspiracy*, 10.

28. Mattson, *When America*, 60–61.

29. Beinart, "An Argument"; Rorty, *Achieving Our Country*; Mattson, *When America*, 8–14.

30. Said, *Culture and Imperialism*, 285.

31. Guilbaut, *How New York Stole the Idea of Modern Art*; Von Eschen, *Satchmo*; Wilford, *The Mighty Wurlitzer*, 106–8.

32. Crossman, "Introduction," 11.

33. Crossman, ed., *The God that Failed*, 26.

34. Ibid., 60.

35. Brennan, *Wars*, 41.

36. Kim, *Ends of Empire*, 37–62. Koestler's use of Orientalism to bolster the alleged superiority of modern, Western dedication to anticommunism is comparable to the Orientalist accounts of modernity Kim traces through key policy documents of the Cold War national security state, including Kennan's "Long Telegram" and NSC 68.

37. Karem, "'I Could Never Really Leave the South,'" 700.

38. Davis, *Livin' the Blues*, 243.

39. Rowley, *Richard Wright*, 263–64.

40. Schrecker, *Age of McCarthyism*, 8–9.

41. Denning, *The Cultural Front*; Gilmore, *Defying Dixie*; Kelley, *Hammer and Hoe*; Wald, *Writing from the Left*.

42. Crossman, ed., *The God That Failed*, 123.

43. Crossman, Introduction, 9.

44. Crossman, ed., *The God That Failed*, 45.

45. Ibid., 120.

46. Ibid., 140.

47. Ibid., 157.

48. Wright, *Black Boy (American Hunger)*, 114.

49. Ibid., 115.

50. Thaddeus, "Metamorphosis," 63.

51. Crossman, ed., *The God That Failed*, 162.

52. Thaddeus, "Metamorphosis," 64, 77.

53. Wright, *Black Boy (American Hunger)*, 383.

54. Crossman, ed., *The God That Failed*, 158.

55. Kinnamon and Fabre, eds., *Conversations with Richard Wright*, 140.

56. Legal Attaché, Paris to Director, FBI, 03/03/1952. Richard Wright FBI File.

57. Kinnamon and Fabre, eds., *Conversations with Richard Wright*, 140.

58. Burns to Wright, October 3, 1951. Richard Wright Papers, Box 100, folder 1412.

59. Frazier, *Black Bourgeoisie*, 183–87.

60. "How to Stop the Russians," *Ebony* 7.1, November 1951, 106.

61. Ctd. in Fabre, *Unfinished Quest*, 364.

62. Ibid., 602.

63. Johnson to Wright, February 2 and 4, 1953, Richard Wright Papers, Box 100, folder 1412; Smith, *Black Boy in France*, 32–36, 39–42.

64. Burns to Wright, September 27, 1950, Richard Wright Papers, Box 100, folder 1412.

65. Burns to Wright, May 1, 1953. Richard Wright Papers, Box 100, folder 1412. Burns apologizes to Wright for the oversight. Wright ceased all communications between them in 1956 after Burns published an essay charging Wright with being an anti-white racist and poisoning Europeans against the United States. See Rowley, 473–74.

66. Wright, "The Shame of Chicago," 28–32.

67. "Return of the Native Son," 100.

68. Wright, "I Choose Exile," 1. Ctd. in Rowley, 398.

69. Wright, "The Shame of Chicago," 32.

70. Ctd. in Kinnamon and Fabre, eds., *Conversations*, 87.

71. Wright, "I Choose Exile," 1. Ctd. in Waligora-Davis, 15.

72. Wright, "I Choose Exile," 2. Ctd. in Fabre, *World of Richard Wright*, 177–78.

73. Ibid.

74. Ibid.

75. Wright, "I Choose Exile," 3.

76. Ibid.

77. Ibid., 4.

78. Ibid., 5. Ctd. in Coles, *Black Writers Abroad*, 107.

79. Lipsitz, *Possessive*, 24–47.

80. Ctd. in Lipsitz, *Possessive*, 26.

81. Dudziak, *Cold War Civil Rights*, 47–78.

82. Wright, "I Choose Exile," 8. Ctd. in Fabre, *The World of Richard Wright*, 179.

83. Ibid.

84. Wright, "I Choose Exile," 16.

85. Ibid., 12.

86. Rowley, *Richard Wright*, 413.

87. Wright, "I Choose Exile," 10–11.

88. Escobar, *Encountering Development*, 23–24.

89. Ibid.

90. Wright, "I Choose Exile," 17; ctd. in Fabre, *The World of Richard Wright*, 178–79.

91. Ibid.

Chapter Three

1. McCarran, *Congressional Record*, 1518.

2. James, *The C. L. R. James Reader*, 234.

3. Trotsky, *Leon Trotsky on Black Nationalism and Self-Determination*, 38–69.

4. Webb, *Not Without Love*, 206–8.

5. James, *Mariners*, 2.

6. Robinson, "James and the World-System," 244–59.

7. James to Padmore, 2. I learned of the existence of this letter from Rachel Peterson, "*Correspondence*: Journalism, Anticommunism, and Marxism in 1950s Detroit," *Anticommunism and the African American Freedom Movement*, edited by Lieberman and Lang, 115–59.

8. Johnson, "Sex and the Subversive Alien," 185–203. Johnson's article provides the best available technical account of James's legal conflict with the US government regarding his immigration status.

9. James, *C. L. R. James Reader*, 183.

10. Cleaver, *Reading* Capital *Politically*, 59–62. Cleaver describes the Johnson-Forest Tendency as part of the autonomous or "workerist" tradition in twentieth-century Marxist thought.

11. Jelly-Shapiro, "C. L. R. James in America," 31.

12. Buhle, *Artist as Revolutionary*, 110–14; Brennan, *At Home*, 208–58; Levi, "Radical West Indian," 492–93; Rosengarten, *Urbane Revolutionary*, 197–203.

13. Nielsen, *Writing*, 28–47; Pease, "Emergence," "*Mariners*," and "Doing Justice"; Robinson, "World-System," and Stephens's *Black Empire*, 241–67.

14. Gair, ed., *Beyond Boundaries: C. L. R. James and Postnational Studies*.

15. James, *American Civilization*, 26.

16. McCarran, *Congressional Record*, 1518.

17. Balibar, *Race, Nation, Class*, 61.

18. Blanchard, *Revolutionary Sparks*, 250.

19. Asch, *The Senator and the Sharecropper*, 155.

20. Buff, "Internal Frontier," 125.

21. Ibid., 137–39.

22. James, *American Civilization*, 37–38.

23. Johnson, "Sex and the Subversive Alien," 197–98; Blackman to Padmore, August 20, 1952, Richard Wright Papers, Box 113, folder 1522.

24. James to Padmore, 2.

25. Truman, "Veto."

26. Žižek, *Did Somebody Say Totalitarianism?*, 3.

27. Melville, *Moby-Dick*, 107. Appearing in multiple of Melville's texts, an "Anacharsis Clootz deputation" alludes to an international assembly that Prussian Baron de Cloots led before the French National Assembly in 1790 in order to pledge worldwide support for the French Revolution.

28. Lauter, "Melville Climbs the Canon," 6.

29. Ibid., 8.

30. Johnson, "Sex and the Subversive Alien," 197.

31. Lauter, "Melville Climbs the Canon," 19.

32. Pease, "*Moby-Dick* and the Cold War," 117–19.

33. Arac, "F. O. Matthiessen," 161.

34. Howard Vincent, "The Man Melville Sheds His Myth," *New York Times*, November 11, 1951, BR1, 25; "Two Studies of Herman Melville," *New York Times*, November 13, 1949, BR9; "The Real Melville?" *New York Times*, March 30, 1952, BR6. ProQuest Historical Newspapers: The New York Times (1851–2009).

35. James, *Mariners*, 3.

36. James, *American Civilization*, 39.

37. James, *Mariners*, 3.

38. Ibid.

39. James, *C. L. R. James Reader*, 236.

40. Ibid., 232.

41. Ibid., 234.

42. Ibid., 236.

43. James, *Mariners*, 3.

44. Warner, *Publics and Counterpublics*, 91.

45. James, *Mariners*, 3.

46. Ibid., 5.

47. Ibid.

48. Ibid.; Melville, *Moby-Dick*, 139.

49. James, *Mariners*, 5.

50. Ibid., 6.

51. Ibid.

52. Cain, "Triumph," 261.

53. Pease, "*Moby-Dick* and the Cold War," 127–44.

54. James, *Mariners*, 13.

55. Ibid.

56. Ibid., 6.

57. Chase, *Herman Melville*, ix.

58. Chase, "Art, Nature, Politics," 590–91.

59. James, *Mariners*, 40.

60. Ibid., 17.

61. Melville, *Moby-Dick*, 103–4.

62. James, *Mariners*, 28.

63. James, *Notes on Dialectics*, 223.

64. James, *Mariners*, 18. For an account of how poet Charles Olson's essay *Call Me Ishmael* also speculates about the frustrated undercurrent of revolutionary potential in Melville's representation of the crew, see my "Charles Olson's American Studies."

65. Arendt, *Origins*, 460.

66. James, *Mariners*, 48.

67. Pease, "C. L. R. James's *Mariners*," xxx.

68. James, *Mariners*, 143n.

69. Ibid., 132.

70. Ibid., 132–33.

71. Pease, "C. L. R. James's *Mariners*," xxi.

72. Schrecker, *Many*, 203–39.

73. Buhle, *C. L. R. James*, 110.

74. Rosengarten, *Urbane Revolutionary*, 197.

75. James to Padmore, 4.

76. Pease, "C. L. R. James's *Mariners*," xv.

77. Ibid., xviii.

78. James, *C. L. R. James Reader*, 154.

79. James, *Mariners*, 164.

80. Marx, "On the Jewish Question."

81. Douzinas, "*Adika*," 83.

82. James, *Mariners*, 157–58.

83. Ibid., 135.

84. Ibid., 136.

85. Ibid., 141; Webb, *Not Without Love*, 256.

86. Boggs, "A Critical Reminiscence," 178.

87. James, *Notes on Dialectics*, 8.

88. Ibid., 67.

89. James, *American Civilization*, 97–98.

90. Bogues, *Caliban's Freedom*, 138–41. Bogues claims James's sequence of Whitman, Melville, and the abolitionists is a dialectical examination of individualism.

91. *James, American Civilization*, 50.

92. Hartz, *The Liberal Tradition in America*.

93. James, *Notes on Dialectics*, 23.

94. James, *American Civilization*, 56.

95. See Schlesinger, *The Age of Jackson*.

96. James, *American Civilization*, 92.

97. Hofstadter, *American Political Tradition*, 177.

98. Ibid., 157.

99. James, *American Civilization*, 96.

100. Ibid., 94–95.

101. Ibid., 93.

102. Kerr-Ritchie, "Forty Acres," 225.

Chapter Four

1. Davis, *Livin' the Blues*, 276.

2. Horne, *Fighting in Paradise*.

3. Tidwell, "Subversive Vision," xv–xxvii.

4. Tidwell, Introduction, xxxv.

5. Davis, *Livin' the Blues*, 243–44.

6. Dolinar, *The Black Cultural Front*, 3–19.

7. Davis, *Livin' the Blues*, 341.

8. Randall, ed., *The Black Poets*, 121–22.

9. "Mystery Poet," 37–48.

10. Mullen, *Popular Fronts*, 43; Smethhurst, *The New Red Negro*, 137–38.

11. Horne, "Rethinking," n.p.

12. Kengor, *The Communist*, 3.

13. Obama, *Dreams from My Father*, 76.

14. Foley, "Rhetoric and Silence," 4. Foley shows that Obama's first memoir "dismisses anticapitalist radicalisms of various kinds with a patronizing shrug."

15. Obama, *Dreams*, 97.

16. Ibid.

17. Ibid., 98.

18. Lejeune, *On Autobiography*, 3–30.

19. Radosh, "Under the Influence."

20. Romney, *No Apology*, 31.

21. Davis, *Livin' the Blues*, 64.

22. Ibid.

23. Kengor, *The Communist*, 27.

24. Kelley, *Hammer and Hoe*, 107.

25. Ibid.

26. Kengor, *The Communist*, 91.

27. Ibid., 207–11.

28. Davis, *Livin' the Blues*, 275–83.

29. Davis, *Writings*, 91–151.

30. Ibid., 91–94, 96–100.

31. Ted Johnson, "*2016* Producers, Investors Sue Dinesh D'Souza," *Daily Variety*, October 24, 2012. variety.com.

32. D'Souza, "Is Racism a Western Idea?"

33. D'Souza, *Obama's America* and *The Roots of Obama's Rage*.

34. Reagan, "Inaugural Address."

35. Timothy Noah, "What We Didn't Overcome," *Slate*, November 10, 2008, www.slate.com/; John Weiner, "The Bad News About White People: Romney Won the White Vote Almost Everywhere," *The Nation*, November 7, 2012, www.thenation.com.

36. D'Souza, *Roots*, 13.

37. William Ayers, "An Open Letter to President Obama from Bill Ayers," *Good: A Magazine for the Global Citizen*, November 8, 2012, magazine.good.is/articles/an-open-letter-to-president-obama-from-bill-ayers.

38. Roberto Mangabeira Unger, "Beyond Obama," *Roberto Mangabeira Unger's Beyond Series*, www.law.harvard.edu/faculty/unger/index.php.

39. Stefano Esposito, "King had a dream, Obama has a drone, Rev. Wright says," *Chicago Sun-Times*, January 15, 2014, www.suntimes.com.

40. D'Souza, *Roots*, 209.

41. Harvey, *A Brief History of Neoliberalism*, 2.

42. Davis, *Livin' the Blues*, 311.

43. Horne, *Fighting in Paradise*, 241.

44. Committee on Un-American Activities, "Report on the *Honolulu Record*," October 1, 1950.

45. Horne, *Fighting in Paradise*, 90.

46. Ibid., 254.

47. Ibid., 239.

48. Davis, "Frank-ly Speaking," 8, 7, May 12, 1949.

49. Ibid., 8.

50. Prashad, *The Darker Nations*, 64–65.

51. Davis, "Frank-ly Speaking," 8, July 28, 1949.

52. *Dred Scott v. Sandford*, 60 US 393 (1856).

53. Davis, "Frank-ly Speaking," April 18, 1949.

54. Ibid., 7.

55. Ibid.

56. Lester, *The Communist Party USA*, vii.

57. Davis, "Frank-ly Speaking," 8, November 22, 1956.

58. "Target is Not Communists but People of Hawaii," *Honolulu Record* IX.17, November 22, 1956, 3. *The Honolulu Record Digitization Project*, www.hawaii.edu/uhwo/clear/Honolulu Record/homepage/homepage.html.

59. "From Eastland's Mouth," *Honolulu Record* IX.17, November 22, 1956, 8. *The Honolulu Record Digitization Project*.

60. Horne, *Fighting in Paradise*, 294.

61. Davis, "Frank-ly Speaking," December 20, 1956, 8.

62. Ibid.

63. Ibid.

Conclusion

1. Heale, *McCarthy's Americans*, 246–53; 256–65. See chapter 1, note 4.

2. Glen, *No Ordinary School*, 217.

3. "Labor Day Weekend."

4. Heale, *McCarthy's Americans*, 259.

5. Ibid.

6. Schrecker, *Many Are the Crimes*, 18.

7. Glen, *No Ordinary School*, 228–29. Glen explains that Highlander's charter was revoked, but for a technicality rather than subversive activities. Horton's accepting contributions for alcohol at the school's social events was deemed an illicit for-profit concession. It reorganized in 1961, and continues to this day as the Highlander Research and Education Center.

8. Menand, "The Color of Law."

9. Ibid.

10. Hall, "The Long Civil Rights Movement."

Bibliography

Adams, Timothy Dow. *Telling Lies in Modern American Autobiography*. Chapel Hill: University of North Carolina Press, 1990.

Adorno, Theodor. *Notes to Literature, Volume 1*. Edited by Rolf Tiedemann. Translated by Shierry Weber Nicholson. New York: Columbia University Press, 1991.

Andrews, William L., and Douglas Taylor, eds. *Richard Wright's "Black Boy (American Hunger)": A Casebook*. Oxford: Oxford University Press, 2003.

Arac, Jonathan. "F. O. Matthiessen: Authorizing an American Renaissance." *The American Renaissance Reconsidered*. Edited by Walter Benn Michaels and Donald Pease, 90–112. Baltimore: Johns Hopkins University Press, 1985.

Arendt, Hannah. *The Origins of Totalitarianism*, rev. ed. San Diego: Harcourt Brace, 1976.

Asch, Chris Myers. *The Senator and the Sharecropper: The Freedom Struggles of James O. Eastland and Fannie Lou Hamer*. 2008. Chapel Hill: University of North Carolina Press, 2011.

Atomic Age Classics Volume 5: "C" Is for Communist. DVD. West Conshohocken, PA: Alpha Home Entertainment, 2006.

Balibar, Étienne, and Immanuel Wallerstein. *Race, Nation, Class: Ambiguous Identities*. New York: Routledge, 1991.

Beinart, Peter. "An Argument for a New Liberalism: A Fighting Faith." *New Republic*, January 13, 2004. 17–24, 29.

Bhabha, Homi K. "DissemiNation: Time, Narrative, and the Margins of the Modern Nation." *Nation and Narration*. Edited by Homi K. Bhabha. London: Routledge, 1990. 291–322.

Blanchard, Margaret A. *Revolutionary Sparks: Freedom of Expression in Modern America*. Oxford: Oxford University Press, 1992.

Boggs, James, and Grace Lee. "A Critical Reminiscence." *C. L. R. James: His Life and Work*. Edited by Paul Buhle. London: Allison & Busby, 1986. 177–79.

Bogues, Anthony. *Caliban's Freedom: The Early Political Thought of C. L. R. James*. London: Pluto Press, 1997.

Branch, Taylor. *At Canaan's Edge: American in the King Years, 1965–68*. New York: Simon & Schuster, 2007.

———. *Parting the Waters: America in the King Years, 1954–63*. New York: Simon & Schuster, 1988.

——. *Pillar of Fire: America in the King Years, 1963–65*. New York: Simon & Schuster, 1998.

Brennan, Timothy. *At Home in the World: Cosmopolitanism Now*. Cambridge, MA: Harvard University Press, 1997.

——. *Wars of Position: The Cultural Politics of Left and Right*. New York: Columbia University Press, 2006.

Buff, Rachel. "Internal Frontier, Transnational Politics, 1945–65: Im/Migration Policy as World Domination." *Postcolonial America*. Edited by C. Richard King. 122–53. Urbana: University of Illinois Press, 2000. 122–53.

Buhle, Paul. *C. L. R. James: The Artist as Revolutionary*. London: Verso, 1988.

Burke, Kenneth. *A Rhetoric of Motives*. Berkeley: University of California Press, 1962.

Cain, William E. "The Triumph and the Will and the Failure of Resistance: C. L. R. James's Readings of *Moby-Dick* and *Othello*." *C. L. R. James: His Intellectual Legacies*. Edited by Selwyn R. Cudjoe and William E. Cain. Amherst: University of Massachusetts Press, 1995. 260–73.

Chase, Richard. "Art, Nature, Politics." *Kenyon Review* 12.4 (Autumn 1950): 580–94.

——. *Herman Melville: A Critical Study*. New York: Macmillan, 1949.

Cherne, Leo. "How to Spot a Communist." *Look: America's Family Magazine* 11.5 (March 4, 1947): 21–25.

Cleaver, Harry. *Reading Capital Politically*, 2nd edition. Leeds, UK and San Francisco: Anti/Theses and AK Press, 2000.

Coleman, Peter. *The Liberal Conspiracy: The Congress for Cultural Freedom and the Struggle for the Mind of Postwar Europe*. New York: Free Press, 1989.

Coles, Robert. *Black Writers Abroad: A Study of Black American Writers in Europe and Africa*. New York: Routledge, 1999.

Committee on Un-American Activities. US House of Representatives. *100 Things You Should Know About Communism*. Washington, DC, 1949.

——. "Report on *The Honolulu Record*." H.R. Rep. 81st Congress, Second Session. Washington, DC, October 1, 1950.

Corber, Robert. *Homosexuality in Cold War America: Resistance and the Crisis of Masculinity*. Durham: Duke University Press, 1997.

Crossman, Richard H., ed. *The God That Failed*. 1950. New York: Columbia University Press, 2001.

——. Introduction. *The God That Failed*. Edited by Richard H. Crossman. New York: Columbia University Press, 2001. 1–11.

Davies, Carole Boyce. *Left of Karl Marx: The Political Life of Black Communist Claudia Jones*. Durham: Duke University Press, 2007.

Davis, Frank Marshall. *Black Moods: Collected Poems*. Edited by John Edgar Tidwell. Urbana: University of Illinois, 2002.

——. "Frank-ly Speaking." *Honolulu Record* May 12, 1949: 8, 7; July 14, 1949: 8, 6; July 21, 1949: 8, 7; July 28, 1949: 8, 7; August 4, 1949: 20, 19; August 11, 1949: 8, 7; August 18, 1949: 8, 7; August 25, 1949: 8, 6; January 20, 1956: 8; November 29, 1956: 8. *The Honolulu Record Digitization Project*. www.hawaii.edu/uhwo/clear/HonoluluRecord/homepage/homepage.html.

———. *Livin' the Blues: Memoirs of a Black Journalist and Poet*. Edited by John Edgar Tidwell. Madison: University of Wisconsin Press, 1992.

———. *Writings of Frank Marshall Davis: A Voice of the Black Press*. Edited by John Edgar Tidwell. Jackson: University of Mississippi Press, 2007.

Denning, Michael. *The Cultural Front: The Laboring of American Culture in the Twentieth Century*. London: Verso, 1997.

Dickson-Carr, Darryl. *The Columbia Guide to Contemporary African American Fiction*. New York: Columbia University Press, 2005.

Dies, Martin. *The Trojan Horse in America*. New York: Dodd-Mead, 1940.

Dolan, Frederick. *Allegories of America: Narratives, Metaphysics, Politics*. Ithaca, NY: Cornell University Press, 1994.

Douzinas, Costas. "*Adikia*: On Communism and Rights." *The Idea of Communism*. Edited by Costas Douzinas and Slavoj Žižek. New York: Verso, 2010. 81–100.

D'Souza, Dinesh, dir. *2016: Obama's America*. DVD. Santa Monica, CA: Lionsgate, 2012.

———. "Is Racism a Western Idea?" *American Scholar* 64.4 (August 1995): 517–39. www.jstor .org/stable/41212409.

———. *Obama's America: Unmaking the American Dream*. Washington: Regnery, 2012.

———. *The Roots of Obama's Rage*. Washington: Regnery, 2010.

Dudziak, Mary. *Cold War Civil Rights: Race and the Image of American Democracy*. Princeton, NJ: Princeton University Press, 2000.

———. "Desegregation as a Cold War Imperative." *Stanford Law Review* 41 (November 1988): 61–120. www.jstor.org/stable/1228836.

Dyson, Michael Eric. *I May Not Get There with You: The True Martin Luther King, Jr.* New York: Free Press, 2000.

Engerman, David C. "Foreword to the 2001 Edition." *The God That Failed*. Edited by Richard H. Crossman. New York: Columbia University Press, 2001. vii–xxxiv.

Escobar, Arturo. *Encountering Development: The Making and Unmaking of the Third World*. Princeton, NJ: Princeton University Press, 1995.

Fabre, Michel. *The Unfinished Quest of Richard Wright*. Translated by Isabel Barzun. Urbana: University of Illinois Press, 1993.

———. *The World of Richard Wright*. Jackson: University Press of Mississippi, 1985.

Fanon, Frantz. *Black Skin, White Masks*. Translated by Charles Lam Markmann. New York: Grove Press, 1967.

Farred, Grant, ed. *Rethinking C. L. R. James*. Cambridge, MA: Blackwell, 1996.

Federal Bureau of Investigation. United States. Frank Marshall Davis file. Assorted documents dated July 5, 1944, to September 9, 1963. File no. 100-328955.

Federal Bureau of Investigation. United States. Richard Wright file. Assorted documents dated November 2, 1942 to May 9, 1963. File no. 100-157464.

Foley, Barbara. *Wrestling with the Left: The Making of Ralph Ellison's Invisible Man*. Durham: Duke University Press, 2010.

———. "Rhetoric and Silence in Obama's *Dreams from My Father*." *Cultural Logic* (2009): 1–46. clogic.eserver.org/2009/foley.pdf.

Foucault, Michel. *The History of Sexuality: An Introduction, Volume I*. Translated by Robert Hurley. New York: Vintage, 1990.

Fraser, Nancy, and Axel Honneth. *Redistribution or Recognition? A Political-Philosophical Exchange*. London: Verso, 2003.

Gaines, Kevin. *African Americans in Ghana: Black Expatriates and the Civil Rights Era*. Chapel Hill: University of North Carolina Press, 2006.

Gair, Christopher, ed. *Beyond Boundaries: C. L. R. James and Postnational Studies*. London: Pluto Press, 2006.

Garrow, David. "The FBI and Martin Luther King." *The Atlantic* (July 2002): 80–88.

———. *Protest at Selma: Martin Luther King Jr. and the Voting Rights Act of 1965*. New Haven: Yale University Press, 1980.

Gilbert, Joel. *Dreams from My Real Father: A Story of Reds and Deception*. Highway 61 Entertainment, 2012. DVD.

Gilmore, Glenda Elizabeth. *Defying Dixie: The Radical Roots of Civil Rights, 1919–1950*. New York: W.W. Norton, 2008.

Glen, John. *Highlander: No Ordinary School*. Knoxville: University of Tennessee Press, 1996.

Goldberg, David Theo. *The Racial State*. Malden, MA: Blackwell, 2002.

Goldfield, Michael. *The Color of Politics: Race and the Mainsprings of American Politics*. New York: New Press, 1997.

Gore, Dayo. *Radicalism at the Crossroads: African American Women Activists in the Cold War*. New York: NYU Press, 2011.

Grimshaw, Anna, and Keith Hart. Introduction. *American Civilization*. Edited by Anna Grimshaw and Keith Hart. Cambridge, MA: Blackwell, 1993. 1–25.

Guilbaut, Serge. *How New York Stole the Idea of Modern Art: Abstract Expressionism, Freedom, and the Cold War*. Translated by Arthur Goldhammer. Chicago: University of Chicago Press, 1983.

Hall, Jacquelyn Dowd. "The Long Civil Rights Movement and the Political Uses of the Past." *Journal of American History* 91.4 (March 2005): 1233–63.

Harrington, Ollie. *Bootsie and Others: A Selection of Cartoons*. New York: Dodd, Mead, 1958.

Harrington, Ollie. "Why I Left America." *Why I Left America and Other Essays*. Edited by M. Thomas Inge. Jackson: University Press of Mississippi, 1993. 96–109.

Harris, Cheryl. "Whiteness as Property." *Harvard Law Review* 106.8 (June 1993): 1710–91.

Hartz, Louis. *The Liberal Tradition in America*. New York: Harcourt, Brace & World, 1955.

Harvey, David. *A Brief History of Neoliberalism*. Oxford: Oxford University Press, 2007.

Heale, M. J. *McCarthy's Americans: Red Scare Politics in State and Nation, 1936–1965*. Athens: University of Georgia Press, 1998.

Higashida, Cheryl. *Black Internationalist Feminism: Women Writers of the Black Left*. Urbana: University of Illinois Press, 2011.

Hill, Robert. "Afterword." *American Civilization*. Edited by Anna Grimshaw and Keith Hart. Cambridge, MA: Blackwell, 1993. 293–366.

Hofstadter, Richard. *The American Political Tradition and the Men Who Made It*. New York: Vintage, 1948.

———. *The Paranoid Style in American Politics and Other Essays*. 1965. New York: Vintage, 2008.

Horne, Gerald. *Black and Red: W. E. B. Du Bois and the Afro-American Response to the Cold War, 1944–1963*. Albany: State University of New York Press, 1986.

———. *Communist Front? The Civil Rights Congress, 1946–1956*. London: Associated University Presses, 1988.

———. *Fighting in Paradise: Labor Unions, Racism, and Communists in the Making of Modern Hawai'i*. Honolulu: University of Hawaii Press, 2011.

———. "Rethinking the History and the Future of the Communist Party." *People's World*, April 6, 2007. www.peoplesworld.org/rethinking-the-history-and-future-of-the-communist-party/.

Jackson, Thomas F. *From Civil Rights to Human Rights: Martin Luther King, Jr., and the Struggle for Economic Justice*. Philadelphia: University of Pennsylvania Press, 2007.

James, C. L. R. *American Civilization*. Edited by Anna Grimshaw and Keith Hart. Cambridge, MA: Blackwell, 1993.

———. *C. L. R. James on the 'Negro Question.'* Edited by Scott McLemee. Jackson: University of Mississippi Press, 1996.

———. *The C. L. R. James Reader*. Edited by Anna Grimshaw. Oxford, UK: Blackwell, 1992.

———. (as J. R. Johnson). "The Lesson of Germany." *New International* (May 1945): 102–6. *Marxists Internet Library*. https://www.marxists.org/archive/james-clr/works/1945/05/lesson-germany.htm.

———. *Mariners, Renegades & Castaways: The Story of Herman Melville and the World We Live In*. Edited by Donald Pease. Hanover, NH: University Press of New England, 2001.

———. Letter to Padmore. MS. Richard Wright Papers. Box 103, folder 1520. Yale Collection of American Literature. Beinecke Rare Book and Manuscript Library.

James, C. L. R., Grace Lee, and Cornelius Castoriadis. *Facing Reality: The New Society: Where to look for it & How to bring it closer*. Chicago: Charles Kerr, 2006.

Jelly-Shapiro, Joshua. "C. L. R. James in America: or, the ballad of Nello and Connie." *Transition* 104 "Souls" (2011): 30–57. doi: 10.1353/tra.2011.009.

Johnson, David. *The Lavender Scare: The Cold War Persecution of Gays and Lesbians in the Federal Government*. Chicago: University of Chicago Press, 2004.

Johnson, W. C. "Sex and the Subversive Alien: The Moral Life of C. L. R. James." *International Journal of Francophone Studies* 14: 1–2 (2011): 185–203. doi: 10.1386/ijfs.14.1&2.185_1.

Jones, Claudia. "An End to the Neglect of the Problems of Negro Women." *Claudia Jones: Beyond Containment*. Edited by Carole Boyce Davies. Oxfordshire, UK: Ayebia Clarke, 2011. 74–86.

Karem, Jeff. "'I Could Never Really Leave the South': Regionalism and the Transformation of Richard Wright's *American Hunger*." *American Literary History* 13.4 (Winter 2001): 694–715. www.jstor.org/stable/3054592.

Keith, Joseph. *Unbecoming Americans: Writing Race and Nation from the Shadow of Citizenship, 1945–1960*. New Brunswick, NJ: Rutgers University Press, 2013.

Kelley, Robin D. G. *Hammer and Hoe: Alabama Communists During the Great Depression*. Chapel Hill: University of North Carolina Press, 1990.

———. *Freedom Dreams: The Black Radical Imagination.* Boston: Beacon, 2002.

Kengor, Paul. *The Communist: Frank Marshall Davis: The Untold Story of Barack Obama's Mentor.* New York: Mercury Ink, 2012.

Kennan, George. "Moscow Embassy Telegram #511: 'The Long Telegram.'" *Containment: Documents on American Policy and Strategy, 1940–1950.* Edited by Thomas Etzhold and John Lewis Gaddis. New York: Columbia University Press, 1978. 50–63.

Kennan, George (as X). "The Sources of Soviet Conduct." *Foreign Affairs* July 1947: 566–82.

Kerr-Ritchie, Jeffrey R. "Forty Acres, or, An Act of Bad Faith." *Redress for Historical Injustices in the United States: On Reparations for Slavery, Jim Crow, and Their Legacies.* Edited by Michael T. Martin and Marilyn Yaquinto. Durham: Duke University Press, 2007. 222–37.

Kim, Jodi. *Ends of Empire: Asian American Critique and the Cold War.* Minneapolis: University of Minnesota Press, 2010.

King, Martin Luther, Jr. "A Time to Break Silence." *A Testament of Hope: The Essential Writings and Speeches of Martin Luther King Jr.* Edited by James Melvin Washington. New York: HarperCollins, 1986. 231–44.

———. "'Face to Face': Television News Interview." *A Testament of Hope: The Essential Writings and Speeches of Martin Luther King Jr.* Edited by James Melvin Washington. New York: HarperCollins, 1986. 394–414.

———. "A Look to the Future." *Martin Luther King Jr. Papers: Volume IV: Symbol of the Movement, January 1957–December 1958.* Edited by Clayborne Carson, Susan Carson, and Virginia Shadron. Berkeley: University of California Press, 2000. 269–76.

———. "If the Negro Wins, Labor Wins." *A Testament of Hope: The Essential Writings and Speeches of Martin Luther King Jr.* Edited by James Melvin Washington. New York: HarperCollins, 1986. 201–7.

———. *Stride Toward Freedom: The Montgomery Story.* 1958. Boston: Beacon Press, 1986.

Kinnamon, Keneth, and Michel Fabre, eds. *Conversations with Richard Wright.* Jackson: University Press of Mississippi, 1993.

"Labor Day Weekend at Communist Training School." Georgia Commission on Education, 1957. Series I., Subseries A, S. Ernest Vandiver collection, Richard B. Russell Library for Political Research and Studies, University of Georgia, Athens, as presented in the Digital Library of Georgia. dlg.galileo.usg.edu/highlander/efhf003.php.

Lasch, Christopher. "The Cultural Cold War." *The Nation* (September 11, 1967): 198–212.

Lauter, Paul. "Melville Climbs the Canon." *American Literature* 66.1 (March 1994): 1–24. doi:10.2307/2927431.

Lejeune, Philippe. *On Autobiography.* Edited by Paul John Eakin. Translated by Katherine Leary. Minneapolis: University of Minnesota Press, 1989.

Lester, Robert E. *The Communist Party USA, and Radical Organizations, 1953–1960: FBI Reports from the Eisenhower Library* [microform]. Bethesda, MD: University Publications of America, 1990. cisupa.proquest.com/ksc_assets/catalog/10834_CPUSAFBID DELib.pdf.

Levi, Darrell E. "C. L. R. James: A Radical West Indian Vision of American Studies." *American Quarterly* 43.3 (September 1991): 486–501. doi: 10.2307/2713113.

Lieberman, Robbie, and Clarence Lang, eds. *Anticommunism and the African American Freedom Movement: "Another Side of the Story."* New York: Palgrave Macmillan, 2009.

Lipsitz, George. *The Possessive Investment in Whiteness: How White People Profit from Identity Politics.* Philadelphia: Temple University Press, 2006.

Lipsitz, George, and Barbara Tomlinson. "American Studies as Accompaniment." *American Quarterly* 65.1 (March 2013): 1–30.

Mailloux, Steven. *Disciplinary Identities: Rhetorical Paths of English, Speech, and Composition.* New York: MLA, 2006.

——. *Reception Histories: Rhetoric, Pragmatism, and American Cultural Politics.* Ithaca and London: Cornell University Press, 1998.

——. *Rhetorical Power.* Ithaca and London: Cornell University Press, 1989.

Marable, Manning. *Race, Reform, and Rebellion: The Second Construction in Black America, 1945–1982.* Jackson: University Press of Mississippi, 1984.

Marqusee, Mike. *Redemption Song: Muhammad Ali and the Spirit of the Sixties.* London: Verso, 1995.

Marx, Karl. "On the Jewish Question." *Early Writings.* Translated by Rodney Livingstone and Gregor Benton. London: Penguin, 1992. 211–42.

Matthiessen, F. O. *American Renaissance: Art and Expression in the Age of Emerson and Whitman.* London: Oxford University Press, 1941.

Mattson, Kevin. *When America Was Great: The Fighting Faith of Postwar Liberalism.* New York: Routledge, 2004.

May, Elaine Tyler. *Homeward Bound: American Families in the Cold War Era.* 2nd edition. New York: Basic Books, 1999.

McCarran, Senator Pat. *Congressional Record.* 2 March 1953: 1518.

McDuffie, Erik S. *Sojourning for Freedom: Black Women, American Communism, and the Making of Black Left Feminism.* Durham: Duke University Press, 2008.

Medovoi, Leerom. *Rebels: Youth and the Cold War Origins of Identity.* Durham: Duke University Press, 2005.

Melamed, Jodi. *Represent and Destroy: Rationalizing Violence in the New Racial Capitalism.* Minneapolis: University of Minnesota Press, 2011.

Melville, Herman. *Moby-Dick.* 2nd edition. Edited by Hershel Parker and Harrison Hayford. New York: Norton, 2002.

Menand, Louis. "The Color of Law: Voting Rights and the Southern Way of Life." *New Yorker* 89.20 (8 July 2013). www.newyorker.com/magazine/2013/07/08/the-color-of-law.

Miller, Keith D. *Voices of Deliverance: The Language of Martin Luther King Jr., and Its Sources.* Athens: University of Georgia Press, 1998.

——. *Martin Luther King's Biblical Epic: His Final, Great Speech.* Jackson: University Press of Mississippi, 2012.

Mills, Charles W. "Racial Liberalism." *PMLA* 123.5 (October 2008): 1380–97.

Morgan, Ted. *Literary Outlaw: The Life and Times of William S. Burroughs.* New York: Henry Holt, 1988.

Mullen, Bill. *Popular Fronts: Chicago and African-American Cultural Politics, 1935–46.* Urbana and Chicago: University of Illinois Press, 1999.

Mullen, Bill, and James Smethhurst, eds. *Left of the Color Line: Race, Radicalism, and Twentieth-Century Literature of the United States*. Chapel Hill: University of North Carolina Press, 2003.

Myrdal, Gunnar. *An American Dilemma: The Negro Problem and Modern Democracy*. 2 vols. New York and London: Harper & Brothers, 1944.

"Mystery Poet: An Interview with Frank Marshall Davis." *Black World* 23.3 (January 1974): 37–48.

Nadel, Alan. *Containment Culture: American Narratives, Postmodernism, and the Atomic Age*. Durham: Duke University Press, 1995.

Nielsen, Aldon. *C. L. R. James: A Critical Introduction*. Jackson: University Press of Mississippi, 1997.

———. *Writing between the Lines: Race and Intertextuality*. Athens: University of Georgia Press, 1994.

Obama, Barack. *Dreams from My Father: A Story of Race and Inheritance*. 1995. New York: Crown, 2004.

Oliver, Melvin L., and Thomas M. Shapiro. *Black Wealth/White Wealth: A New Perspective on Racial Inequality. Tenth-Anniversary Edition*. New York: Routledge, 2006.

Omi, Michael, and Howard Winant. *Racial Formation in the United States: From the 1960s to the 1990s*. 2nd edition. New York: Routledge, 1994.

O'Reilly, Kenneth. *Hoover and the Unamericans: The FBI, HUAC, and the Red Menace*. Philadelphia: Temple University Press, 1983.

———. *Racial Matters: The FBI's Secret File on Black America, 1960–1972*. New York: Free Press, 1991.

Pease, Donald. "C. L. R. James, *Moby-Dick*, and the Emergence of Transnational American Studies." *The Futures of American Studies*. Edited by Donald Pease and Robyn Wiegman. Durham and London: Duke University Press, 2002. 135–63.

———. "C. L. R. James's *Mariners, Renegades and Castaways* and the World We Live In." *Mariners, Renegades & Castaways: The Story of Herman Melville and the World We Live In*. Edited by Donald Pease. Hanover, NH: University Press of New England, 2001. vii–xxxiii.

———. "Doing Justice to C. L. R. James's *Mariners, Renegades and Castaways*." *boundary 2* 27.2 (summer 2000): 1–20.

———. "*Moby-Dick* and the Cold War." *The American Renaissance Reconsidered*. Edited by Walter Benn Michaels and Donald Pease. Baltimore: Johns Hopkins University Press, 1985. 113–55.

———. *The New American Exceptionalism*. Minneapolis: University of Minnesota Press, 2009.

Phelan, James. *Living to Tell about It: A Rhetoric and Ethics of Character Narration*. Ithaca, NY: Cornell University Press, 2005.

Plummer, Brenda Gayle. *Rising Wind: Black Americans and U.S. Foreign Affairs, 1935–1960*. Chapel Hill: University of North Carolina Press, 1996.

Prashad, Vijay. *The Darker Nations: A People's History of the Third World*. New York and London: New Press, 2007.

Radosh, Ronald. "Under the Influence." *National Review* (October 29, 2012): 45–46. *Lexis Nexis Academic*.

Rampersad, Arnold. "Note on the Text." *Black Boy (American Hunger): A Record of Childhood and Youth*. New York: Harper Perennial, 1998. 407–8.

Randall, Dudley, ed. *The Black Poets*. New York: Bantam, 1971.

Reagan, Ronald. "Inaugural Address." January 20, 1981. *The American Presidency Project*. www.presidency.ucsb.edu/ws/?pid=43130.

Reed, Adolph. "Nothing Left: The Long, Slow Surrender of American Liberals." *Harper's Magazine* (March 2014): 28–36.

"Return of the Native Son." *Ebony* (December 1951): 100–101.

Richard Wright Papers. Yale Collection of American Literature. Beinecke Rare Book and Manuscript Library.

Robbins, Bruce. "Socialism, Elitism, Progress, and Other Transgressions: On Edward Said's 'Voyage In.'" *Social Text* 40 (fall 1994): 25–38. doi: 10.2307/466794.

Robinson, Cedric J. *Black Marxism: The Making of the Black Radical Tradition*. 1983. Chapel Hill: University of North Carolina Press, 2000.

———. "James and the World-System." *C. L. R. James: His Intellectual Legacies*. Edited by Selwyn R. Cudjoe and William E. Cain. Amherst: University of Massachusetts Press, 1995. 244–59.

Roediger, David. *How Race Survived U.S. History: From Settlement and Slavery to the Obama Phenomenon*. London: Verso, 2008.

Rogin, Michael. *Ronald Reagan, the Movie: And Other Episodes in Political Demonology*. Berkeley: University of California Press, 1987.

Romney, Mitt. *No Apology: The Case for American Greatness*. New York: St. Martin's Press, 2010.

Rorty, Richard. *Achieving Our Country: Leftist Thought in Twentieth-Century America*. Cambridge, MA: Harvard University Press, 1997.

Rosengarten, Frank. *Urbane Revolutionary: C. L. R. James and the Struggle for a New Society*. Jackson: University Press of Mississippi, 2008.

Ross, Andrew. "Civilization in One Country? The American James." *Rethinking C. L. R. James*. Edited by Grant Farred. Cambridge, MA and Oxford, UK: Blackwell, 1996. 75–84.

———. *No Respect: Intellectuals and Popular Culture*. London: Routledge, 1989.

Rowley, Hazel. *Richard Wright: The Life and Times*. New York: Henry Holt, 2001.

Rubin, Andrew. *Archives of Authority: Empire, Culture, and the Cold War*. Princeton, NJ: Princeton University Press, 2012.

Said, Edward. *Culture and Imperialism*. New York: Alfred A. Knopf, 1993.

———. "Reflections on Exile." *Granta* 13 (1984): 159–72.

———. *Representations of the Intellectual*. New York: Vintage, 1994.

———. *The World, The Text, and The Critic*. Cambridge, MA: Harvard University Press, 1983.

Saunders, Frances Stonor. *The Cultural Cold War: The CIA and the World of Arts and Letters*. New York: New Press, 1999.

Schlesinger, Arthur Jr. *The Age of Jackson*. Boston: Little, Brown, 1946.

———. "The U.S. Communist Party." *Life* 21.5 (July 29, 1946): 84–96.

———. *The Vital Center: The Politics of Freedom.* 1949. New York: Da Capo Press, 1988.

Schrecker, Ellen. *The Age of McCarthyism: A Brief History with Documents.* Boston: Bedford/ St. Martin's, 2002.

———. *Many Are the Crimes: McCarthyism in America.* Boston: Little, Brown, 1998.

Scott-Smith, Giles. *The Politics of Apolitical Culture: The Congress for Cultural Freedom, the CIA, and Postwar American Hegemony.* London: Routledge, 2002.

Selby, Gary. *Martin Luther King and the Rhetoric of Freedom: The Exodus Narrative in America's Struggle for Civil Rights.* Waco: Baylor University Press, 2008.

Siegel, Don, dir. *Invasion of the Body Snatchers.* Los Angeles: Walter Wanger Productions, 1956.

Singh, Nikhil. *Black Is a Country: Race and the Unfinished Struggle for Democracy.* Cambridge, MA: Harvard University Press, 2004.

Smethhurst, James Edward. *The New Red Negro: The Literary Left and African American Poetry, 1930–1946.* Oxford, UK: Oxford University Press, 1999.

Smith, William Gardner. "Black Boy in France." *Ebony* 8.9 (July 1953): 32–36, 39–42.

Sommer, Doris. "Irresistible romance: the foundational fictions of Latin America." *Narration and Nation.* Edited by Homi Bhabha. London: Routledge, 1990. 71–98.

Stephens, Michelle. *Black Empire: The Masculine Global Imaginary of Caribbean Intellectuals in the United States, 1914–1962.* Durham: Duke University Press, 2005.

Storrs, Landon. *The Second Red Scare and the Unmaking of the New Deal Left.* Princeton, NJ: Princeton University Press, 2012.

Thaddeus, Janice. "The Metamorphosis of *Black Boy.*" *Richard Wright: Critical Perspectives Past and Present.* Edited by Henry Louis Gates, Jr., and K. A. Appiah. New York: Amistad, 1993. 272–84.

Tidwell, John Edgar. "Introduction: Weaving Jagged Words into Song." *Black Moods: Collected Poems.* Frank Marshall Davis. Edited by John Edgar Tidwell. Urbana: University of Illinois Press, 2002. xxi–lxv.

———. "The Subversive Vision of Frank Marshall Davis: An Introduction." *Writings of Frank Marshall Davis: A Voice of the Black Press.* Edited by John Edgar Tidwell. Jackson: University Press of Mississippi, 2007. xiii–xxxii.

Trotsky, Leon. *Leon Trotsky on Black Nationalism and Self-Determination.* Edited by George Breitman. New York: Pathfinder Press, 1978.

Truman, President Harry. "Veto of the Internal Security Act." September 22, 1950. Truman Library. trumanlibrary.org/publicpapers/viewpapers.php?pid=883.

Von Eschen, Penny. *Race after Empire: Black Americans and Anticolonialism, 1937–1957.* Ithaca, NY: Cornell University Press, 1997.

———. *Satchmo Blows up the World: Jazz Ambassadors Play the Cold War.* Cambridge, MA: Harvard University Press, 2006.

Wald, Alan. *Writing from the Left: New Essays on Radical Culture and Politics.* London: Verso, 1994.

Waligora-Davis, Nicole A. *Sanctuary: African Americans and Empire.* Oxford: Oxford University Press, 2011.

Warner, Michael. *Publics and Counterpublics*. New York: Zone Books, 2005.

Webb, Constance. *Not without Love: Memoirs*. Hanover, NH: University Press of New England, 2003.

Weigand, Kate. *Red Feminism: American Communism and the Making of Women's Liberation*. Baltimore: John Hopkins University Press, 2000.

Whitfield, Stephen J. *The Culture of the Cold War*. 1991. Baltimore: Johns Hopkins University Press, 1996.

Wilford, Hugh. *The Mighty Wurlitzer: How the CIA Played America*. Cambridge, MA: Harvard University Press, 2008.

Winant, Howard. *The World Is a Ghetto: Race and Democracy Since World War II*. New York: Basic Books, 2001.

Woods, Jeff. *Black Struggle, Red Scare: Segregation and Anti-Communism in the South, 1948–1968*. Baton Rouge: LSU Press, 2003.

Wright, Richard. *Black Boy (American Hunger): A Record of Childhood and Youth*. New York: Harper Perennial, 1998.

———. "I Choose Exile." MS. Richard Wright Papers. Box 6. Folder 110. Yale Collection of American Literature, Beinecke Rare Book and Manuscript Library.

———. "I Tried to Be a Communist." *Atlantic Monthly* 159 (August 1944): 61–70, (September 1944): 48–56.

———. "The Shame of Chicago." *Ebony* (December 1951): 24–32.

———. *Black Power: Three Books from Exile: Black Power; The Color Curtain; and White Man, Listen!* New York: Harper Perennial, 2008.

Ybarra, Michael J. *Washington Gone Crazy: Senator Pat McCarran and the Great American Communist Hunt*. Hanover, NH: Steerforth Press, 2004.

Zeigler, James. "*Call Me Ishmael* and the Cold War: Charles Olson's American Studies." *Arizona Quarterly* 63.2 (summer 2007): 51–80.

Žižek, Slavoj. *Did Somebody Say Totalitarianism? Five Interventions in the (Mis)use of a Notion*. London: Verso, 2001.

Index

Page numbers in **bold** indicate an illustration.

9 781496 809711